D1443043

Decided on the

BATTLEFIELD

DAVID ALAN JOHNSON

Decided on the

BATTLEFIELD

GRANT, SHERMAN, LINCOLN
and the Election of 1864

 Prometheus Books

59 John Glenn Drive
Amherst, New York 14228–2119

Published 2012 by Prometheus Books

Cover images of Grant, Sherman, and Lincoln courtesy of
National Archives and Records Administration

Battle of Chickamauga by Kurz & Allison ca. 1890 courtesy of Library of Congress

Jacket design by Nicole Sommer-Lecht

Inquiries should be addressed to
Prometheus Books
59 John Glenn Drive
Amherst, New York 14228–2119
VOICE: 716–691–0133
FAX: 716–691–0137
WWW.PROMETHEUSBOOKS.COM

16 15 14 13 12   5 4 3 2 1

Library of Congress Cataloging-in-Publication Data

Johnson, David, 1950–
      Decided on the battlefield : Grant, Sherman, Lincoln, and the election of 1864 / by David Alan Johnson.
            p. cm.
      Includes bibliographical references and index.
      ISBN 978–1–61614–509–5 (cloth : alk. paper)
      ISBN 978–1–61614–510–1 (ebook)
      1. Presidents—United States—Election—1864. 2. United States—History—Civil War, 1861–1865—Campaigns. 3. United States—Politics and government—1861–1865. 4. Lincoln, Abraham, 1809–1865. 5. Grant, Ulysses S. (Ulysses Simpson), 1822–1885. 6. Sherman, William T. (William Tecumseh), 1820–1891. I. Title.

E458.4.J733 2011
973.7—dc23

                                                                                                    2011039394

Printed in the United States of America on acid-free paper

CONTENTS

Chapter One

GENERALS AND POLITICIANS

TWO FRIENDS AND A GRAND STRATEGY

To the desk clerk at the Burnet House, Cincinnati's leading hotel, the two officers did not have anything in common except the blue uniforms they both wore. One of the men was striking in appearance—tall, with red hair and a short beard. He would have stood out anywhere. The other one also had a beard, but was short and stocky. There was nothing impressive about the shorter man at all; he could have disappeared into any crowd without ever being given a second look. The tall, redheaded man was talkative and highly strung, chattering away almost continuously in nervous, energetic bursts. The shorter man did not say very much—later on, people would say that he could be silent in several languages—and was much calmer and more reserved than his animated friend.

The short, stumpy officer was Ulysses S. Grant, the Hero of Vicksburg, Shiloh, and Chattanooga, who had been given his commission as lieutenant general by President Abraham Lincoln less than two weeks before. His talkative red-haired friend was Major General William Tecumseh Sherman, who had known General Grant since their days at West Point and had been with him at Shiloh and Vicksburg. The differences in their manner and appearance never had any effect on how well they got along with each other. But the relationship between the two was about to take a new turn. Their meeting in Cincinnati would change the lives of both men, and would also alter the course of the Civil War and forever change the future of the United States.

Grant and Sherman had come to the Burnet House to discuss strategy—how the war would be waged from then on. It was March 1864, a month or two before the roads would be dry enough to let the spring campaigns begin. The North had won major victories at Gettysburg, Pennsylvania, and Vicksburg, Mississippi, but that had been eight months earlier and the Confederacy was far from finished. General Robert E. Lee's Army of Northern Virginia and General Joseph E. Johnston's Army of Tennessee were still in the field, and were the main topic of discussion between the two generals.

The war had been going on for nearly three years. People in the North were becoming tired of the endless fighting and everything about it. Because of the tactics and weaponry employed by both sides, the number of men being killed and wounded in every battle was enormous—at Fredericksburg, Virginia, three months before, more than 12,000 Union soldiers had been killed or wounded. War weariness was hardening into opposition against Lincoln's war to restore the Union.

There is no record of whether Grant and Sherman discussed the upcoming presidential election in November—probably not, because it was still a long way off and the Democrats would not even name a candidate until summer. Neither of them could have known it, but the outcome of their strategy meeting in that smoke-filled Cincinnati hotel room would alter public opinion concerning the war, as well as public opinion of Abraham Lincoln as a war president. The decisions reached by the two generals, the short and stumpy Grant and the tall and nervous Sherman, would also determine the outcome of the November election, in ways that no one could possibly have guessed.

In their hotel room, Parlor A, Grant and Sherman talked about how they should go about destroying the two Confederate armies. For two days, they spread out their big war maps, discussed Lee and Johnston, thrashed over possible troop movements, and smoked endless cigars—after two days and dozens of cigars, the air in that room must have been absolutely fetid. Lee was still preventing the Army of the Potomac from capturing Richmond, just as he had been doing since the beginning of the war, and Johnston was in Georgia reorganizing his forces. Both armies would have to be overcome and shattered before the war could be won and the rebellion could be brought to an end. Both Grant and Sherman were well aware that defeating two armies and ending the rebellion would require a great deal of hard planning, and even harder fighting.

Ulysses S. Grant and William Tecumseh Sherman had both graduated from West Point; Grant in 1843 and Sherman in 1840. They had not been close friends—Grant was a new plebe when Sherman was in his final year at the academy—but they remembered each other. They met again in St. Louis before the war, after both men had left the army and had been civilians for several years. Both of them were having a very hard time earning a living—at one point, Grant was reduced to selling firewood in the street. One of their topics of conversation was how a West Point education left them unsuited for any sort of career outside the army. But when the war began in 1861, West Point graduates were very much in demand by the War Department. Grant and Sherman began their second military careers, and their hard times were over forever.

The two men understood each other, and they understood what had to be done. They also liked each other, and had stood by one another during troubled times. In February 1862, during Grant's attack on Fort Henry, Tennessee, Sherman had been given the job of sending boatloads of supplies and replacement troops to reinforce Grant's assault. When nearby Fort Donelson was taken later in the same month, along with its stash of weapons and ammunition, Sherman asked if there was anything else he could do for Grant. At the time, Sherman was senior to Grant; this total lack of ego on Sherman's part was much appreciated, and would be well remembered. More than 20 years afterward, Grant recalled that "every boat that came up with supplies or reinforcements brought a note of encouragement from Sherman . . . saying that if he could be of service at the front I might send for him and he would waive rank."[1]

Sherman came to Grant's rescue again a few months later, but in a completely different way. Early in April, Confederate troops surprised Grant's forces at Shiloh, on the Tennessee River. Sherman was one of Grant's subordinates in the Shiloh campaign, commanding one of his divisions, and was appalled by the losses during the first day's fighting. In a conversation that has become legendary, Sherman told Grant that it had been the devil's own day that day. He expected Grant to order a withdrawal. But Grant did not want anything to do with retreating or withdrawing, a trait he would often show in Virginia two years later. "Yes," he said quietly. "Lick 'em tomorrow, though."[2]

Grant was right. Union reinforcements arrived during the night and, in a series of attacks the next day, they forced the Confederates into full retreat. Grant turned Shiloh into a victory for the Union, although a very costly one. Once again, Grant was a hero. But the euphoria did not last long. Soon after the battle, Grant began to receive criticism for having been taken completely off guard by the Confederate attack—which was true. He was also accused of not being on hand to lead his troops, which resulted in unacceptably high casualties. The *New York Times* and the *Chicago Tribune* both reported Union losses at between 500 to 1,000 killed and 3,000 to 4,000 wounded. Actual casualties were even worse than this: over 13,000, with more than 1,700 killed and 8,000 wounded.[3] This would not be the last time that Grant would be accused of allowing an unacceptably high number of killed and wounded.

Grant was stung and humiliated by this criticism; he had gone from national hero to bungling murderer within a matter of days. When Sherman heard about all the disapproval and criticism, he was livid. Grant had given him a command when just about everybody else in the army, and everybody in Washington, had dismissed him as mentally unfit for command, if not absolutely insane. When a news reporter wrote an article accusing Grant of being stupid and inept, Sherman wrote a letter to the reporter in which he called him a liar. Sherman had a temper to match his red hair. The two indulged in a war of words that went on for weeks, with Sherman defending Grant and calling the reporter any number of unflattering names, while the news reporter retaliated by printing news articles attacking both Grant and Sherman.

While all this was going on, Grant was replaced as commander of the armies of the West by Major General Henry Halleck for reasons of seniority and was demoted to "assistant commander." For all intents and purposes, Grant had lost his job—"assistant commander" was a meaningless title, without any duties or responsibilities, and Grant was reduced to just sitting around camp all day. This was too much for him. After winning at Fort Fisher, Fort Donelson, and Shiloh, during a time when Union victories were few and far between, he was rewarded first by having his competence called into question, and then by having his job taken away. Grant was thoroughly disgusted, and he decided that the best thing for him to do was leave the army. He had vague plans of going back to St. Louis. If nothing else, he could always go back to work in his father's harness shop in Galena, Illinois.

Sherman did not want to hear any of this. He gave Grant a good talking to, telling him that the collective memory of the press, the general public, and Washington was only as long as the next battle. He managed to persuade Grant that he belonged in the army, and convinced him to stay on. Grant was both moved and encouraged by Sherman's support. He wrote to his wife, Julia, that William Tecumseh Sherman was a gallant defender of the country, and was also a true friend.

During the course of the two-day strategy conference in Cincinnati, these incidents were very likely mentioned in conversation, if only in passing. Shiloh, and its casualties, would have been only one topic covered. Two subjects that would not have been brought up, which may have been whispered in private but never brought into the open, were Sherman's mental illness and Grant's problem with alcohol.

Grant's reputation as a drunk began before the war. He had to resign from the army in 1854 because he had been drinking while on duty—he had shown up obviously drunk at pay parade one day. Everyone in camp had seen him while he was under the influence, and nearly everybody in the army, including Sherman, had heard about it. When Richard Henry Dana, the author of *Two Years Before the Mast*, met Grant, he saw a seedy, run-down nobody who looked as though he drank a little too much. "He had no gait, no station, no manner," Dana recalled. "Rough light brown whiskers, a blue eye and a rather scrubby look.... The look of a man who did, or once did, take a little too much to drink."[4] When Congress passed the act creating the rank of three-star general, one question lurked at the back of everybody's mind: could someone with Grant's reputation for drunkenness be trusted with that much rank?

Actually, this reputation was completely overblown. The main reason that Grant drank, when he drank to excess, was because he was bored. He was not a habitual drunkard; basically, he drank to escape the boredom of a remote army post's dull routine or, as had happened at Vicksburg, the boredom of a long siege. There was nothing for him to do, and his wife, Julia, and their children were not on hand to keep him company. At Vicksburg, Grant went on a two-day binge, but this happened only after weeks of sitting outside the city and waiting for the Confederates to give up.

Grant's drinking was never really held against him, probably because of the fact that he was not a chronic drunk and could control his drinking. Whether or not he brought a bottle with him to Cincinnati during his meeting with Sherman has never been mentioned, just all those cigars. But the officers of the US Army knew better than to fault Grant, or anyone else, for drinking—it was a matter of people living in glass houses throwing stones. If getting drunk disqualified anyone from being an officer, probably 80 percent of the Union's officer corps would have been disqualified, from General Grant down to the most junior lieutenant. The army had more than its share of officers who drank.

But the army was not nearly as forgiving in the case of William Tecumseh Sherman. Sherman was not a drunk; he had mental problems. That was a completely different matter. Grant chose to overlook Sherman's troubles and tribulations, and concentrated on his friend's strengths instead of his weaknesses. This attitude toward any sort of mental illness was a revolutionary attitude, just about unheard of in the 1860s.

Sherman inherited his mental problems from his mother's side of the family. His maternal grandmother had actually been sent to an asylum. Gossip about Sherman and his mental troubles began to circulate in the autumn of 1861, a few months after he rejoined the army and while he was in command of the Department of the Cumberland. Sherman told Secretary of War Simon Cameron that if he had 60,000 men, he would be able to drive the enemy out of Kentucky. If he had 200,000 men, Sherman went on, he could finish the war in that part of the country. Sherman was not demanding this many troops; he was only suggesting that 200,000 men would give him a large enough army to destroy all opposition. But

Cameron was absolutely astonished by these numbers, which he considered fantastic if not absolutely insane, and he told reporters that Sherman must be mentally unhinged to have come up with them. Newspapers released the story that General William Tecumseh Sherman was demanding 200,000 men, and that he was not in a sound state of mind.

At the time, Sherman was in a highly nervous state—he was nervous and highly strung by nature and disposition to begin with. The Union's losses up to that time—including at the first battle of Bull Run, about 30 miles southwest of Washington, DC, where he had taken part in the battle as a colonel in the 13th US Infantry—worsened his condition, making him depressed and irritable. When he was in that state of mind, Sherman tended to talk in a loud voice, and he sometimes paced about the room when he talked. In other words, his natural nervousness became much more noticeable, and also became disconcerting to anyone who happened to be in the same room with him.

Sherman had only been in command of the Department of the Cumberland a short time. Anxiety over his new appointment, as well as the resulting stress and lack of sleep, were pushing him into a debilitating state of depression—he was prone to these periods of black despondency that bordered on something more ominous. His wife, Ellen, once commented that she had seen Sherman when he was extremely depressed and agitated, on the verge of insanity, when they had been in California.

The reports concerning Sherman's mental state reached General George B. McClellan, commander of Union forces, and were taken seriously. McClellan sent one of the officers on his staff to observe Sherman and his activities. The officer made his observations and reported that Sherman was on the edge of a nervous breakdown.

Sherman saw what was coming and asked McClellan to relieve him of his command by placing him on medical furlough. He was already tense and overly anxious; the talk about his mental condition, and the report by McClellan's staff officer, made his condition worse. McClellan sent Sherman home; Sherman's wife, Ellen, was telegraphed to come and get him. When they arrived back home in Lancaster, Ohio, Sherman was very nearly in a state of complete mental collapse.

Going back to Ohio, and getting away from the army for a while, was probably the best thing for Sherman in his current mental state. His nerves calmed down and his morale began to take a decided turn for the better. But while he was recovering, some news reporters got wind of his condition.

Sherman hated reporters and was not shy about letting his hatred show. He would not allow any newsmen anywhere near his headquarters, and any reporter who got close enough to him to ask a question usually received a snarling insult for a reply. When he received information that two Northern reporters had been executed as spies by the Confederates, Sherman was absolutely delighted—it was something he had always wanted to do himself. Now members of the news media went out of their way to let Sherman know that the feeling was mutual.

The *New York Times* reported that Sherman's mental disorders had caused him to be removed from command of the Department of the Cumberland, perhaps permanently. Although this was true, having his mental state reported to the public in a prominent New York newspaper both upset and depressed him. But at least the *New York Times* tried to be factual. The *Cincinnati Daily Commercial* published an article under the headline "GENERAL WILLIAM T. SHERMAN INSANE," which went on to declare that Sherman was "stark mad," and that any previous criticisms of the general would now be replaced by "feelings of deepest sympathy for him and his great calamity."5 The *Daily Commercial* had the largest circulation of any newspaper in Ohio. None of these things helped calm Sherman's nerves or settle his state of mind.

After his medical furlough ended during the early part of 1862, Sherman was ordered to report to General Henry Halleck at the Department of the West headquarters in St. Louis. By this time, still more newspapers picked up the story of Sherman's mental difficulties; their editors seemed to take a perverted glee in printing stories about how Sherman was "crazy" and not fit to command. Sherman was ashamed and humiliated. Although he was welcomed warmly by General Halleck and his headquarters staff, no one would trust him with any responsibilities. The only assignment that Sherman could get was a training command—working with raw recruits at nearby Benton Barracks. General Halleck wanted to be able to keep an eye on Sherman, just in case he started to "act crazy" again. It would also keep Sherman's mind occupied and would keep him from any type of combat command until General Halleck thought he was ready—if Halleck thought he would ever be ready.

But General Halleck began to receive letters from influential people on General Sherman's behalf, insisting that Sherman be given a real assignment and not just some little job designed to keep him occupied. Sherman's brother, Senator John Sherman, and his father-in-law, Secretary of the Interior Thomas Ewing, asked Halleck to consider Sherman for another job, something better than overseeing recruits drilling on the parade ground. General Halleck began to have second thoughts about Sherman—he even sat down with him to confer about a future campaign in the West.

Sherman was slowly coming out of his nervous state by this time. He also seemed to have a flair for training troops. Although he may not have been the model parade-ground officer—on at least one occasion, he showed up for inspection wearing an old brown overcoat and a stove pipe hat—at least he was no longer insane. Or at least General Halleck had been persuaded to think so.

At the beginning of 1862, General Halleck gave General Ulysses S. Grant permission to attack Fort Henry in Tennessee. It was at this time that he also ordered Sherman to go to the river port of Paducah, Kentucky, for the purpose of sending Grant supplies and reinforcements. After Fort Henry would come Fort Donelson, Shiloh, Vicksburg, and a relationship that would change the course of the war. Sherman would later say, "Grant stood by me when I was crazy, and I stood by him when he was drunk, and now we stand by each other."[6]

By March 1864, after many battles had changed both men and had also changed the country's opinion of them, Grant and Sherman sat in their room at the Burnet House and mapped out what they hoped would be the final campaign of the war. Or, rather, Grant sat and listened while Sherman talked and stomped about the room to relieve his nerves. Ultimately, the decision was to split up and wage war on two separate fronts. Grant would go to northern Virginia to face Robert E. Lee, and Sherman would move south to fight Joseph E. Johnston's army and do as much damage as possible to the Confederacy's ability to make war. In summing up the two-day meeting, Sherman offered another quotable, and much-quoted, observation: "He was to go for Lee and I was to go for Joe Johnston."[7]

"You I propose to move against Johnston's army, to break it up and to get into the interior of the enemy's country as far as you can, inflicting all the damage you can against their war resources,"[8] Grant wrote officially, and somewhat awkwardly, to Sherman. The Army of the Potomac, commanded by General George Gordon Meade, would "go for Lee." As general in chief, Grant would go along with General Meade.

Grant made it plain that his objective, and Meade's, was the destruction of Lee's army and not the capture of Richmond. There had been too many "On To Richmond" drives already, all of which had fallen far short of their objective. During the War of Independence, the British had fallen in love with the idea of capturing cities—they took New York early in the war, and also captured Philadelphia—instead of destroying Washington's army in the field. Grant did not intend to make the same mistake. "Lee's army will be your objective point," Grant instructed General Meade. "Wherever Lee goes, you will go also."[9]

The two armies, Sherman's and Meade's, with Grant overseeing both, would be "acting as a unit so far as such a thing was possible over such a vast field." Grant would stay in communication with Sherman via "magnetic telegraph," one of the electronic wonders of the era. "All other troops were employed exclusively in support of these movements"—namely, the destruction of Lee's and Johnston's armies.[10]

President Lincoln was not in attendance during the meeting, but he would have approved of what Grant and Sherman had decided to do. The president had not even been invited, but probably would not have come if he had been. He was well aware that his military background was limited in the extreme and preferred his generals to act independently—especially Grant and Sherman, who were among the few Union generals in whom he had confidence. If anyone could bring victory to the Union—and help him get re-elected to the White House in November—it was Ulysses S. Grant and William Tecumseh Sherman.

After two days of talking and deciding and looking at maps, the two men said good-bye to each other. They shook hands warmly and affectionately, like the good friends they were. They had drawn up their grand strategy, and had nothing else to say. Grant and Sherman left Cincinnati on separate roads and would not see each other again for a year. Their journeys would take them to Cold Harbor, Spotsylvania, and Petersburg, Virginia, and Resaca, Jonesborough, Atlanta, and Savannah, Georgia. All their roads would ultimately lead to the sitting room of a man named Wilmer McLean in a little Virginia town called Appomattox Court House.

At the time, neither could have had any idea that their strategy meeting in Cincinnati would have far-reaching effects well beyond the battlefield. Their plans would also have a vital impact on the election, still months in the future, and on who would occupy the White House for the rest of the war. That question was very much in doubt. Lincoln may have been the incumbent, but his re-election as president was anything but a sure thing.

COPPERHEADS AND RADICALS

Abraham Lincoln had only one strategy for the November 1864 election: win another four years in the White House and then win the war. But to accomplish this goal, he would not only have to fight the Democrats, but would also have to do battle with several leading members of his own party.

A good many leading Republicans did not want Lincoln as their candidate. They were resigned to the fact that he probably would be renominated, but they would have preferred somebody else. "The opposition to Mr. Lincoln was secretly cherished by many of the ablest and most patriotic men of the day," wrote Congressman George W. Julian, a Republican from Indiana. "Of the more earnest and thorough-going Republicans in both Houses of Congress, probably not one in ten really favored [Lincoln's renomination]."[11]

The reason behind this opposition was simple: the Republicans thought that Lincoln was going to lose the November election. If the results of the midterm elections of 1862 were anything to go by, Lincoln would not only be defeated, but would be defeated by a very wide margin and would take many other Republicans down with him. The congressional elections of 1862 resulted in a stunning setback for President Abraham Lincoln and the incumbent Republican Party. The Republicans lost 23 seats in the House of Representatives, lowering their percentage of seats from 59 percent to 46 percent, which meant that they also lost control of the House.

Until November 1862, the war had not produced very much cause for celebration in the North. Most of the battles had either been outright defeats or costly victories: First Bull Run in July 1861; Shiloh, Tennessee, in April 1862; the Peninsula Campaign, in Virginia, during June and July 1862; Second Bull Run, August 1862; and Antietam, Maryland, in September 1862. The public reaction to these battles, and the number of dead and wounded they produced, was a combination of shock, anger, and utter disappointment.

Every newspaper account of every battle told the same story—General Robert E. Lee had outfought and outthought and outmaneuvered every general that Lincoln sent to oppose him. Lincoln had fired more than a half dozen generals since the beginning of the war, but every general seemed to be as bad as his predecessor. The only Union general that seemed capable of winning battles was Ulysses S. Grant, but he did not have a very good reputation, either. Everyone was saying that he was a drunk who had no regard for how many of his men were killed in battle.

The public blamed Lincoln and the Republicans for all this: the bad generals, the horrendous casualties, and the continuation of the war. By the spring of 1864, the overall opinion of Lincoln and his party had not improved since 1862. The year and a half that had passed since the midterm elections had produced Union victories at Gettysburg and Vicksburg, but had also seen humiliations at Fredericksburg and Chancellorsville. The fighting went on, the number of dead and wounded continued to increase alarmingly, but the end of the war never seemed to come any nearer.

Lincoln and the Republicans were unpopular for other reasons as well. Thousands considered Lincoln a dictator and a tyrant—he imprisoned dissenters who spoke out against the government and suspended the writ of habeas corpus. Others opposed the draft, which had gone into effect during the spring of 1863. Also, the price of everything, from food to clothing to just about any other item needed to carry on with day-to-day life, had sky-rocketed since the beginning of the war. And many thousands opposed the Emancipation Proclamation—fighting to restore the Union was one thing, but sending men out to be killed to free the slaves was something else again. But the major objection to Lincoln and the Republican Party was the war and the way it was being run.

For the Democrats, this turning of public opinion was nothing short of miraculous. When Abraham Lincoln was elected in 1860, the future of the Democratic Party looked anything but encouraging. Prospects became even less encouraging when the Southern states seceded from the Union and took all their Democratic voters with them. To make matters even worse, one of the stalwarts of the party, Stephen A. Douglas, died in June 1861. Douglas had been one of the three losing presidential candidates in 1860. His death left a gaping hole in the Democratic Party's leadership. It began to look as though the Republicans would control Congress and the White House at least until 1868. But the 1862 elections, coupled with the way public opinion had turned against Lincoln, gave the Democrats a new burst of hope.

Democratic hopes for the 1864 election were bolstered even further by infighting within the Republican Party. A splinter group, calling themselves the Radicals, had broken away from the main body of the party. The Radical Republicans separated themselves from Lincoln and the rest of the party on the grounds that Lincoln was not antislavery enough to suit them and was not pursuing a more forceful all-out war against the South. Most of the Radicals were even more anti-Lincoln than the Democrats.

One of the most outspoken and ruthless of the anti-Lincoln Republicans was the party's floor leader, Thaddeus Stevens, of Pennsylvania. Thad Stevens was one of the leaders of the Radicals, and he was proud of it. He did not like Abraham Lincoln or any of his policies, especially his policy of leniency toward the Confederacy. Lincoln wanted to bring the South back into the Union as gently as possible and to forgive all past differences when the war was over. Not Thad Stevens. Stevens wanted a Carthaginian peace; his goal was to crush the rebel states and devastate the South. He wanted no part of Lincoln's promise of peace with charity and forgiveness. Lincoln offered amnesty to any Confederate who would take an oath of allegiance. Stevens made it clear that he intended to hang Jefferson Davis and any other Confederate that he could get his hands on.

The Radicals detested Lincoln because he did not think like them—he was not radical enough. Besides wanting to wipe out the Confederacy and either execute or imprison every one of its leaders and politicians, the Radicals also wanted to free all the slaves immediately, wherever they happened to be, and they thought that Lincoln did not go far enough with his Emancipation Proclamation. Thad Stevens wanted a more relentlessly antislavery Republican candidate for president in 1864, and all his fellow Radicals agreed. If Stevens and his Radical friends were to have their way, Abraham Lincoln would not be the party's candidate in November.

Author Carl Sandburg called Stevens "a gnarled thorn tree of a man"; he was as tough and nasty as he looked.[12] He had a clubfoot, which gave him a pronounced limp and did not help to sweeten his disposition. He also had a malicious and sarcastic tongue. Anyone who did not agree with him became a potential target for his withering mockery. When Secretary of State William Seward made a speech in 1861, calling for the reconciliation of the North and the South, Stevens reacted to both Seward and his speech with contempt. He said that he listened very carefully to every word that Seward had to say and did not hear one damned thing. Stevens did not want anything to do with reconciliation with the South or with anybody who supported it.

His sarcasm was not just used against political enemies. Hardly the soul of tact or discretion, Stevens had reached the point in his life and political career where he was too old and too powerful to care whether or not he offended anyone. At one point in time, a Pennsylvania woman approached him and asked him for a lock of his hair—Stevens was very popular in Pennsylvania, and won his re-election in 1860 by an overwhelming majority. Stevens was nearly 70 at the time, and he wore a famously ill-fitting wig to cover his bald head. In response to the woman's request, he took his wig off and handed it to his startled admirer.

Stevens preferred to use his mockery and his considerable skills as a faultfinder against Abraham Lincoln. When Lincoln announced that he had ordered a naval blockade of Southern ports, Stevens informed Lincoln that he had as good as recognized Confederate independence. A country does not blockade its own ports, Stevens went on to say, which meant that Lincoln had just implied the sovereignty of the Confederate States of America. Lincoln was not all that impressed by Stevens's remarks, or by what the blockade might imply. Lincoln told Stevens that he did not know anything about international law himself, and that he intended to keep the blockade. This was not exactly a dismissal of Stevens and his point of view, but it came as close to it as Lincoln intended.

Thaddeus Stevens and the Radicals did not think much of Lincoln, either as a candidate or as a president. As far as Stevens was concerned, Lincoln was a dead candidate. Or, as he put it, a dead card in the political deck. When he found out that Lincoln would be going to Gettysburg in November 1863 for the dedication of the national cemetery, Stevens could not resist making another of his sarcastic remarks. He said that Lincoln's trip to Gettysburg would be entirely appropriate—the dead would be eulogizing the dead.

Along with a good many other Republicans, the candidate Stevens wanted to represent the party in November was Salmon P. Chase. Salmon Chase had been one of the potential Republican nominees in 1860 and had also served two terms as governor of Ohio. Chase was in full agreement with Thad Stevens—he wanted to be president more than anything else. At the 1860 Republican convention, he had done his best to obtain the party's nomination, and had received 49 votes out of 465 on the first ballot. But he did not have the necessary support to advance any closer to his goal, so, giving in to the inevitable, he decided to turn his backers and their votes over to Lincoln.

But Salmon Chase never really gave up on the idea of being president. Lincoln appointed him to the post of secretary of the treasury, on the premise that it would be better to have Chase on his side than against him. He became one of the most effective treasury secretaries in American history and left his permanent mark on the US economy. Among his accomplishments was the establishment of a legal paper currency—the first "greenback" notes were printed in 1862. Chase also made certain that his own picture appeared on the one dollar bill—he was already thinking ahead to the 1864 presidential campaign and intended that the humble dollar bill would serve as his election poster, probably the most widely circulated election poster of all time.

Salmon Chase did his best to use the Treasury Department as a stepping-stone to the White House. He did not want a cabinet position, not even a vitally important one. Salmon P. Chase wanted to be the seventeenth president of the United States.

Everybody, including Lincoln, was well aware of the fact that Salmon Chase planned to be the next president in the White House. He certainly made no secret of his ambition. In 1860, he thought that he was the best-qualified candidate for president, and he still thought so. He certainly was the best known of all the challengers to Lincoln, thanks to his appointment as secretary of the treasury, and he was the most electable of all the Radicals. No one would have voted for Thad Stevens—outside of Pennsylvania, his voter appeal was extremely limited, to put it diplomatically. Others were also mentioned as possible candidates for the Republican nomination, including General John C. Fremont and General Benjamin Butler; even Ulysses S. Grant was mentioned. But only Salmon Chase was given a real chance of unseating Lincoln, at least among the Radicals.

As for the Democrats, their prospects entering the 1864 November election could not have looked any brighter—public sentiment had turned against Lincoln and the Republicans because of the war, and, to make the situation even more favorable, the Republicans were turning against each other. The only trouble was that the Democrats were having internal problems of their own, and the war was at the bottom of the problems. The party had been split into two rival factions: the peace faction and the war faction.

The War Democrats backed the Lincoln government's war objectives. Had he lived, Stephen A. Douglas would have been a War Democrat. Douglas openly supported Lincoln, and spoke out for the president and his conduct of the war on more than one occasion. In May 1861, Douglas told a large crowd in Chicago that every man must either be for the United States or against it; there were either patriots or traitors. Many of Douglas's fellow Democrats became War Democrats because of his influence, including Illinois congressman John A. Logan. Quite a few War Democrats merged with the Republicans. Other Democrats supported Lincoln's war efforts and his intention to restore the Union but would not go along with the Republican policy on slavery. These were called Regular Democrats; they would not join with the Republicans.

The Peace Democrats opposed both Lincoln and the War Democrats. They also opposed the war itself. As far as they were concerned, the war with the South had been a total fiasco. The Peace Democrats sounded very much like the anti–Vietnam War Democrats in 1968. The only option that Peace Democrats would consider was to end the war as quickly as possible —stop all fighting immediately, let the Southern states have their independence, and let them keep their slaves.

Peace Democrats were also known as Copperheads, a comparison with the poisonous snake. It was meant to be an insult, but they decided to take it as a compliment. Copperheads wore the head of Liberty, cut from a copper penny, in their lapel buttonholes—a copperhead in the most literal sense. The Peace Democrats had been in existence since the beginning of the war—they were originally known as "Doughfaces"—but thought it best to keep their opinions to themselves in the days immediately following Fort Sumter. A great wave of patriotic feeling had passed through the North at the very beginning of the war. Pro-Southern sympathizers were considered traitors, even worse than the rebels themselves. But after First Bull Run and subsequent Union disasters, the Copperheads began condemning Lincoln and the war openly and publicly, and found a great many voters who shared their point of view.

The champion of the Peace Democrats, their equivalent of Thaddeus Stevens, was Congressman Clement Vallandigham of Ohio. Vallandigham was not nearly as old and gnarled as Thad Stevens—he would turn 44 in July 1864, and is usually described as tall and handsome—but he was just as much of a curmudgeon and was just as outspoken. He was also self-righteous—he was thoroughly convinced that his views on the war, and on every other subject, were the only correct views.

And Clement Vallandigham firmly believed that the war should be brought to an immediate end. "Ought this war to continue?" he shouted to the rest of the House. Answering his own question, he went on: "no—not a day, not an hour."[13] Stop the war right now, Vallandigham insisted. Stop the fighting, declare an immediate armistice, and withdraw all Union troops from the seceded states. Let them have their slaves. Do anything to end the war as soon as possible.

Shortly after this address in the House of Representatives, on May 1, 1863, Vallandigham made another anti-war speech to a sizeable gathering of Democrats in Mount Vernon, Ohio. Quite a few of these loyal Democrats wore copper Liberty heads in their lapels. Vallandigham denounced President Lincoln in ringing tones for not ending the war. Lincoln and his government were damned and blasted for other things as well—the draft, the slavery issue, the suspension of habeas corpus—but the war was Vallandigham's main objection. The crowd certainly liked his delivery, breaking into cheers repeatedly as he called for an immediate end to the war.

This sort of talk was bound to get him into trouble. Four days after his Mount Vernon speech, Vallandigham was rousted out of a sound sleep in the middle of the night by soldiers pounding on his door. He discovered that his house in Dayton had been surrounded by an entire company of men wearing blue uniforms. After breaking down the door—Vallandigham fired a few shots at the soldiers, with no result—the officer in charge informed the bleary-eyed Vallandigham that he was under arrest for violating General Order No. 38.

Vallandigham knew all about General Order No. 38; in Mount Vernon, he said that he opposed the order and also that he spit on it. The first section of the order stated: "The habit of declaring sympathy for the enemy will not be tolerated in this department."

It went on to declare that anyone violating the order would be arrested for treason, tried, and, if found guilty, would either be imprisoned for the duration of the war or "sent beyond our lines into the lines of their friends"—in other words, deported to the Confederacy.[14]

Vallandigham's arrest had been ordered by Major General Ambrose Burnside, who had also issued General Order No. 38. General Burnside had been given command of the Department of the Ohio after the disaster at Fredericksburg and the "Mud March" of January 1863, a failed offensive against Robert E. Lee in the winter rains. He was replaced by Major General Joseph Hooker as commander of the Army of the Potomac. Burnside could not get anywhere near Lee's Army of Northern Virginia from Ohio, which is exactly what Lincoln had in mind, but he could take action against the defeat-talking Copperheads.

A military tribunal heard Vallandigham's case. Vallandigham had very little to say for himself, only insisting that a military court had no right to try him because he was a civilian. The tribunal paid no attention, finding Vallandigham guilty of all charges and sentencing him to be imprisoned for the duration of the war.

Lincoln had just returned from a visit to General Hooker's headquarters when he heard about what had happened to Vallandigham. The news took Lincoln by surprise. He did not particularly like what Burnside had done—he already had enough problems with the Supreme Court because of his suspension of habeas corpus, and he did not want another confrontation. But he did not want to condemn Burnside, either; Burnside believed that he was acting on the president's behalf.

After mulling the problem over, Lincoln remembered the part of General Order No. 38 mentioning that anyone found guilty of violating it could be sent "into the lines of their friends." That struck Lincoln as a neat piece of poetic justice. He decided to send Vallandigham to Tennessee, where he would be safely out of the way but could not be made into a martyr by the Copperheads. As someone later pointed out, Vallandigham was only being sent where his heart already was.

When Vallandigham arrived in Tennessee, the Confederates did not know what to do with him—which is just what Lincoln supposed would happen. The exile did not stay in the South for very long. He went to the West Indies via blockade runner, with the full blessing of Richmond, and turned up in Nova Scotia in July 1863. The Ohio Democratic Convention nominated Vallandigham for governor, and Vallandigham returned to his home state to campaign for the office—Lincoln discreetly looked the other way, not wanting to cause another incident that might make Vallandigham into a Copperhead hero or a martyr. But when Vallandigham lost the election, Lincoln breathed a sigh of relief.

Even with Vallandigham safely disposed of, Lincoln still had a lot to worry about. The Democrats, especially the Peace Democrats, were doing their best to arouse public opinion against both the Emancipation Proclamation and the war—they opposed freeing the slaves just as intensely as they opposed the war. At the other extreme, the Radical Republicans wanted to see the South absolutely crushed and every slave freed immediately. Both sides wanted Lincoln out of the White House.

Lincoln worried about both sides, and what effect they would finally have on the November election. But most of all, Lincoln worried about the war and how he could win it. With the appointment of Ulysses S. Grant as general in chief, he hoped that he had finally found the man who would outfight and outgeneral Robert E. Lee. If Grant could do that, Lincoln would be able to take care of all political doubts and anxieties without any distractions. If Grant would take care of Lee, Lincoln would be free to deal with the Copperheads and the Radicals.

A REAL GENERAL

As far as Lincoln was concerned, Ulysses S. Grant was the first real general he ever had—no matter how much anybody complained about the amount of whiskey he drank. He explained this to William O. Stoddard, a member of the White House staff, shortly after Grant was awarded his third star. Stoddard found Lincoln stretched out on a sofa one Sunday in early 1864, looking completely relaxed and at ease. Lincoln seemed even taller and lankier than usual, which probably had something to do with his loose and easy manner that day. An English magazine described Lincoln as "about six feet in length and thin in proportion, with long, bony arms and legs, which somehow seem always to be in the way."[15] Lincoln did not seem to care about his appearance on that particular Sunday, or about anything else.

Lincoln explained to Stoddard why he felt so free from worry—it was because the weight of the army had been taken from his shoulders by General Grant. All his previous commanders had wanted *him* to be the general, Lincoln said. They had all had the rank and the authority to run the army, but by presenting their plans for campaigns to him for final approval, they had attempted to shift responsibility for the success or failure of their operations from their own shoulders onto his. But Grant was not that way.

Grant did not even inform Lincoln of what he had in mind for his campaign against Lee. Which was fine with Lincoln—he did not want to know. He was glad to find a general who could act on his own and get along without him, a truly independent commander.

As an example, Lincoln told Stoddard about how Grant had reacted to the state of affairs involving a cavalry unit that was stationed near Harper's Ferry, Virginia. The problem with this particular cavalry unit was that it had no horses—about 15,000 cavalrymen and no horses. When Grant took command, Lincoln expected him to complain about this. But the only thing Grant did was to ask if he should disband the men or turn them into infantry. He did not grumble or complain or ask for more men. Grant was the first general who did not do one or the other. Grant also won battles, which was another welcome change from Lincoln's other generals. Just knowing that Grant was going to command came as a great and welcome relief, putting Lincoln in a calmer and more genial mood than Stoddard had ever seen him in.

Abraham Lincoln certainly had more than his share of trouble with just about every one of his generals prior to Ulysses S. Grant. He had gone through seven generals before Grant—eight, if George B. McClellan's two terms were counted separately. In order of their tenure as commander, Lincoln's generals were Winfield Scott, Henry Halleck, and George McClellan as general in chief; John Pope, George McClellan again, Ambrose Burnside, Joseph Hooker, and George Meade as commanders of the Army of the Potomac. George Meade would stay on as commander of the Army of the Potomac, with Grant as his superior.

When Lincoln became president in 1861, General Winfield Scott was commander of the army. Winfield Scott had been a hero of two wars: the War of 1812 and the Mexican War. In 1847, when his army captured Mexico City, Scott was acclaimed as the greatest living general by the Duke of Wellington. But by the time of Fort Sumter, Winfield Scott was a very old 75 years, in poor health, grossly overweight, lacking in energy and

enthusiasm, and falling asleep at staff meetings. He handed Lincoln his res-
ignation from the army in November 1861, citing poor health as the reason.
General Scott was in no condition, physically or mentally, to command the
Union army.

The general who preceded Ulysses S. Grant as general in chief was Major
General Henry W. Halleck, Grant's superior at Fort Henry and Fort
Donelson. Halleck was known as "Old Brains," because he was an expert on
military studies and wrote textbooks on the subject. But after his appointment as commander of the army, and his lack of aptitude as a commander
became readily apparent, the nickname took on a sarcastic meaning. Regulars
called Halleck "Old Brains" in the same way that someone without a hair
on his head is called "Curly," or someone six foot four is called "Shorty."

Halleck tended to look at his appointment as general in chief as a
Washington desk job—just the opposite of Grant, who did not want to
have his headquarters in Washington for fear that he might be trapped
behind a desk for the rest of the war. Even though Halleck was a West Point
graduate, he was no soldier. Lincoln said that he was little better than a first-
rate clerk, and Halleck thought of himself as nothing more than an adviser
to the president and to Secretary of War Edwin M. Stanton. This is one of
the main reasons why Halleck distrusted Grant. Grant was a fighter; Halleck was an administrator, a glorified clerk who could never see anything
Grant's way.

Because of his failure to command the armies in the field, everybody
lost patience with Henry W. Halleck. Gideon Welles, the secretary of the
navy, said that Halleck "originates nothing, anticipates nothing . . . takes no
responsibility, suggests nothing, is good for nothing."[16] Halleck did not
even have the talent for motivating his field commanders, who sometimes
ignored him and his instructions. When Grant received his commission as
lieutenant general, Halleck was demoted to chief of staff, a post that suited
his mind and temperament. In this job, his administrative skills would be
put to work supporting Grant. By demoting Halleck, Lincoln had lost a
general in chief but had now officially gained a first-rate clerk.

Major General Ambrose E. Burnside was another general who turned
out to be a disappointment for Lincoln. A West Point graduate, he seemed

to have all the qualifications for a first-rate commander. In March 1862, Burnside impressed his superiors with his successes at the battles of Roanoke Island and New Bern, North Carolina, and was promoted to major general. He also impressed Lincoln, who was looking for officers who might be able to win a few victories. Roanoke Island and New Bern were among the first Union victories in the East.

Although he was only 38 years old, Burnside gave the appearance of being older. This was largely because of the muttonchop whiskers he wore, which also lent him an air of authority and competence. With his mutton-chops and his high, bald forehead, Burnside gave the impression of being self-assured and confident. Lincoln convinced himself that Ambrose Burnside was not only capable enough to command the Army of the Potomac, but was also the best man for the job.

Burnside did not agree—he did not think he had the talent, the experience, or the ability to command an army, and he refused Lincoln's offer twice. In spite of his appearance, Burnside was anything but self-assured and confident. But Lincoln kept after Burnside until he reluctantly accepted. It was a decision both men would come to regret.

On November 7, 1862, Burnside became commander of the Army of the Potomac and began to plan an offensive against Lee. His strategy for the offensive was to march his army to Fredericksburg, Virginia, capture the heights outside the town, overpower Lee's army, and begin a quick movement south toward Richmond. Lincoln approved the plan with misgivings, advising Burnside to move with all possible speed—he knew from past experience that Robert E. Lee could always be counted upon to do something to outsmart, outthink, and outmaneuver his opponent, no matter how brilliant the plan might seem to be at the time.

Lincoln's misgivings were well founded. The Battle of Fredericksburg, on December 13, 1862, turned out to be another Union disaster. Because of delays in Burnside's attack—some his fault, some not—General Lee had time to concentrate his defenses and repulse every one of the Union army's repeated frontal attacks. The Army of the Potomac suffered almost 13,000 casualties—dead, wounded, and missing—in the fighting. Lee sustained just over 5,000 casualties, and held his position on the heights outside Fredericksburg.

Even though General Burnside insisted that all the blame for Fredericksburg be placed on him and him alone, the public thought that the disaster was Lincoln's fault. Radical Republicans shared this opinion and used Fredericksburg as another reason for replacing Lincoln as the Republican candidate in November. The Radicals wanted a more aggressive and assertive—and destructive—war against the Confederacy, and did not think that Lincoln had it in him to conduct that kind of war. Salmon Chase wanted Secretary of State William H. Seward to resign—Chase thought that Seward had too much influence on Lincoln, and that another Radical should be secretary of state.

The Radicals declared that something had to be done, and quickly, to reverse the succession of Union military setbacks. In other words, if the Republicans seriously intended to win the November election, the North had better start winning battles and Lincoln had better find a general who could outfight Robert E. Lee. Lincoln could not have agreed more. He knew he had the men and the resources to defeat the Confederacy, but he lacked the commanding general who was up to the job. He was doing his best to find that general.

After the Battle of Fredericksburg, Lincoln knew that Ambrose E. Burnside was not the general he was looking for. Fredericksburg cost General Burnside the confidence of Lincoln, as well as of his subordinate officers. His next campaign after Fredericksburg lowered Burnside's reputation even further.

In January 1863, Burnside began another offensive against Lee's army. His plan was to cross the Rappahannock River and attack the Confederate flank above Fredericksburg. But the campaign literally bogged down in the heavy rain and resulting mud that turned all the roads into swamps. The aborted attack—Burnside turned back after two days—became known as the Mud March. It was another fiasco for Burnside, but at least this one was a bloodless fiasco.

At this stage, the morale of the Army of the Potomac had reached its lowest point, along with Lincoln's confidence in Ambrose Burnside. When Burnside resigned his command, Lincoln accepted his resignation. He assigned the hapless general to the Department of the Ohio, where his arrest of Clement Vallandigham would cause Lincoln embarrassment of a different sort. Burnside had been in command of the Army of the Potomac from November 7, 1862, to January 25, 1863, less than three months. The Army of the Potomac needed another commander; Lincoln hoped for better luck with his next choice.

Lincoln chose Major General Joseph Hooker to replace Burnside. Hooker would at least be a fighting general, it seemed to Lincoln—even his nickname, "Fighting Joe," was encouraging. Hooker's credentials seemed encouraging as well—a West Point graduate, a veteran of the Seminole War and the Mexican War, and also a veteran of Antietam, Fredericksburg, and the Peninsula Campaign. Throughout the army he was known as courageous and aggressive, but he also had a reputation for being coarse, vulgar, and a heavy drinker. Lincoln knew all about Hooker's defects, but hoped that his fighting qualities would counterbalance the darker side of his personality. Lincoln needed a general who could win, who could beat Robert E. Lee, and he was willing to overlook any and all negative personality traits from anyone who could bring him a victory.

As the Army of the Potomac's new commander, Hooker certainly got off to an excellent start. Throughout the late winter and early spring of 1863, Hooker saw to it that all worn-out equipment was replaced, everything from boots to artillery caissons, and he also made certain that the men were well fed with top-quality rations. He did everything possible to raise the army's morale after it had been crushed following the Fredericksburg disaster.

In April, Lincoln paid a visit to Hooker. He wanted to talk about the army's spring campaign, and also wanted to know exactly what Hooker had in mind regarding Robert E. Lee and his Army of Northern Virginia. The Army of the Potomac was well rested by this time, and Lee was still dug in at Fredericksburg. Lincoln wanted Hooker to be aware that his main objective was Lee's army, and not Richmond. The details of Hooker's spring offensive were not all that important to him, as long as Hooker was going after Lee. The destruction of Lee's army was the only thing that mattered.

Hooker gave a great deal of thought about what to do, and finally decided that his best course of action would be to split his force. He would keep part of his force in reserve to attack Lee's front at Fredericksburg, and he would send the main body, about 70,000 men, up the Rappahannock to attack the Confederates from the rear. On May 1, the flanking force crossed the river west of Fredericksburg and began advancing toward Lee's army.

But General Lee guessed what Hooker was up to. He divided his own force as well—about a quarter of his men were kept at Fredericksburg, while Thomas J. "Stonewall" Jackson's corps moved to block Hooker's advance. When the Confederates reached the edge of a part of Spotsylvania County, Virginia, known as the Wilderness, Hooker's troops moved out to meet them. The Wilderness was a dense thicket of underbrush, sapling trees, and malevolence that could break an advancing line and hide everything from view, including enemy troops that were only 100 yards ahead. But the fighting had only just started when Hooker ordered a retreat to Chancellorsville, which consisted of the large house owned by the Chancellor family near the Wilderness. Hooker had lost his nerve, and Lee gained the initiative. At the Chancellorsville house, Hooker set up a defensive position. But he left his right flank "in the air"—unprotected and vulnerable to attack.

On the following day, Lee sent Stonewall Jackson's corps, about 28,000 men, through the Wilderness to attack Hooker's exposed right flank. Hooker received several reports that a large rebel force was approaching, but he ignored them. Jackson hit Hooker's men late in the day, taking them completely by surprise, and chased them for two miles. The rout was ended only because of nightfall. This would not be the last time the Army of the Potomac would find itself tangled up in the Wilderness. A year later, it would fight another battle there, under a very different commanding general.

Lee attacked Hooker again on May 3. Hooker was hurt when a shell hit Chancellorsville house, splitting a beam he was leaning against. Even though he was stunned by the impact of the shell, he refused to relinquish command. His troops put up a good fight, but Hooker seemed to have been paralyzed both physically and mentally and did not shift infantry reinforcements to areas where they were vitally needed. Having lost all confidence in his troops, as well as in himself, Hooker ordered a retreat. On May 6, in spite of objections from his officers, he recrossed the Rappahannock during a driving rainstorm. His defeat had been total. To Lincoln's disappointment, Fighting Joe certainly did not live up to his nickname.

Lee's victory had been as dazzling as Hooker's defeat had been humiliating. But the Battle of Chancellorsville had been a pyrrhic victory—Chancellorsville cost Lee much more than he could afford to pay. Hooker lost 17,000 men, but Lee lost 13,000, which was almost a quarter of his army. The South could not replace its men nearly as easily as the North, and Lee felt his losses much more desperately.

But the most urgently felt loss of all was Stonewall Jackson, Lee's best corps commander and his most gifted tactical commander. Jackson had been shot by his own pickets while returning to the Confederate lines after a night reconnaissance. Two bullets shattered his left arm, which was amputated on the following day. He died of pneumonia on May 10. Lee knew all too well that Jackson was irreplaceable—he said that Jackson might have lost his left arm, but he had lost his right arm.

President Lincoln did not focus on Lee's losses, however; he was too preoccupied with his own. During the first days of May, Lincoln waited anxiously for news about Hooker and his army—there had been word that fighting had started, but there had been no definite news regarding the battle's progress. The lack of information struck Secretary of the Navy Gideon Welles as a bad sign; if Hooker had succeeded in his attempt to trap Lee and his army, somebody would have heard about it. Lincoln was beginning to have doubts of his own, but he kept them to himself, hoping against hope that no news was good news.

On the afternoon of May 4, a telegram from Hooker's chief of staff ended the mystery along with any remaining optimism. The Union forces had been decisively defeated and had recrossed the Rappahannock, the telegram reported. The Battle of Chancellorsville had been another fiasco. Lincoln's newspaper correspondent friend Noah Brooks was with Lincoln at the White House when the news came through. Brooks had never seen the president so shaken; as he read the telegram, Lincoln paced back and forth across the room, saying, "My God! My God! What will the country say! What will the country say!"[17]

The country—that is, the North—was shocked and disappointed by another defeat, and another bloodbath. "Another terrible battle has been fought, and more fields crimsoned with human blood," began an article in the May 5, 1863, edition of the *New York Times*. "Few more days such as this will find no enemies left on either side to fight battles."[18] Four days later, the *New York Times* ran a full-page "List of Killed and Wounded at the Washington Hospitals." The list, which consisted of more than six columns of names, tightly spaced, gave an even more graphic image of the carnage at Chancellorsville than any of the previous articles describing the battle.[19]

Lincoln was as upset by the casualty list as everybody else, but he had an additional reason for being upset—the Copperheads and the Radical Republicans, each to further their own agendas, were using the dead and wounded to stop Lincoln's re-election in November.

The men of the Army of the Potomac were looking for the same thing as Abraham Lincoln—a general who had the brains and the will and the tenacity to stand toe to toe with Robert E. Lee and beat him. They knew that they were much better than they had shown so far, and that the failures they had suffered on the battlefield were not their fault. After Chancellorsville, everyone knew that it was only a matter of time before Hooker was replaced. When Lincoln appointed General George Gordon Meade as the army's commander on June 28, the men were not exactly elated—no soldier is ever elated by a new commanding officer. They knew that Meade had a reputation for being crusty and bad tempered, but they hoped that he would at least represent an improvement over Hooker and Burnside. Lincoln hoped so as well.

Everyone would find out soon enough just how good General Meade really was. By the time he had been appointed as the Army of the Potomac's newest commander, Robert E. Lee and his army had already left Virginia and were moving north into Pennsylvania. Nobody knew exactly where Lee was headed—Lincoln himself thought his objective was to sack Philadelphia—but now it was up to Meade to stop him. Lincoln knew what was being said about Meade, that his men called him a "goddamned goggle-eyed old snapping turtle," but he did not care about that. All that mattered was that Meade stop Lee before he could get as far as Philadelphia or any other Northern city. Lincoln's campaign for the White House, and his political career, depended upon it.

The two armies, Lee's and Meade's, came together at the small seminary town of Gettysburg. "Gettysburg was an act of fate," historian Bruce Catton wrote, "a three-day explosion of storm and flame and terror, unplanned and unavoidable."[20] At the end of the third day, July 3, 1863, Lee had been decisively defeated. Both armies had mauled each other—the Union had lost about 23,000 men and the Confederates had lost about 28,000. But Lee got the worst of it, and withdrew across the Potomac and into Virginia. Lincoln could breathe a sigh of relief, at long last. He finally had a victory to celebrate.

But he had expected more. Meade had not gone after Lee as the Confederates retreated toward the Potomac, and had allowed the Army of Northern Virginia to escape. Lincoln hoped and expected that Meade would destroy Lee's army, not just chase it out of Pennsylvania. When he was told what happened, Lincoln was furious—Meade had the enemy in his grasp, he complained, but let him get away.

After thinking about the battle and its outcome, however, Lincoln had second thoughts. Although he was still unhappy that the final result of the battle had not been more conclusive and that Meade had not been more aggressive—Lincoln compared Lee's escape to planting an enormous crop and then not harvesting it—he reached the conclusion that Meade had done his best. He was grateful that General Meade had done so much, and he decided not to censure the general for not having done more. He might have wondered what Burnside or Hooker would have done at Gettysburg. After some initial misgivings by Lincoln, Meade stayed on as commander of the Army of the Potomac.

By the time of Gettysburg, Lincoln was glad to have someone like Meade at the head of the army. He may not have been brilliant, but at least he was competent. This was more than he could have said about most of his generals. All of them seemed capable enough until the shooting started, but all of them—Hooker, Halleck, Burnside, and Major General John Pope, who was thoroughly routed at the second battle of Bull Run—turned out to be anything but capable. Every one had either been too cautious, too inept, or both.

But the general who had given Lincoln the most anxiety and sleepless nights was George B. McClellan, who had looked so utterly brilliant at the beginning of the war. If anyone had seemed the natural commander of all the Union forces, it was George Brinton McClellan. He was another West Point graduate with a glittering résumé: he served with distinction in the Mexican War; he had been appointed major general only a month after Fort Sumter; and he won two impressive, although small, battles in western Virginia. After the Union army's first major setback at the first battle of Bull Run, Lincoln sent for McClellan to reorganize the badly beaten and demoralized army. McClellan certainly rose to the occasion.

General McClellan not only reorganized the army, he transformed it. He instilled discipline into the unruly and despondent men, and he made certain that infantry noncommissioned officers drilled their men hard. Cavalrymen learned how to wheel their horses and ride formations. Artillerymen had their own drill, and learned how to fire their guns efficiently and effectively. Everybody seemed inspired by their new general; the men affectionately called him Little Mac. Morale went from rock bottom to superlative; the army was gaining the confidence it would need in the coming campaign against the Confederates. The Army of the Potomac was McClellan's army; he created it.

When the weary and infirm old General Winfield Scott retired as general in chief of all the Union armies, Lincoln appointed McClellan to replace him. To Lincoln, Little Mac seemed the best man for the job, an opinion that McClellan shared completely and wholeheartedly. McClellan thought the appointment was fitting—he *should* be general in chief because he was so brilliant. People had been telling him how smart, talented, and clever he was for so many years that he had come to believe it himself. McClellan certainly was greatly talented. He did have a flair for organizing and for administration, as well as for motivating and inspiring his men. But, as he would soon find out, it would take a lot more than that to lead an army into battle, especially against Robert E. Lee.

The first campaign that McClellan commanded, which would be known as the Peninsula Campaign, was a gigantic expedition. It had two objectives—capture Richmond and overwhelm any Confederate force that came out to confront the Army of the Potomac. But the only thing it actually accomplished was to point out McClellan's two most glaring weaknesses: his indecision and his overcautiousness.

McClellan's grand campaign certainly started out grandly enough. He moved his army by steamboat to the peninsula in Virginia between the York and the James Rivers. From there he planned to march it up the peninsula and then on to Richmond. McClellan's force was massive: more than 120,000 men and 15,000 horses. As he began his move toward the Confederate capital, he came face to face with an enemy force that had dug in at Yorktown. Even though he had more than twice as many men as the Confederate commander, Joseph E. Johnston, McClellan managed to convince himself that he was vastly outnumbered. Instead of attacking, he settled down to a methodical siege of the enemy trenches. Nobody but George B. McClellan would have hesitated to launch a major assault, which would have driven the enemy out of Yorktown. This would have given President Lincoln, and the North, a morale-building victory.

The Union army stayed in front of the trenches at Yorktown for a month while McClellan brought up mortars and other siege equipment. Lincoln ordered McClellan to do something, to make some sort of attack on the enemy position. McClellan ignored Lincoln and continued to prepare his siege. Joseph E. Johnston waited until McClellan had completed all of his siege preparations before vacating the trenches and moving up the peninsula. McClellan declared that he had won a victory for the Union.

Following the Peninsula Campaign, things only got worse for McClellan—and for Lincoln. McClellan, still convinced that he was outnumbered, refused to attack Johnston's army and advance on Richmond. Johnston attacked McClellan on May 31 at Seven Pines and Fair Oaks Station. At Fair Oaks, General Johnston was severely wounded; his injuries left him unable to carry on as commander. President Jefferson Davis replaced him with Robert E. Lee. The Confederate forces facing McClellan were renamed the Army of Northern Virginia.

Johnston had allowed McClellan the luxury of moving as slowly as he wanted and doing as little as possible. But Lee had no intention of letting the Union army remain at large in Virginia. In the Seven Days' Battles—as the week's fighting between June 26 and July 2 came to be known—Lee and

Stonewall Jackson outfought and outmaneuvered McClellan and his army, even though McClellan managed to inflict higher losses—Lee lost 20,000 men while McClellan lost 15,000. McClellan had the chance to break through to Richmond, but Lee had guessed that his opponent was much too cautious to try anything that daring. Instead, the Union forces retreated; McClellan wanted to bring his troops under the protection of navy gunboats that occupied the lower James River. His officers pleaded with him to counterattack, but McClellan refused.

By this time, Lincoln was totally exasperated. Although McClellan had more men and better equipment than Lee, he did not have the nerve to do anything with them. Lincoln's brilliant young general had turned out to be anything but. McClellan would not follow orders, would not listen to suggestions, and would not take advantage of opportunities to defeat Lee. The newspapers once lionized McClellan, referring to him as "Little Napoleon." But after the Peninsula and the Seven Days battles, they called him things like "Mac the unready." A subordinate called McClellan the Virginia Creeper. Lincoln said that McClellan suffered from a malady known as the Slows. Hoping that he might be able to provide some motivation and incentive to his overcautious general, Lincoln went to visit McClellan in the field. But McClellan stubbornly refused to be inspired or motivated. Instead, he demanded another 50,000 men if Lincoln and the War Department expected him to mount another offensive against Lee.

Lincoln had already suspended McClellan as general in chief on March 11, hoping that limiting his authority to the command of the Army of the Potomac might make him more effective. Since that had not worked, Lincoln's next step was to relieve McClellan from commanding the Army of the Potomac, replacing him with General John Pope. McClellan thought that Lincoln was making the biggest mistake of his life.

When General Pope faced Lee at the second battle of Bull Run, the Army of the Potomac was routed again and driven back to the fortifications around Washington. Lincoln rapidly reached the conclusion that Pope was not the solution to the McClellan problem but was just another problem. He sent Pope off to Minnesota to put down a Sioux uprising and recalled McClellan. It was not a decision he made with any enthusiasm. He hoped that McClellan might be able to restore the army's self-confidence. Little Mac had done it once before; maybe he could do it again.

The men of the Army of the Potomac certainly were happy to see their old commander; they still thought of themselves as members of McClellan's army. McClellan was overjoyed to be back. In his humble opinion, the army could not have been placed in better hands. But, as Lincoln would soon find out, McClellan had not changed at all.

Early in September 1862, General Lee took his army across the Potomac into Maryland. He was hoping to inflict another Bull Run on the Union forces, except this time on their own ground. Another Union setback might even convince Great Britain to grant official diplomatic recognition to the Confederacy. But his battle plans had been discovered and turned over to McClellan and his staff—the document was found in an envelope, wrapped around three cigars. McClellan knew exactly where Lee was going, and also that Lee had divided his army into two sections. If he moved fast enough, McClellan would be able to destroy each section separately and end the war.

But moving fast was never one of McClellan's strong points. Even though he had Lee's orders and knew his intentions, McClellan did not attack. For 18 vital hours, he did absolutely nothing. On September 17, the armies of McClellan and Lee met near the town of Sharpsburg, Maryland, above Antietam Creek. McClellan totally mismanaged his forces. Among other things, he withheld about one-third of his army, which did not fire a shot during the entire battle, and he also failed to support an attack by General Burnside. As one of Lee's officers later remarked, McClellan brought superior forces to the battle but, unfortunately for the Army of the Potomac, he also brought himself.

Superior Union forces saved the day for the Army of the Potomac, not its commanding general. McClellan lost more than 12,000 men at Antietam; Lee lost over 10,000. But even though the Union forces suffered heavier losses, Lee lost a higher percentage of his troops—about 25 percent of his 40,000 men. More Americans were killed and wounded at the Battle of Antietam than on any other single day during the entire Civil War, or any other war—including D-Day in June 1944.

With one-quarter of his army out of the fight, Lee had no choice but to withdraw to Virginia. Tactically, the fight had been a draw. But strategically it had been a Confederate reversal, and Lee knew it. His invasion of the North had ended. He retreated toward the Potomac and waited for McClellan to attack his depleted army.

President Lincoln waited for McClellan to attack as well. But, as usual, McClellan did nothing. Lee recrossed the Potomac on the night of September 18–19; McClellan let him go. Even though Lincoln now had the victory he needed to issue the Emancipation Proclamation—actually, he would issue an announcement that the final proclamation would go into effect on January 1, 1863—it was not the victory that he wanted.

After Antietam, McClellan refused to follow Lee into Virginia, in spite of orders from both Lincoln and the War Department. All anybody heard from McClellan were excuses and complaints. He complained that he did not have enough men—McClellan always complained that he did not have enough men. He complained that he did not have enough horses and that the horses he did have were sore and fatigued. He complained that he did not have enough supplies, even though his own quartermaster said that the army was already very well supplied.

When McClellan finally did decide to move into Virginia, it took nine days for the army to cross the Potomac. And once in Virginia, the army moved so slowly that Lee was left to move at will. For all the good he had done, McClellan might just as well have stayed in Maryland.

Lincoln had seen enough and had had enough of George B. McClellan. On November 7, he finally relieved McClellan of the command of the Army of the Potomac. McClellan took it graciously enough, although he wrote to his wife that he feared for the country now that he was no longer commanding the army. He said good-bye to the troops and left for New Jersey, where he would wait for orders from the War Department. The orders would never come. When McClellan finally did receive his summons, it would be from the Democratic Party, not the army.

As Lincoln said to Secretary of State William O. Stoddard one year and four months after firing McClellan, Ulysses S. Grant was the first real general he ever had. He had had just about everything else: incompetents, glorified clerks, nervous Nellies, bunglers, and complainers. Grant was none of these things, Lincoln told Stoddard. Grant was a fighter. Lincoln had given him a free hand, and had complete faith in his new general in chief. If Grant could win in Virginia like he had done at Shiloh, Fort Donelson, and Vicksburg, Lincoln was not going to worry about how he planned to go about it.

Stoddard pointed out that Virginia was not Vicksburg, and also that Grant had not faced Robert E. Lee at Shiloh, Fort Donelson, or Vicksburg, but Lincoln did not seem to be worried by this observation. He was sure that Grant would carry on in Virginia just as he had done in the West, Lee or no Lee. The president was content that Grant was the man—and the general—that he had been looking for all along. Grant would take care of the fighting, and would leave Lincoln to take care of politics. If everything went the way he expected it to go, Grant would win the war, and he would win another four years as president.

Stoddard had often seen Lincoln when he was tired and preoccupied, lost in thought about the war. This had been especially true during the preceding weeks, when the coming spring campaign against the South began occupying so much of his time. But on this particular Sunday, the president did not seem to have a care in the world. His face beamed with contentment and confidence.

Chapter Two

CAMPAIGNS BEGINNING

NO TURNING BACK

At the end of April 1864, while he was waiting for something to happen on both the political and military fronts, Abraham Lincoln's nerves began to get the better of him. He was well aware that General Grant would be setting off against Robert E. Lee very soon, now that spring had finally arrived, and Lincoln wanted to send him a message of encouragement. Grant had not issued any orders as yet, not to General Meade, the commander of the Army of the Potomac, or to anybody else. But the president knew that it would be only a matter of days before Grant set the armies in motion, and he wanted to say a few things to his general. He also knew exactly what effect Grant's campaign in Virginia would have on his own drive to be re-elected in November.

The letter that President Lincoln sent to Grant, dated April 30, 1864, is an odd mixture of motivation and anxiety. "Lieutenant General Grant: Not expecting to see you again before the Spring campaign opens, I wish to express, in this way, my entire satisfaction with what you have done up to this time, so far as I understand it. The particulars of your plan I neither know, or seek to know."

Although Lincoln wanted to express his faith in his new lieutenant general, he also remembered that Grant had not yet faced Lee. "You are vigilant and self-reliant, and, pleased with this, I wish not to obtrude any constraints or restraints upon you," he went on, before coming to the point. "While I am very anxious that any great disaster, or the capture of our men in great numbers, shall be avoided"—the possibility of another disaster in Virginia weighed on Lincoln's mind—"I know these points are less likely to escape your attention than they would be mine—If there is anything wanting which is within my power to give, do not fail to let me know it." Lincoln wanted to do everything possible to help Grant succeed, knowing that if Grant succeeded, he would also succeed.

Lincoln closed with: "And now with a brave army, and a just cause, may God sustain you. Very truly yours, A. Lincoln."[1]

He would never have sent such a letter to any of his previous generals—not to the overcautious McClellan, the overmatched Burnside, the inept Hooker, or any of the others. And he was profoundly glad that he would not have to depend upon Hooker, Burnside, or McClellan in the days and months to come, when the success or failure of the Union armies would determine his own political future.

On May 3, General Meade finally received the orders that he—and President Lincoln—had been waiting for. He was notified by General Grant to begin moving the Army of the Potomac out of its winter quarters and to prepare to move south. The order was passed down the chain of command: to the commanders of the many units within the army and down to the colonels and the captains and the lieutenants and the noncoms, and the great body of men began to stir. Regiment after regiment formed up and, on May 4, started moving out of their camps near Culpeper and Brandy Station and headed toward Chancellorsville and the Wilderness.

General Henry Halleck also received notice from General Grant, short and terse, like the general himself. "The army moves to-morrow morning. Will occupy Germanna, Ely's and Culpeper Mine Fords by daylight the morning of the 4th."[2] Going after Lee meant crossing the Rapidan River. Grant took possession of all three fords early on May 4, and his engineers built pontoon bridges across them. The Wilderness was just south of the Rapidan fords. Later in the day, the Army of the Potomac surged across the narrow bridges to meet its old enemy, the Army of Northern Virginia.

On the same day, over 300 miles to the southwest, General William Tecumseh Sherman also began moving south, into Georgia. Grant's long-awaited spring campaign had started at last. Nobody realized it at the time, but this would also turn out to be the first day of Abraham Lincoln's re-election campaign.

By early May, the roads of northern Virginia had thoroughly dried from the winter rains, but the spring sunshine had turned the heavy, sticky mud into about three inches of dirt. The thick coating of dust was as much of a problem as the mud had been—at the end of even the shortest of marches, everyone found themselves covered with it. One private thought that everybody "looked like walking dirt heaps" at the end of the day.[3] The clouds of dust churned up by the men also served as a warning to enemy observers—the great brown haze could be seen from miles away.

The weather had been warm and sunny for over a week, which made marching much easier than it would have been in the rain, in spite of the dust. It would almost have been a pleasure to go hiking in such weather if they had been going someplace else. But everybody knew exactly where they were going, and what would be in store for them when they got there. An officer on Meade's staff wondered how it would look if every man destined to be killed in the coming campaign wore a large badge.

At around noon on May 4, General Grant himself crossed the Rapidan at Germanna Ford. He came to an abandoned farmhouse on the south side of the river and dismounted his big bay horse, Cincinnati, to sit on the porch and watch the army pass by. By that time, a sizable portion of the army had already crossed at Germanna Ford and nearby Ely's Ford, six miles away. It took a while to move an army that size—between 116,000 and 122,000 men, depending upon which source is consulted, along with 50,000 horses—and the last wagon would not make its crossing until the afternoon of May 5.

While the line of wagons was still making its crossing, at 7:30 in the morning, Grant received his first message regarding the Confederate army. "The enemy have appeared in force on the Orange Pike, and are now reported forming line of battle in front of Griffin's Division, Fifth Corps," General Meade reported from Wilderness Tavern. "I have directed General Warren to attack them at once with his whole force." Meade went on to say that he thought the enemy was only trying to delay the army's movement and would not stand and fight, "but we shall see."[4]

Less than an hour later, Grant sent his reply. "Burnside's advance is now crossing the river," he said. "As soon as I can see Burnside I will go forward." He closed by telling Meade, "If any opportunity presents itself for pitching into a part of Lee's army, do so without giving time for disposition."[5] It was typical Grant—hit the enemy as soon as you can and as hard as you can, and do not let anything distract you from making your attack.

Grant was hoping to move right through the Wilderness and confront Lee in the open country to the south. He definitely did not want to fight in the Wilderness, an area of about 64 square miles of underbrush, saplings, and roots in which it was difficult to walk and impossible to ride a horse. The word most often used to describe the Wilderness is "tangled"—it was a tangle of roots and vines and brambles and tree branches. "No one but the devil himself would choose such ground for a field of battle," veterans of the Union army said, "the devil and old man Lee."[6]

Lee had a good reason for picking the Wilderness as his battlefield. He knew very well that the tangle of the woods would negate Grant's numerical superiority in troops. Veterans who had fought in the Wilderness at the battle of Chancellorsville a year earlier remembered that the woods were so dense that nobody could see more than 50 yards in front of him. In those surroundings, the Union advantage in numbers meant nothing—it was impossible to keep any kind of unit formation, or to bring any concentration of firepower to bear. The soldiers came across many skeletons from the previous May's battle, uncovered from their shallow graves by the rains, and had a bad feeling about fighting in this forbidding place again.

But Grant was not one to back away from a battle—if Lee wanted to fight in the Wilderness, he would give Lee what he wanted. As the two sides made contact, and the fighting became louder and heavier, Meade gave orders to bring units up. The men arrived at the edge of the Wilderness, but because of the gun smoke and the undergrowth no enemy could be seen. The muzzle flashes of the rifled muskets started brush fires, which made visibility even more limited. No one could see anything; men simply fired at what they hoped was the enemy.

General Meade was wrong when he told Grant that the enemy was only trying to delay the army's movement. Lee was making a full-scale fight of it.

Major General Gouverneur K. Warren's 5th Corps attacked in force, as Meade had ordered, but his men were having a hard time just locating the enemy. They were told to move toward the heaviest firing, but that did not help at all—the firing seemed to be coming from everywhere at once.

Men did their best to take cover wherever they could—behind fallen trees or stumps, or lying flat on the ground if they could not find anything to shelter behind. Anyone who stood up or wandered out into the open was almost certain to be shot. Everyone on both sides loaded and fired as fast as they could. Their bullets hit saplings and cut them in half, hit the ground like rainfall—and hit men, killing and wounding by the hundreds. More officers were hit than enlisted men; the gold trim on their uniforms and their shiny swords stood out in the gloom, making them more inviting targets. A Zouave unit, some of General Warren's men, suffered especially heavy losses. The Zouaves' bright red and yellow uniforms, patterned on those worn by French units in North Africa, were just as conspicuous as the officers' gold braid. Their gaudy trousers and tunics probably made them the most visible soldiers in the Wilderness.

"The toll and crackle of the musketry was something terrible, even to the veterans of many battles," recalled Private Warren Goss of the 2nd Massachusetts Artillery. "The lines were very near each other, and from the dense underbrush and the tops of trees came puffs of smoke, the 'ping' of the bullets, and the yell of the enemy." Private Goss went on to describe what it was like to fight in the Wilderness. "The underbrush and briars scratched our faces, tore our clothing, and tripped our feet from under us constantly."[7]

Through all of this, General Grant remained outwardly cool and composed. He was dressed in his best uniform and frock coat—he is usually described as being all dressed up—with a sash around his waist and a sword at his side and tan dress gloves. It looked as though he had come for a parade instead of a battle. Throughout the morning, he sat on a tree stump and smoked one cigar after another. While he was smoking, he also kept busy by whittling twigs with a pocketknife he always carried—whittling helped to calm his nerves. His pocketknife kept snagging the fingers of the gloves and soon left them frayed and ragged. While he sat whittling and smoking, staff officers kept him informed of the battle's progress. Grant kept a cool eye on the fighting as it developed, reading dispatches and sending new units into the fray.

In spite of the smoke and the tangle of underbrush, the Union forces were not only standing their ground but were beginning to push the Confederates back. Major General Winfield Scott Hancock's corps pressed forward with their attack in spite of heavy losses. General George W. Getty's division alone lost over 1,000 men in the fighting, and Confederate Major General A. P. Hill was forced to give way to the determined Union attacks.

Brushfires had started among the dead leaves and in the dense scrub; they began to merge into larger fires, which were fanned into a roaring forest fire by the wind. The smoke added to the confusion, making it even more difficult to locate the enemy. Wounded men, soldiers who had been shot and were too badly injured to walk, desperately tried to drag themselves away from the approaching flames. Some were able to crawl to safety; the lucky ones were rescued by their comrades. But not everyone managed to get away. A Union general estimated that a least 200 Federal troops were burned alive by the Wilderness fires.

"The uproar of battle continued through the twilight hours," Private Goss from Massachusetts later wrote. "It was eight o'clock before the deadly crackle of musketry died gradually away and the sad shadows of night, like a pall, fell over the dead in these ensanguined thickets." After the firing stopped, the "groans and cries" of the wounded replaced the sound of gunfire. "This ended the first day's fighting of the Army of the Potomac under Grant."[8]

The second day did not offer any respite. Grant wanted to begin the attack at four o'clock in the morning, on May 6. He knew that another 14,000 Confederates under General James Longstreet would be reinforcing Lee sometime during the morning, and he wanted to attack before Longstreet arrived. But Meade persuaded Grant to postpone the attack for an hour to give his commanders more time to put his disorganized troops in order— they were still exhausted and disordered from the previous day's fighting.

As soon as the troops began moving forward, they ran into the enemy. Winfield Scott Hancock's 40,000 men charged into the remains of A. P. Hill's corps and began pushing them back. Hancock shouted to a staff officer, "We are driving them, sir—tell General Meade we are driving them most beautifully."[9]

By late morning, Hancock had pushed A. P. Hill more than two miles, and had also inflicted heavy casualties. Ambrose Burnside was coming south with his corps and was supposed to take part in the attack. But even though Burnside had not yet arrived, Hancock kept pushing Hill farther and farther back.

Just when it began to look as though the Confederates would break altogether, Longstreet and his men arrived at around midday. Men on both sides heard them before they saw them—the high-pitched, quavering rebel yell announced the dramatic arrival of the Texas brigade. Lee became so carried away by the appearance of the Texans that he attempted to lead them into battle himself. He waved his hat and encouraged them forward, but the men refused to move until Lee withdrew to a safer distance, out of harm's way. Everyone knew all too well that if Robert E. Lee died, the Confederacy would die. To an increasing number of Confederates, especially Confederate soldiers, Lee *was* the Confederacy. The general allowed himself to be persuaded, and withdrew from the front lines.

Longstreet's attack gave the Confederates the advantage and, for the time being, the momentum. Now it was the Federals' turn to give ground. But Winfield Scott Hancock, like Grant, was not a man to give up, and he pushed reinforcements forward into the battle. Also, Burnside's 9th Corps began to make their appearance. The Union forces held, and the fighting went on. In the confusion of the twilight attack, Longstreet was shot by his own men, not far from where Stonewall Jackson had been shot a year earlier. Unlike Jackson, Longstreet did not die from his wounds. But it would be five months before he would be back with the Army of Northern Virginia.

Although not very much artillery had been used by either side, mainly because the dense underbrush of the Wilderness made artillery unfeasible, the Confederates managed to bring a few guns forward. Some of them began shelling the knoll where Grant was sitting, still whittling and smoking. A staff officer suggested that the general move himself and his headquarters out of range. Grant had a suggestion of his own—move some of their own guns forward, start firing back, and hold their present position instead of giving ground. As is usually the case with three-star generals, Grant's suggestion was put into effect: the guns were brought up, the position was held, headquarters stayed right where it was, and Grant went on whittling and smoking.

The fighting had died down toward late afternoon, until Brigadier General John B. Gordon from Georgia discovered that Grant's extreme right flank had been left exposed. Lee gave his personal permission for Gordon to attack. The Confederates hit the Union flank hard and pushed the shaken Federal troops back for about a mile. Two generals were captured during the rampage, and panic began to set in. But corps commander John Sedgwick brought up reserves and, combined with the coming darkness, stopped the attack.

Because it was too dark to see, and because the men were too tired to do anything but sleep, the fighting finally ended for the day. By this time, everybody on both sides was overcome with fatigue, including General Grant. Grant knew how much the Army of the Potomac would be needing its sleep on this particular night. No one else but Grant knew exactly what was in store for tomorrow, or what the army was going to do next. Not even President Lincoln had any idea what his new lieutenant general had in mind.

Lincoln had not been getting very much sleep ever since Grant and the army had crossed the Rapidan. Throughout May 5 and past midnight on May 6, he haunted the telegraph room and read through all the "flimsies," the dispatches from the Wilderness. But these scant reports were all the information Lincoln had—he received no word from General Grant.

A reporter named Henry E. Wing was scheduled to interview Lincoln at two o'clock in the morning on May 7. Because of his insomnia, Lincoln often kept odd hours. Young Mr. Wing had also interviewed General Grant just after the battle ended on May 6. Because of this, Lincoln was as anxious to speak with Henry E. Wing as Mr. Wing was to speak with Lincoln.

During their two-hour interview, Lincoln probably asked more questions than Wing, and had a much more urgent reason for asking them. The president wanted to know everything the young reporter had seen and heard while he was with Grant in the Wilderness. Wing told Lincoln everything he could about the battle, and also delivered a personal message from Grant: "If you do see the president, see him alone and tell him that General Grant says there will be no turning back."[10] This was exactly what Lincoln wanted to hear.

It was what everyone in the Army of the Potomac wanted to hear, as well, although nobody would find out about Grant's intentions until much later in the day. On the morning of May 7, it looked as though another day of fighting would be in store for the army. In a letter to his father, Sergeant Major William Burroughs Ross of the 14th New Jersey Volunteers said, "I write this as we lie behind our entrenchments" in the Wilderness near Chancellorsville "expecting at every moment a charge from the enemy.... The Rebs have been shelling us all day but they can't seem to get the proper range and therefore don't do much harm." Ross went on to report that the 1st New Jersey Brigade had suffered heavy losses the previous day, but seemed optimistic in spite of it. "I will write more when I have an opportunity for I think trusting in God and General Grant we are sure to be successful."[11]

The optimism of Sergeant Ross and the entire Army of the Potomac was about to take a gigantic leap. Both armies kept firing at each other all day long on May 7, although the shooting was mainly limited to picket line skirmishing. After sundown, the entire army was ordered to begin making preparations to move out—men, horses, supply wagons, artillery, everything. The question in everyone's mind was, which way would the army be marching, north or south?

After the battle of Chancellorsville a year earlier, General Hooker had taken the army back north across the Rapidan to regroup and re-equip. In other words, he had retreated north to lick his wounds. A good many veterans of Chancellorsville expected General Grant to follow Hooker's example and retire beyond the north bank of the Rapidan, to "skedaddle" from Lee and his army. The men of the Army of the Potomac did not yet know their new commander.

As soon as night arrived, the army slung its packs, shouldered its muskets, and began walking. It was a routine night march until the lead column reached the first crossroad. At the crossroad, the men expected to turn right and head back toward the Rapidan. Instead, they turned left, heading south. It was a moment of revelation—the army was not going to retreat after all. They were finding out that this man Grant did not frighten very easily and had no intention of retreating. When they realized what was happening, the men began cheering and kept on cheering until Grant himself ordered them to stop—the enemy would hear the noise and realize that the army was on the move. The Army of the Potomac found out what Abraham Lincoln already knew—that there would be no turning back. Grant's friend William Tecumseh Sherman would comment that Grant's decision to turn south was one of the most important of his life. It was certainly one of the most important of the war.

The Battle of the Wilderness was a tactical victory for the Confederacy, but a strategic victory for the Union forces. Grant suffered much higher casualties than Lee, but he also lost a much smaller percentage of his army. Union losses are usually given at around 17,500 killed, wounded, or missing, although the National Park Service's figure is 18,400. Confederate casualties are estimated at around 11,000.[12] The Confederacy did not have the men or the resources to replenish Lee's losses, which Grant fully understood. Grant intended to use his superior numbers, along with the wealth of the North, to grind down Lee's army. At the Wilderness, he had accomplished his intentions, although he wished that he could have done it with fewer losses. Unlike Lincoln, Grant did not have to worry about public opinion or an impending national election; his entire focus would be on destroying Lee and his Army of Northern Virginia.

The fighting in the Wilderness set the tone for the battles still to come. Grant would continue to fight Lee throughout the coming weeks with the same single-mindedness he had shown at the Wilderness, never admitting defeat or turning back in spite of how many killed and wounded the army might suffer. He would continue to go after Lee, and would hammer the Confederates until they could no longer stand and fight.

The soldiers of the Army of the Potomac were in high spirits as they marched south on May 8. General Grant had sent them walking toward Spotsylvania Court House, a small town about ten miles to the southeast of the Wilderness. "Make all preparations during the day for a night march to take Spotsylvania C. H.,"[13] Grant ordered General Meade. Grant's plan was to get to Spotsylvania before Lee, which would place the Army of the Potomac between Lee and Richmond. If he succeeded, Lee would be in a very precarious position, but the gods of war were not on Grant's side. The Confederates managed to reach the small country town first. The resulting battle went on for 13 days—relentless fighting, like in the Wilderness, except longer and even more vicious. Grant kept on trying to get around Lee's flank and put his army between the Confederate army and Richmond.

Grant's men broke through the Confederate line on May 12, in a place that would become known as the "Bloody Angle." Ferocious hand-to-hand fighting went on all day long around the Bloody Angle; Union troops did their best to drive a wedge into the Southern lines and break Lee's army in two, but the attempt fell short.

Every morning, from May 8 to May 21, the battle resumed; every day, the casualties on both sides increased. Among those killed was Major General John Sedgwick, commander of the 6th Corps, who was killed by a sniper. "General Sedgwick commanding our Corps was killed about half an hour ago," Sergeant Major William Burroughs Ross wrote to his father in Freehold, New Jersey. "He was standing right by our Regiment and was shot directly under the left eye, the blood flying on some of our boys." Hundreds of others were killed that day besides General Sedgwick.[14]

Another kind of fighting was taking place at Army of the Potomac headquarters. At one point during the battle, General Meade started an argument with Major General Philip H. Sheridan over the role Sheridan's cavalry was playing. Meade accused Sheridan's cavalry of interfering with General G. K. Warren's infantry. The energetic and hard-driving Sheridan had a short temper, as short people often have, and did not take kindly to Meade's criticism. He contended that Meade ought to stay out of his way, and the cavalry's, and allow him to command the cavalry corps using his own methods. If Meade would let him use his cavalry as an independent fighting unit, instead of just for scouting and reconnaissance, Sheridan claimed that he would be able to beat Jeb Stuart himself.

Although Phil Sheridan commanded the Army of the Potomac's entire cavalry corps, which was composed of three full cavalry divisions, he was junior to Meade. General Meade outranked everyone but Grant. He did not like being told off by one of his corps commanders, and went off to complain to Grant about Sheridan's insubordination.

Grant listened to what Meade had to say, although he did not seem very interested. But when Meade mentioned Sheridan's claim that he could beat Jeb Stuart if he were allowed to operate as an independent force, Grant's attitude changed instantly. James Ewell Brown "Jeb" Stuart was one of the most celebrated commanders of the war, and was both a legend and a bogeyman among the Union cavalry. His exploits made headlines and raised morale at home, and outraged enemy commanders. Getting the best of Jeb Stuart would be as much a psychological victory as a tactical one. Grant was just waiting for the chance to rout Stuart, to beat him at his own game, and was willing to take a risk. "Did he say that?" Grant asked, brightening. "He usually knows what he is talking about. Let him go ahead and do it."[15]

Meade was not entirely happy with Grant's response—he thought that Sheridan should at the very least have been reprimanded for insubordination. But Grant did not really care what Meade thought. He wanted to make war against Lee every way possible, and with all of his resources. If Sheridan said that he could beat Jeb Stuart, who had been a thorn in the side of every Union commander since the beginning of the war, he should be given the chance.

General Meade did what Grant ordered him to do, even though he did not particularly like it. He issued new instructions: Sheridan was to take his 13,000 mounted men, plus horse artillery, and go after the Confederate cavalry. In other words, Sheridan was to look for trouble: disrupt communications, interfere with Lee's line of supply, and fight Jeb Stuart when he came out to stop him.

In accordance with their new orders, Sheridan's cavalry created all the mischief and injury they could against Lee and his army, just as Jeb Stuart had done against Union forces: his men wrecked trains, tore up rail lines, and released several hundred prisoners that had been captured at the Wilderness. But this is not what Sheridan said he would do—he said that he would beat Jeb Stuart.

Stuart and his cavalry came after the Union cavalry and tried to stop its destructive binge against Confederate property, without very much success. Jeb Stuart was not the type to take any sort of setback lightly—defeats damaged his reputation, and he was as vain as he was brilliant and daring. He decided to stand and fight Sheridan at a place called Yellow Tavern, about six miles north of Richmond, on May 11. But the Union forces outnumbered Stuart's men two to one, and were also equipped with rapid-fire Spencer repeating carbines. Sheridan's troopers overwhelmed the Confederates, driving them off and mortally wounding Jeb Stuart. Stuart died on the following day.

It took Phil Sheridan only a couple of days to do what he promised—he not only defeated Jeb Stuart and his vaunted cavalry, but also killed Stuart himself. Stuart's death was another loss that Lee could not afford. The relentless Grant was well satisfied that his faith in Phil Sheridan had not been misplaced.

Grant was confident that the fighting around Spotsylvania was going against Lee, in spite of his own losses. "We have lost at this time eleven general officers killed, wounded and missing, and probably twenty thousand men," he said in a letter to General Henry Halleck.[16] Halleck was his chief of staff; anything Grant said to Halleck would reach the president. Based on the fact that the Federals had taken over 4,000 prisoners so far, Grant went on to report that the enemy's losses must be even greater than his own. This was pure wishful thinking on Grant's part. Lee had suffered far fewer losses than Grant and Meade, although he could afford them less.

Grant went on with his letter to Halleck, sitting in his tent writing and smoking, in the same optimistic manner. The most famous part came about halfway through: "I am now sending back to Belle Plain all my wagons for a fresh supply of provisions and ammunition, and propose to fight it out on this line if it takes all summer."[17]

Newspaper editors took a particular liking to this sentence and frequently used it as part of a subheading, especially the last part. The phrase was usually changed so it would stand on its own: "I propose to fight it out on this line if it takes all summer." It would be used as a catchphrase to signify Grant's determination, and became famous throughout the North. It became so well known that Lincoln paraphrased it during one of his campaign speeches: "I say we are going through on this line if it takes three years more." He hoped that it would not take until November.[18]

The fighting on the Spotsylvania Court House line went on until May 21. By that time, the Army of the Potomac had lost over 17,000 men, while Lee's losses are estimated at 11,000.[19] While at Spotsylvania, Grant received news that Lee was falling back on Richmond. The news turned out not to be true. On May 26, he informed General Halleck—and President Lincoln—that the Army of the Potomac would be moving south in an attempt to get between Lee and Richmond.

The two armies moved south in wide semicircles—with Grant and Meade always moving to their left, closer to Richmond—out of Spotsylvania to the North Anna River, then across the Pamunkey River, then north of the Chickahominy River, and finally to a little crossroads called Cold Harbor. Once again, Lee got there first and immediately began digging in. "The enemy well knew the importance of Cold Harbor to us," Grant would say, "and seemed determined that we should not hold it."[20]

Between June 1 and 3, Grant did his best to break through Lee's lines at Cold Harbor. The first day's fighting had not been very successful, although the day did net 750 Confederate prisoners. Another attack was planned for June 2, but Winfield Scott Hancock's 2nd Corps did not arrive until nearly daybreak and were exhausted after an all-night march. Instead, the all-out frontal attack on Lee's lines was postponed until dawn on June 3.

Although Grant and Meade planned the strategies and issued the orders, it was the soldiers who did the fighting. And the veterans, the men who had been at the Wilderness and Fredericksburg and Gettysburg, could sense what was coming. On the night before the attack, officers noticed men writing their names and addresses on slips of paper and pinning them to the backs of their coats. They did not want to be buried in an anonymous grave or dumped into an open pit with other "unknowns." At least they could be certain that their bodies would be identified, and that their families back home would be notified of their death.

As it turned out, these fears were more than well founded. One writer called the battle of Cold Harbor "a wild chain of doomed charges, most of which were smashed in five or ten minutes and none of which lasted more than half an hour."[21] The Union army lost more than 7,000 men. Confederate losses came to about 1,500. Grant admitted that the attack of June 3 was a mistake: "I have always regretted that the last assault at Cold Harbor was ever made," he wrote in his memoirs, going on to say that "no advantage whatever was gained to compensate for the heavy loss we sustained."[22]

But even though his (and Meade's) army had taken a terrible beating, Grant refused to withdraw. Instead, he held his ground in the trenches at Cold Harbor before moving south again, this time toward the James River. Grant intended to cross to the south side of the James and capture Petersburg, a major rail link with Richmond. Doing so would cut all supply lines to Lee's army, thereby forcing it out into the open. Grant felt certain that if he could force the Army of Northern Virginia out from behind its fortifications he would be able to destroy it once and for all. It was a good plan— if he could make it work.

Since Grant's campaign had begun in early May, with so much hope, the Army of the Potomac had lost half as many men as it had since 1861, when the war began. The Overland Campaign, as it came to be called, was the costliest campaign in the history of the United States, resulting in far more dead, wounded, and missing than any battle of either the First World War or the Second World War. All of Ulysses S. Grant's predecessors put together—Irvin McDowell, George McClellan, Ambrose Burnside, Joseph Hooker, and George Meade—lost just over 100,000 men in all of their battles combined. During the Overland Campaign, the Army of the Potomac lost about 55,000 men (7,600 killed). The estimated Confederate losses are 32,600 (4,200 killed).[23]

But Grant was doing exactly what he had planned to do—he was grinding Lee's army down, which is something that none of his predecessors had been able to do. He had also forced Lee into fighting a defensive battle. Even though Richmond was not Grant's primary objective, Lee had no choice but to defend it. The Confederates would no longer move freely and maneuver on open ground, the way they had done at Chancellorsville and at so many other battles. The Union army was now close enough to Richmond that the troops could hear the city's church bells on Sunday. (One writer pointed out that the bells could only be heard when there was no shooting, which was not very often.) Grant had restricted Lee to a defense of the capital of the Confederacy, which was the kind of battle that Lee did not want and had tried to avoid. He knew that he could not win it.

Grant knew that Lee and the Confederacy would never be able to withstand the relentless pressure of his attacks, and would have to cave in eventually. In other words, the war was gong his way. But the North only saw the losses and the casualties. The Wilderness and Spotsylvania and Cold Harbor had not produced a Gettysburg; they had only produced more dead and wounded. Throughout the North, the optimism of May, when Grant first crossed the Rapidan, had turned into discouragement and despair.

Newspapers helped spread the word of the horrible casualties. "The day has closed upon a terribly hard-fought field, and the Army of the Potomac has added another to its list of murderous conflicts," reported the *New York Times* on the fighting in the Wilderness. "We have no official reports from the front, but the Medical Director has notified the Surgeon General that our wounded were being sent to Washington and will number from six to eight thousand." Other reports also went on about very heavy losses on both sides.[24]

Residents of Washington did not have to read newspaper reports to tell them about the wounded; they could see them for themselves. The injured from the Virginia battlefields arrived by the thousand every day, by boat and by ambulance. Some came with arms or legs in a sling, others missing arms or legs, still others barely able to limp along. Crowds gathered to watch the boats and ambulances arrive, standing in silence as they unloaded their ghastly cargo.

Sometimes, letters from men at the front brought home the immediacy of the fighting in a way that news reports could not. "We are now 8 miles from Richmond near Cold Harbor and nothing but the wail of musketry and roar of artillery wrecks the ear from morning till night." Major Peter Vredenburgh of the 14th New Jersey Volunteers sat under a tree and wrote this letter on June 2. "Such terrible sights Mother as I have never seen. Oh and how I wish this war was over. Even now while I am writing men are being carried by on stretchers by the dozens, for the firing is very severe about 300 yards in front."[25]

President Lincoln appreciated Grant's tenacity and persistence, knowing full well that any of his predecessors would have retreated beyond the Rapidan if they had gone through what the Army of the Potomac had gone through since the beginning of May. But even though he approved of what Grant was doing, he was as shaken by the casualties of Virginia as everyone else. Congressman Schuyler Colfax visited Lincoln at the White House during the fighting at the Wilderness and was shocked by Lincoln's appearance. "I saw [Lincoln] walk up and down the Executive Chambers, his long arms behind his back, his dark features contorted still more with gloom," Colfax recalled, "as he looked up I thought his face the saddest one I had ever seen."[26]

Lincoln knew that Grant would not let up in his war against Lee and the Army of Northern Virginia, regardless of the cost. Grant intended to wear down Lee and his army, not only in numbers but also mentally and psychologically. He was not going to let up. As one of Lincoln's biographers pointed out, "A new mental and psychic factor was entering the war."[27]

In spite of the horrible casualties from the Wilderness, Spotsylvania, and Cold Harbor, Lincoln did not lose faith in Grant. He hoped that Grant's plan would work as much as Grant did, only he had a time frame to worry about. The casualty lists were having a negative effect on public opinion, and the Democrats were already using the dead and wounded as political ammunition against Lincoln. Newspapers that backed the Democrats were calling Grant a drunken butcher, among other things, and saying that the worst was yet to come if Lincoln was re-elected in November.

But Lincoln knew that if he were to have any hope of winning in November, the Union would have to win a major battle, something along the lines of Gettysburg or Vicksburg. And as far as Lincoln was concerned, Lieutenant General Ulysses S. Grant was the only general capable of accomplishing this. In order for Lincoln to win in November, either Grant would have to win against Lee in Virginia or Sherman would have to do something spectacular in Georgia. Lincoln was putting his faith and hope in Grant. Cynics might say that Lincoln was putting all of his eggs in one basket.

By June 15, the entire Army of the Potomac had moved out of its Cold Harbor entrenchments and was on its way to Petersburg. Grant sent his chief of staff, General Halleck, a dispatch to inform him of his intentions. The army would begin crossing the James River that day, Grant said. If all went well, Federal troops would capture Petersburg before Lee and his army arrived to oppose them. Grant ended by saying that the army's movement from Cold Harbor to the James had been made quickly and without loss or accident.

President Lincoln read the dispatch with as much hope as trepidation—he knew exactly what was at stake in Virginia, as well as what was riding on Grant's strategy. The outcome of the war could result from Grant's success or failure in this campaign, not to mention the outcome of the presidential election in November. He studied the message carefully, his face thoughtful rather than sad, reading it over and over again.

On the following day, Lincoln sent a telegram to Grant, acknowledging the message to General Halleck: "HAVE JUST READ YOUR DISPATCH OF 1 PM YESTERDAY. I BEGIN TO SEE IT. YOU WILL SUCCEED. GOD BLESS YOU ALL."[28]

Lincoln's nerves were making themselves known again. Although his good wishes were much appreciated by General Grant, what Lincoln was actually saying was that he hoped that Grant would succeed by November.

TWO IGNORANT BACKWOODS LAWYERS

Abraham Lincoln may have been nervous and anxious over the war, and may have paced the White House corridors over the casualties of the Wilderness and the stalemate at Cold Harbor, but he did not lose any sleep at all over the coming Republican convention. When it came to the fighting in Virginia, he had no choice but to put his faith in General Grant, but in the political battlefield he knew that he did not have to rely upon anyone but himself and his own political instincts and abilities. He certainly knew a lot more about political infighting than he knew about battlefield tactics and gunnery, and he knew his limitations.

The Republican National Convention—called the National Union Party Convention, to accommodate the War Democrats who supported Lincoln's war aims—would convene in Baltimore on June 7. Lincoln knew very well that he had his share of detractors, and even haters, in the Republican Party, people who would use any dubious means to stop his nomination for a second term as president. But he also knew that he had all the support he needed to win the nomination. A Republican Party official calculated that Lincoln already had enough delegates lined up to give him the nomination.

Other possible candidates had been mentioned as replacements for Lincoln on the ticket. General Ulysses S. Grant was one name that was being bandied about. Grant was a war hero and an instantly recognizable name. As would be the case with General Dwight D. Eisenhower 88 years later, it was hoped that Grant's name alone would attract massive amounts of voters and produce a landslide. But unlike Eisenhower, Grant was not interested in being president, at least not yet. He assured Lincoln that his one and only objective was to win the war. His goals would change after the war was over but, for the time being, Grant had no interest in the White House.

Grant was not the only general to be suggested as an alternative to Lincoln. A week before the National Union Party Convention was called to order, a splinter Republican party, calling itself the Radical Democracy, convened in Cleveland to nominate its own candidate. Four hundred delegates nominated Major General John C. Fremont, a well-known frontiersman and explorer who had fought Stonewall Jackson at the Battle of Cross Keys in 1862, as their choice for president.

Lincoln laughed off this convention as nothing but a congregation of malcontents. When he received a telegram informing him that Fremont had been nominated by 400 Radicals, he picked up a Bible and thumbed his way through to the first book of Samuel: "And every one that was in distress, and every one that was in debt, and every one that was discontented, gathered themselves unto him," Lincoln read out loud, "and he became captain over them: and there were with him about four hundred men."[29]

Lincoln could afford to make jokes about his rivals—he knew that there was nothing they could do to stop him. John C. Fremont and his 400 did not have the support or the political muscle to derail his campaign; neither did anyone else. He was not worried about the nomination or the outcome of his party's convention. What worried Lincoln was what was going to happen after he was nominated, in the battles that were certain to come in Georgia and Virginia after the convention had ended.

The National Union Party's convention was supposed to have been held in Baltimore's large convention hall; at least, that is what the planners had in mind. But the hall had already been booked by someone else, a Radical congressman from Maryland named Henry W. Davis. Congressman Davis had absolutely no use for Lincoln, and had hired the hall just to spite him. So the National Union Party planners rented the Front Street Theatre, which was inadequate for the occasion at best. But it was the largest hall that was available on such short notice, and it would have to do.

The number of delegates that would be attending the convention would have made the theater uncomfortable at any time of the year, but an early June heat wave made a bad situation even worse. Cynics would say that the speeches of all the politicians generated enough hot air to create another heat wave inside the Front Street Theatre. A rainstorm on the evening before the convention did not help matters—the rain increased the humidity and made the air seem even hotter than before.

All the delegates, about 500 of them, along with alternates, visitors, and members of the press, who were "numerously represented and suitably accommodated," began filing in to the Front Street Theatre on the morning of June 7.[30] Senator Edwin D. Morgan of New York, the Republican executive chairman, called the convention to order at about eleven o'clock and made a short opening speech.

In his speech, the senator gave a short history of the eight-year-old Republican Party, and also called for a constitutional amendment prohibiting "African slavery" in the United States. The antislavery amendment was a deliberate attempt to placate the Radicals within the party. Lincoln wanted to do his best to unite his party before the campaign against the Democrats began, and he did not want the Radicals to rock the boat.

Having done his job as executive chairman by opening the proceedings, Morgan turned the floor over to Reverend Dr. Robert J. Breckinridge of Kentucky, the temporary chairman of the convention. Reverend Breckinridge was known by one and all as the "Old War Horse of Kentucky," and he certainly looked the part—grizzled, white-haired, and white-bearded, he looked like an Old Testament prophet. He was also a microcosm of the divided country. The Breckinridge family was well known throughout Kentucky and Virginia, and Robert J. Breckinridge was the only member who had not joined the Confederacy. Just about everyone present knew they were looking at a man who had two sons and a nephew in the Confederate army who were fighting for the South at that very minute.

Reverend Breckinridge's speech set the tone for what President Lincoln hoped would be the theme of the convention: the preservation of the union and the abolition of slavery. He spoke about the "political principles" that the National Union Party should stand for: "Now, amongst those principles, if you will allow me to say it, the first and most distinct is that we do not intend to permit this nation to be destroyed." He went on to tell the convention, "You are for the preservation of the Union and the destruction of this rebellion, root and branch." This was exactly what everyone wanted to hear.[31]

But Lincoln also wanted everyone present to receive a message regarding the abolition of slavery, which Reverend Breckinridge conveyed very eloquently: "I join myself with those who say away with it forever; and I fervently pray God that the day may come when, throughout the whole land, every man may be as free as you are, and as capable of enjoying regulated liberty."[32]

This was another attempt to appease the Radical element within the party, the almost fanatical abolitionists who opposed Lincoln because he was not antislavery enough for them. What the Radicals did not understand was that Lincoln's first priority was to win the war, not free the slaves. After the war was over, *then* he would take action to end slavery throughout the United States. Lincoln knew very well that the Emancipation Proclamation did not go far enough to suit the Radicals—they wanted slavery abolished everywhere, including the border states, and not just in the South—but this was as far as he was prepared to go until the Confederate armies had been destroyed.

Following another prayer, a suggestion was made that the convention should determine which states had sent delegates, and also what authority these delegates actually possessed. It was an innocent enough suggestion, but it brought Thaddeus Stevens to his feet. Thad Stevens feared that some of the states that were "in secession" would be admitted to the convention. Stevens had no use for the South; in fact, it is fairly safe to say that he hated the Confederacy. He did not want any states that had seceded from the Union to be admitted, and he especially did not want any of the damned rebels to have any voting rights. "I think we ought to march with great caution in this matter," he said, ". . . it is a question which ought to be settled before we commit ourselves at all, whether they are entitled to be represented here or not."[33]

In response to Thaddeus Stevens's remarks, Horace Maynard of Tennessee took the floor. Maynard was head of the Tennessee delegation, and he did not like what Thad Stevens had to say. He was a tall, lean man who had been given the nickname "Narragansett Indian." Somebody once decided that he looked like an Indian because of his fierce and warlike appearance, and the name stuck. But Maynard decided that his reply to Thad Stevens would be neither warlike nor fierce—he would counter Stevens's challenge with a soft voice. It had been a noisy day, with delegates shouting above each other since morning. Maynard thought that a quiet response would be a lot more effective than more screaming and shouting.

Maynard began by reminding the delegates that Tennessee was as divided as the rest of the country, and that he had been sent "by the loyal Union portion of the population of that old State," and also pointed out that the sixteenth star of the American flag, which occupied a central place at the Front Street Theatre, "symbolizes the existence of Tennessee." Having made his point about loyalty, Maynard came to the main part of his argument.[34]

"I rose simply for the purpose of entering, in behalf of those much-enduring, long-suffering men who sent us here, a protest that you should not pass us by, or forget or ignore our existence." He was on the verge of tears as he spoke, explaining that he represented the people of Tennessee who had not joined the Confederacy but supported the "common government" of the country. "Their sons are dying in the field under the national flag. Their blood has scarcely even now dried upon the sand." Maynard concluded by telling the delegates, "In the name of these heroes, we call upon you to receive us among the friends of the Union here assembled."[35]

The convention seemed genuinely stirred by Maynard's speech, a rare happening among such hard-bitten politicians. "A storm of applause swept the main floor and galleries when Maynard finished," according to one account.[36]

After Maynard sat down, a Virginia delegate wanted to know why his state should not also be given full recognition. Thaddeus Stevens had a quick answer for him—"may I ask the gentleman when I ever recognized Virginia, since her Ordinance of Secession, as being in the Union?"[37] Virginia was a state in secession and in armed rebellion against the Union and, as far as Thad Stevens was concerned, therefore should not be recognized as anything other than being beneath contempt.

In spite of what Horace Maynard and Thaddeus Steven had to say, whether or not Virginia and Tennessee would be admitted was up to the Credentials Committee, the committee that decided who had the right to vote. The committee members would be reporting their recommendations on the following morning. Maynard's eloquence and Stevens's sour temper would probably not have much of an effect on this hardheaded lot.

Before the convention adjourned for the day, a permanent chairman was appointed to replace Reverend Breckinridge. He was William Dennison of Ohio, who made a short acceptance speech in which he thanked the convention for their confidence in him. At the end of the first day's political scheming and maneuvering, everyone went back to their hotels and did their best to sleep in the sweltering heat.

It began all over again at ten o'clock on the following morning. Among the first things to be settled was the matter of which states would be seated and—more to everyone's interest—which states would not. Of the controversial Southern states, the committee agreed that the delegates from Virginia, Tennessee, Louisiana, Florida, and Arkansas should be admitted to the convention with all the rights and privileges of delegates, except the right to vote. The delegates from South Carolina had been completely denied admission, which made Thaddeus Stevens's day, at least up to that moment. South Carolina was considered the birthplace of the rebellion; barring its delegates gave the vengeance-minded Stevens at least a small measure of satisfaction.

The delegation from Missouri began a controversy of its own. Missouri had come to Baltimore with two delegates: a conservative delegate and a Radical delegate. It was obvious that both of them could not be seated—the delegation had to be either all Radical or all conservative—which meant that the convention would have to choose one or the other. The choice was not going to be an easy one—the two opposed each other and, whichever side won, the losing side was going to be angry and insulted. The vote could split the convention, and the National Union Party, wide open.

Abraham Lincoln was not present at the convention, but his influence certainly was. Lincoln had already sent a message of conciliation to the Radicals via Senator Edward D. Morgan, prompting Morgan to call for a constitutional amendment to prohibit African slavery. (No other form of slavery was mentioned.) Now, in another attempt to extend an olive branch to his foes, Lincoln wanted to seat Missouri's radicals. He began campaigning for the radicals through his personal secretary, John Nicolay, who circulated through the Front Street Theatre saying good things about the radicals and making it known to all that seating Missouri's radical delegation was something to be desired.

The other delegates had the sense to know where Nicolay's comments were really coming from, and began to see things the way Lincoln wanted them to see things. Lincoln has often been referred to as a master politician, somebody who knew how to get his own way subtly but effectively. One writer said that Lincoln had "a maddening habit of being, in a kind of tooth-sucking way, wiser and sharper than you."[38] He knew all too well that he was going to need all the help he could get if he was going to be re-elected in November, including help from the radicals. If Missouri's radical delegates were excluded from the convention, the radical movement throughout the country would be insulted and would take its anger out on Lincoln in November.

Lincoln did not like the radicals very much, any more than they liked him, but he needed their support. Allowing the radical delegation from Missouri to be seated at the convention was one way to keep all the Radicals pacified, and to keep them from voting against him in November. Or so Lincoln hoped.

Reverend Breckinridge was among those who saw what Lincoln was up to, but Breckinridge was not happy about it. He did not want the Radicals seated. The conservative delegates, who had supported Lincoln, would be denied seats, while—"as I understand the English language," is the way he put it—the Radicals, who had done nothing but make life as miserable as possible for the president, were to be admitted.[39] Breckinridge made it plain that he had no intention of voting to seat the Radical delegation from Missouri.

He was as good as his word—he refused to vote for the Radical delegation from Missouri. Neither did three other delegates, all of whom were from Pennsylvania. But everybody else who had voting privileges—440 delegates, out of 444—voted to seat the Radicals. Lincoln got his way in a landslide vote.

Following another round of arguing, motioning, and political chess, the delegates voted to allow Tennessee, Arkansas, and Louisiana full voting rights. Horace Maynard had gotten his way, as well.

With that bit of business out of the way, the next item for consideration was the report from the Committee on Resolutions, the men who drew up the party's platform. The report was read by Henry J. Raymond, the head of New York's 66 delegates. New York had the most delegates of any state, making the leader of the New York delegation one of the most powerful and influential men at the convention. The resolutions—which in later times would be called the planks of a party's platform—addressed most of the issues that were on everybody's mind, Radical and non-Radical alike. Raymond read all 11 of them.

1. The party resolved to unite and to do everything in its power "to aid the Government in quelling by force the Rebellion . . . and in bringing to the punishment due their crimes the Rebels and traitors" in revolt against the Union.

2. The war would be prosecuted with a determination "not to compromise with the Rebels, or to offer them any terms of peace, except . . . unconditional surrender."

3. In deference to the Radicals, at the convention and throughout the

country, an amendment to the Constitution that would "terminate
and forever prohibit the existence of Slavery within the limits or
the jurisdiction of the United States" would be ratified.

4. A gesture of thanks would be made to "the soldiers and sailors of the
   Army and Navy" and provisions would be made for the wounded so
   that "the memories of those who have fallen in [the country's]
   defense shall be held in grateful and everlasting remembrance."

5. The party resolved to "approve and applaud" Abraham Lincoln
   and "the measures and acts which he has adopted to defend the
   nation against its open and secret foes" and to express its confidence in Lincoln's ability to carry out all other measures "essential
   to the salvation of the country."

6. To ensure harmony in the national councils and the government,
   only those who "cordially endorse" the party's resolutions should
   be entrusted with "the administration of the government."

7. A resolution giving "full protection of the laws of war" to all soldiers and sailors, regardless of race, was deemed appropriate.

8. A resolution fostering and encouraging foreign immigration was
   passed.

9. A resolution was passed supporting "the speedy construction of
   the railroad to the Pacific coast."

10. The party addressed the economy, taxation, and the public debt,
    and vowed "rigid responsibility" in "public expenditures."

11. The final resolution dealt with approving the use of military force
    against any European power "that might attempt to overthrow . . .
    any Republican Government on the Western Continent."[40]

The National Union Party platform was an attempt to please just about
everyone, with special consideration given to the Radicals. There was a
salute to Abraham Lincoln; a pledge to put down the rebellion, with no
compromise with the rebels; a proposed constitutional amendment to
outlaw slavery; protection for all men under arms, regardless of race; and
even a resolution to encourage foreign immigration. One phrase in the first
resolution, which called for punishing the rebels and traitors, would prob-

ably have been seen as going too far to appease the Radicals, even by Lincoln. But when the time came, Lincoln probably would have conveniently overlooked this particular passage. He had no desire for a Carthaginian peace against the South, no matter what Thad Stevens and his friends wanted.

With the platform hammered out to the satisfaction of almost everyone, the next order of business was the nomination of the party's candidate for president. Simon Cameron, of Pennsylvania, made the formal motion to nominate Abraham Lincoln for president and Hannibal Hamlin for vice president. The nomination of Lincoln and Hamlin was the signal for general mayhem to break out inside the Front Street Theatre, from the floor to the uppermost balcony. The noise of several hundred delegates, each one shouting at the top of his lungs, made enough of an uproar to startle anyone on the street who happened to be passing by.

"Almost every delegate was on his feet, objecting or hurrahing," commented one observer. "For a few minutes, pandemonium reigned, and in the midst of it Cameron stood with his arms folded, grim and smiling, regarding with composure the storm he had raised."[41]

Thaddeus Stevens called for a vote by states, a roll call vote. Others wanted President Lincoln and Vice President Hamlin nominated by acclamation. Nobody could make themselves heard above all the noise and shouting. Henry Raymond of New York, who was also an editor for the *New York Times*, also called for a roll call vote, which was accepted after some more shouting. The roll call vote would only be for the nomination of Lincoln, not for Hamlin.

Maine voted first: "Her entire vote for Abraham Lincoln, of Illinois—14 votes."[42] Every other delegation followed suit: New Hampshire, Vermont, Massachusetts, Rhode Island, Connecticut, New York, New Jersey, Pennsylvania, Delaware, Maryland, Louisiana, and Arkansas. Some states voted with a flourish. Connecticut's delegate said that his state gave her 12 votes to "that pure and patriotic statesman, Abraham Lincoln, of Illinois."[43] New Hampshire's delegate gave a little speech along with his state's 10 votes—much to the displeasure of the other delegates, who did not want to hear any more speeches. Pennsylvania made an attempt at comedy. "Pennsylvania gives her entire vote, forty-two, to Abraham Lincoln, 'nigger' troops and all."[44]

Every state voted for Lincoln, right down the line, until it became Missouri's turn to cast its vote. J. F. Hume said that it was "a matter of much regret" that he had to differ from the rest of the convention, but explained that he had his instructions from back home. And his instructions were to cast Missouri's 22 votes "for the man who stands at the head of the fighting Radicals of the Nation, Ulysses S. Grant."[45]

Ulysses S. Grant probably had no idea that he was the head of the fighting Radicals. In fact, he probably never even heard of them. But Missouri had stunned the convention—they were not voting for Lincoln, they were voting for Ulysses S. Grant.

Following Missouri's interruption, the voting went on: Tennessee, Kentucky, Ohio, Indiana, Illinois, Michigan, Wisconsin, Iowa, Minnesota, California, Oregon, Kansas (Radical Kansas casts her six votes for "Honest Old Abe"), West Virginia, Colorado, Nevada. All the states and territories except Missouri cast their votes for Abraham Lincoln.

When it became evident to everybody that the vote would have otherwise been unanimous, the Missouri delegation decided to change its vote. Mr. Hume rose to declare, "I move that the nomination of Abraham Lincoln, of Illinois, be declared unanimous."[46] After the vote was officially announced—484 for Lincoln and Missouri's 22 votes for Ulysses S. Grant—Hume was allowed to change Missouri's vote. The secretaries then announced that the vote was unanimous—506 for Abraham Lincoln.

Missouri was not the only Radical delegation that voted for Lincoln either as an afterthought or against its better judgment. A good many Radicals did not like the fact that Lincoln would be the nominee. He just did not hate the South enough to please Thad Stevens. Stevens would have preferred someone who advocated not only the destruction of the Confederate armies, but also the total obliteration of the entire South and everyone in it. Stevens's passionate wish was to lay waste to the land and kill every last damned rebel, leave nothing behind but scorched earth and burnt buildings. Radical abolitionists thought that Lincoln did not have enough fire in his soul when it came to opposing slavery, and agreed with British prime minister Lord Palmerston's verdict on the Emancipation Proclamation:

that Lincoln undertook "to abolish slavery where he was without power to do so, while protecting it where he had power to destroy it."[47]

Lincoln knew that the Radicals were against him and that they had only backed him for the good of the party. He also knew that many Republicans had no faith in him and thought that he was sure to lose the White House in November. But he was happy to be renominated. At least the news from the convention took his mind off the disastrous fighting at Cold Harbor. Throughout the convention, he haunted the telegraph office, reading every dispatch from Virginia with foreboding, hoping against hope for some good news.

"I will neither conceal my gratification, nor restrain the expression of my gratitude, that the Union people, through their convention . . . have deemed me not unworthy to remain in my present position."[48] This is what he said when he was officially informed of the unanimous vote on June 8. Later on the same day, June 9, he told a delegation from the National Union League basically the same thing, but seasoned his gratitude with one of his famous Lincolnisms—he was reminded of a story about an old Dutch farmer who said that it was best not to swap horses while crossing streams. He probably wished that he could think of something funny to say about what Grant was trying to accomplish outside of Richmond.

The next item on the National Union Party's convention was the nomination of the vice presidential candidate. The obvious choice was Hannibal Hamlin, who had been Lincoln's vice president throughout his first term. A good many delegates thought that Hamlin would be renominated without any opposition. Hamlin thought so as well. But some political insiders had heard that Hamlin was on his way out and that another candidate, Andrew Johnson of Tennessee, would be Lincoln's new running mate.

Nobody had anything against Hannibal Hamlin, including Lincoln. He had been faithful to the Republican Party. Although he had started his political life as a Democrat, Hamlin had been a Republican congressman for two terms, a US senator, and the governor of Maine, an important state for the Republicans. He was also a tall and distinguished candidate, looking very much the part of statesman and elected official. But there were some—including Lincoln himself—who thought that Hamlin was a little *too* faithful to the Republican line and not faithful enough to Lincoln. For one thing, Hamlin tended to side with the Radicals too often to suit Lincoln. The talk was that Lincoln preferred Andrew Johnson to Hamlin.

From Lincoln's point of view, Johnson's strongest recommendations to be his vice presidential candidate were that he was strongly pro-Union and, especially, that he was a Southern War Democrat. Johnson had been a Democratic senator from Tennessee when Lincoln appointed him as military governor in 1862. Being a Lincoln-appointed governor in a Southern state made Johnson widely hated throughout the South, second only to Lincoln himself. Lincoln used to say that Hannibal Hamlin was his insurance against assassination—no Confederate in his right mind would ever shoot him, because he would immediately be replaced by the Radical Hamlin. With Johnson as his vice president, Lincoln's insurance would double. No Southerner would want a pro-Union, Lincoln-appointed military governor from a seceded state as president.

Other powerful Republicans also preferred Johnson to Hamlin. Three of the New York delegates, including Henry J. Raymond, wanted Andrew Johnson as their nominee. Actually, Raymond and his fellow New Yorkers would have preferred Daniel S. Dickinson, another New Yorker. But if Dickinson received the nomination, Secretary of State William Seward— also from New York—would be relieved of his office. Lincoln would never allow New Yorkers to be both vice president *and* secretary of state. To remove Seward would very probably incite another Radical-conservative battle over who would succeed him as secretary of state, which was exactly what the party was trying to avoid. So New York stood by Andrew Johnson of Tennessee.

Strangely enough, the newly renominated Abraham Lincoln would not let on which vice presidential candidate he liked best. Although Andrew Johnson would be a good candidate, Lincoln did not endorse him. But he did not endorse Hannibal Hamlin, either. He liked the idea of a War Democrat balancing the ticket, but would not give any indication whether he preferred Johnson or Hamlin. Lincoln decided to allow the delegates to go their own way.

Indiana formally nominated Andrew Johnson as the National Union

Party's candidate; Iowa seconded the nomination. Hannibal Hamlin was nominated by Pennsylvanian Simon Cameron. Daniel S. Dickinson's name was presented by a New York delegate, "in behalf of a portion of the New York delegation."[49] Seven other candidates were also nominated, but they had no chance at all.

Horace Maynard, the Narragansett Indian, gave a speech in support of Andrew Johnson, making him sound like a Union folk hero—he "met the leaders of treason face to face, and denounced them" while he was a Tennessee senator, "for which he was hanged in effigy in the city of Memphis."[50] Lyman Tremaine, another New Yorker, spoke for Daniel S. Dickinson in a long-winded speech. When he ran out of time, he was denied ten more minutes of speaking time—everybody had heard enough speeches at this stage. The delegates were hot and tired; they wanted to cast their votes and go home. Nobody made a speech supporting Hannibal Hamlin, which probably came as a surprise to the delegation, but a welcome one.

Next, with all the preliminaries out of the way, a motion was made for a roll call vote. The vote was taken quickly, with no speeches and no fanfare. When the results of the vote were announced, Hannibal Hamlin and his supporters had a very nasty shock in store: Andrew Johnson had received 200 votes; Hamlin 150 votes; and Dickinson 108 votes. The other seven candidates had received only 61 votes among them. All but David Tod of Ohio quickly disappeared from all further voting. (Former governor David Tod was another War Democrat, who has been described as "an old Douglas Democrat," after Stephen A. Douglas. This gives an indication of how the delegation was leaning.)[51]

Even before all the votes were tallied, delegates began changing their votes—everyone could see which way the wind was blowing and no one wanted to be caught on the wrong side. After all the changes had been made, the results were even more ominous for Hamlin: 494 votes for Johnson; 17 votes for Dickinson; 9 votes for Hamlin; and one lone vote for David Tod.

Immediately after the results were announced, Andrew Johnson was officially named the vice presidential nominee of the National Union Party. "Gentlemen of the convention—Andrew Johnson, having received a majority of all the votes, is declared duly nominated as the candidate of the

National Union Party for the Vice-Presidency." Lyman Tremaine of New York moved that the nomination be made unanimous. The motion "was agreed to unanimously, amid great enthusiasm."[52]

The convention had produced a coalition ticket: a Republican for president and a Democrat for vice president. Not everybody in the country was happy about the combination. The *New York World* complained that Lincoln and Johnson were nothing but "two ignorant, boorish, third-rate backwoods lawyers."[53] The *Richmond Dispatch*—as might be expected—called Lincoln an ass, but neglected to issue any insults directed at Andrew Johnson. But the *New York Times* commented that the result of the convention was received in Washington, DC, with the utmost satisfaction by all classes of Union citizens. A clergyman in Middletown, Connecticut, gave his opinion via a quotation from the book of Genesis, 22:15—"The angel of the Lord called unto Abraham out of heaven a second time."[54]

Like it or not, and for better or worse, the Republican/National Union Party would have a pro-war Democrat for its second spot on the ballot in November. "The selection for the Vice-Presidency strikes dismay into the ranks of the Copperheads," said the *New York Times*, "who feel that it has strengthened the Union cause tremendously." Abraham Lincoln hoped that the *New York Times* was right.[55]

With the nomination of Andrew Johnson, the National Union Party's convention was all but over. There were still a few details to be dealt with. A committee was formed to inform both Abraham Lincoln and Andrew Johnson of their nomination, and the territory of New Mexico asked that their delegates be allowed to record their votes for Lincoln and Johnson, a motion that was denied. But everybody was anxious to adjourn and go home. After approving a motion to thank the city council of Baltimore for its hospitality, the convention was formally adjourned at 4:30 on the afternoon of June 8.

Abraham Lincoln was glad that the convention was behind him, and that he had been renominated. He probably did not put all that much emphasis on the fact that Andrew Johnson would be his running mate. He hoped that a War Democrat would strengthen the ticket—and would also strengthen his chances of being re-elected. As far as his personal feelings were concerned, he neither liked nor disliked Andrew Johnson; he never sent Johnson a telegram to congratulate him on his nomination. (Johnson never sent Lincoln a congratulatory telegram, either.) Both Lincoln and Johnson were fully aware that this would be strictly a political marriage and that they had been teamed up together solely to get votes.

Now that the convention had ended, Lincoln could look ahead. He was not encouraged by what he saw in his immediate future. This was partly because he was gloomy and melancholy by nature and partly because he was realistic enough to see that there would be rough going ahead and that the war was far from being won. His nomination in Baltimore had been fairly straightforward, but he could see that being re-elected in November was not going to be nearly as easy.

TWISTING AND TURNING

While Abraham Lincoln fretted and lost sleep over the Army of the Potomac and the thousands of dead and wounded it had lost since the first week of May, General Grant's old friend William Tecumseh Sherman was having problems of his own in northwestern Georgia.

Along with much of the population in the East, and most of the politicians in Washington, Lincoln tended not to pay nearly as much attention to Sherman's campaign in Georgia as he did to General Meade and General Grant's activities in Virginia. This seems a very odd point of view, since the campaign in Georgia was every bit as vital to the Union's strategy for winning the war as anything that happened in Virginia. Maybe it was because Georgia seemed so far away, while Virginia was just across the Potomac. Whatever the reason, Sherman's fight against Joseph E. Johnston's Army of Tennessee was considered to be something of a sideshow when compared with Grant's campaign against Robert E. Lee. Lincoln should have worried as much about Sherman as he did about Grant, particularly in view of the effect that Sherman would have on his re-election.

"I am going to move on Joe Johnston the day Grant telegraphs me he is going to hit Bobby Lee," Sherman told an officer.[56] Sherman was fretting as well, but not for the same reason as Lincoln. While he waited for Grant's telegram, Sherman impatiently stomped about his headquarters, smoking one cigar after another. Grant had originally given April 30 as the day of their simultaneous advance, but changed the date to May 5. Always nervous and anxious, this postponement must have caused Sherman no small amount of anxiety.

The long-awaited telegram arrived on May 5, just as Grant had promised. No sooner had the Army of the Potomac crossed the Rapidan and began their gloomy trudge into the Wilderness than Sherman also began moving south. Three armies under Sherman, totaling 98,000 men, headed out from their camps around Chattanooga, Tennessee, and began moving toward Dalton, Resaca, and other points along the way to Atlanta.

Grant had ordered Sherman "to move against Johnston's army, to break it up, and to get into the interior of the enemy's country as far as you can, inflicting all the damage you can against their war resources."[57] The way Grant put it, the whole venture sounded very simple. But both Grant and Sherman knew that the Georgia campaign would be anything but simple.

Joseph Eggleston Johnston and William Tecumseh Sherman were another study in contrasts—the stately Virginian and the lanky redhead from Ohio. General Johnston was courtly, courteous, and patient. With his well-trimmed beard and flowing moustache, he looked like a Kentucky colonel out of Hollywood casting. A classmate of Robert E. Lee, his bearing at West Point was so tall and erect that he was called Colonel Johnston, even though he was still a cadet.

Nobody ever described Sherman as being either stately or courtly. Friends and family called him "Cump," a nickname he had acquired as a child—he could not wrap his mouth around his middle name, and "Cump" was the best he could come up with. He was tall, angular, and energetic, with a scruffy, close-cropped red beard. When he walked, he tended to slouch over and keep his hands in his pockets. Sometimes, the look in his eyes or the expression on his face gave a hint of his mental problems.

Sherman's first brush with Joe Johnston came on May 8, at a place called Rocky Face Ridge. The town of Dalton, about 15 miles south of the Tennessee border, was on the other side of Rocky Face Ridge. To the north and west of Dalton a gap known as Buzzard's Roost, at least to the locals, split the mountain ridge and was the only access to Dalton from the north. Johnston ordered his men to dig in at Buzzard's Roost—he planned to give the Federals a hotter reception than they ever could have imagined when they tried to get to Dalton by way of that gap.

But Sherman was no Ulysses S. Grant. He saw Buzzard's Roost for what it was—he called the gap "the doors of death."[58] Instead of attacking the Confederate position in a full frontal assault, as Grant probably would have done, Sherman decided to outmaneuver Johnston. He did attack the dug-in force at Buzzard's Roost, but it was only a diversionary attack. At the same time, he sent Major General James B. McPherson's 25,000-man Army of the Tennessee off to the right to attack Resaca, about 12 miles south of Dalton and at Johnston's rear. Sherman intended to outflank the enemy instead of outfighting him.

"I had no purpose to attack Johnston's position at Dalton in front," Sherman later wrote, "but marched from Chattanooga to feign at his front and make a lodgment in Resaca ... on 'his line of communication and supply.'"[59] Not everything went Sherman's way. When General McPherson sent word that he was approaching Resaca and was not meeting with any significant opposition, Sherman pounded the table, rattling the crockery, and shouted, "I've got Joe Johnston dead!"[60] But McPherson was too slow in his advance toward Resaca, which gave Johnston enough time to send reinforcements to stop the Federal attack.

Meanwhile, the diversionary attack at Buzzard's Roost was beginning to develop into a full-scale battle. Federal troops—the Army of the Cumberland, 60,000 men commanded by General George Thomas—gave a good account of themselves, but were turned back twice by Confederates under General Carter Stevenson. General Stevenson probably thought that he had a major fight on his hands, which is exactly what Sherman wanted him to think. Instead, Stevenson was about to become a victim of Sherman's ability to outmaneuver and outthink his opponents.

When the sun came up on May 11, General Stevenson was surprised by the quiet—the almost-constant gunfire of the past three days had stopped completely. Stevenson immediately knew that something had happened, and he contacted General Johnston. Johnston had his own suspicions and sent General Joseph Wheeler's cavalry to investigate. Wheeler confirmed Stevenson and Johnston's fears—the entire Federal force, all 60,000 men, had withdrawn from Rocky Face Ridge and were heading south. Sherman had disengaged General Thomas's men from the fighting and had sent them south to reinforce McPherson. It was not the last time that Sherman would use movement and guile, rather than frontal assault, to achieve his objective.

Johnston knew that he had been outmaneuvered, and also faced the hard fact that he had no choice but to withdraw to Resaca. "The movement was partly, not wholly, successful," Sherman would later say about his feint at Rocky Face Ridge, it "compelled Johnston to let go Dalton and fight us at Resaca where, May 13th–16th, our loss was 2,747 and his 2,800."[61]

Johnston had to "let go" Resaca, as well, after Sherman outflanked him again. On May 15, his army retreated south in the middle of the night. Federal troops entered Resaca on the morning of May 16. "He then fell back to Calhoun, Adairsville, and Cassville," Sherman wrote about Johnston, who "continued his retreat behind the next spur of mountains to Allatoona," steadily moving back toward Atlanta.[62]

The battles of Rocky Face Ridge and Resaca were not major battles, but they did set the tone for the fighting between Joseph E. Johnston and William Tecumseh Sherman. Sherman would advance and, invariably, would find Joe Johnston's men blocking his way. Instead of mounting a full-scale attack against Johnston, Sherman would send George Thomas and his army forward to keep Johnston busy while McPherson's men would go around the Confederate flank. With Thomas at his front and McPherson trying to attack from the rear, Johnston had no choice but to retreat.

Sherman kept at it, always trying to go around Joe Johnston and his army, always trying to catch his opponent out in the open. But Johnston was not about to be caught off guard—he was too cautious for that—and always met Sherman's maneuver with a countermaneuver of his own. Both generals "went down through northern Georgia in a series of movements that were almost formalized," one writer said, "like some highly intricate and deadly dance."[63]

"The enemy commenced moving from our front this morning, to our left, and have kept it up all day," noted Private John S. Jackman of the 1st Kentucky Brigade, also known as the "Orphan Brigade." "The supply train noticed yesterday still moving towards Resaca and sharpshooting and shelling kept up all day by both sides."[64] Two days later, on May 17, Private Jackman wrote, "At 2 o'clock A.M. fell in and marched for Adairsville, 12 or 15 miles." After a day of skirmishing and shelling, the Orphan Brigade moved out again: "At 10 P.M., fell in and marched through Adairsville towards Kingston."[65]

Both sides kept twisting and turning, always heading south toward Atlanta. As a young lieutenant, Sherman had surveyed much of northern Georgia for the army. He claimed that he knew the territory better than the rebels, which was probably true. He certainly had a thorough knowledge of the terrain—the rivers, the valleys, the mountains—and how to use the lay of the land to his advantage.

Sherman did not attack Dalton in a direct assault because he knew the area around Dalton. He was well aware that the only access to the town was over Rocky Face Ridge or through Buzzard's Roost, both of which would be well fortified by the Confederates. Instead of attacking Dalton, he decided to bypass it.

Sherman's tactics were working. He was gaining ground, moving closer to Atlanta every time he sidestepped Johnston. But Sherman actually wanted give the Confederates a real battle—Federal forces outnumbered the Confederates by a margin of two to one. Johnston refused to cooperate, though, and always managed to slip away. And in spite of the fact that Sherman was literally getting closer to his objective every time he faced Johnston, he was still being criticized. In the North, particularly in Washington, Sherman was faulted for not bringing the Confederates to battle and for not destroying Johnston's army. In other words, he was not aggressive enough to suit some of his critics.

Johnston was also coming under criticism. Jefferson Davis was disappointed that Johnston was allowing Sherman to move closer to Atlanta without putting up a fight. It seemed to President Davis that Johnston should be more aggressive, and that he was misusing the Army of Tennessee. Throughout the South, more and more people agreed with Davis. News reporters reflected public opinion and were also increasingly outspoken against what they saw as Johnston's lack of aggressiveness. Diarist Mary Chesnut noted, "Every newspaper (except some Georgia ones) in the Confederacy is busy as a bee, excusing Joe Johnston's retreats. He gives up one after another of those mountain passes where one must think he could fight and is hastening down the plain."[66]

The two armies, Sherman's and Johnston's, continued to move south, always closer to Atlanta, throughout the month of May. At New Hope Church, the Confederates managed to turn back an attack led by Joseph "Fighting Joe" Hooker, the same Joe Hooker who had been humiliated at Chancellorsville. The fighting went on for two days, May 25 and May 26. Sherman made a very costly mistake when he sent only Hooker's 20th Corps to attack; he was under the impression that Johnston had only a small, token force at New Hope Church. In the ensuing battle, the Federals suffered severe casualties—about 665 killed, wounded, and missing, while the Confederates lost fewer than half that number. "It is fun," a Confederate lieutenant wrote to his sister, "for our troops to stand in their trenches and mow down [the Yankees'] lines as they advance."[67]

New Hope Church was only 25 miles away from Atlanta—a fact noted by Jefferson Davis with alarm. It was also noted by the citizens of Atlanta, with even more alarm. The battlefield was close enough for the sounds of gunfire to be heard in the streets, which frightened and upset the populace— Atlanta never thought that the dreaded Yankees would ever get that close.

Although many people were worried and anxious, there was no widespread panic—at least not yet. Some of the more apprehensive residents made preparations to evacuate the city, but few actually left. When Sherman did not come storming into Atlanta, as some gossipmongers had been predicting, the fear subsided. People began to put their faith in General Johnston—Old Joe would stop Sherman and his damn Yankees! But in Richmond, President Davis was not as confident in Johnston as some residents of Atlanta.

President Lincoln had more faith in General Sherman than Jefferson Davis had in Joe Johnston. But Lincoln did not really have much choice. The public was slowly becoming aware that it was as important for

Sherman to win in Georgia as it was for Grant and Meade to destroy Lee's Army of Northern Virginia. Lincoln was beginning to reach this conclusion as well—winning the war would depend upon both men. Lincoln had to believe in Sherman, just as he had to believe in Grant.

If either Sherman or Grant failed, the Democrats would win in November and the war would be over. The Peace Democrats were actually hoping for a disaster for the Union forces, a defeat along the lines of Chancellorsville or Fredericksburg. Another major catastrophe, either in Virginia or Georgia, should convince voters throughout the North that the war was as good as lost, and should also convince them to vote against Lincoln, and the war, in November. There were a good many Northerners who considered this line of thinking to be nothing less than high treason, but to the Democrats it was only smart politics—get their own candidate into the White House by turning public opinion against the president. After the election, the new president, a Democrat, would grant the Confederacy its independence and withdraw all Federal troops from Southern states.

The North was becoming increasingly disillusioned with the war, and its horrible casualties, and wanted it to end. If the war could not be ended with a victory, the North was becoming increasingly willing to give the South what it wanted. The public at large was becoming more and more inclined toward the Democratic point of view—which was to let the South secede and take their slaves with them. Northerners wanted to win the war, but, unless a major victory took place, voters were fully prepared to elect a Democrat and cut their losses. Lincoln knew that restoring the Union depended just as much upon Sherman as Grant. One of them would have to win a major victory if the Democrats were to be turned away from the White House.

Chapter Three

OMINOUS ROADS AHEAD

MISSED OPPORTUNITIES

Neither Ulysses S. Grant nor Robert E. Lee was very happy about the situation at Petersburg. Grant expected to be in Petersburg, about 23 miles south of Richmond, by mid-June. Instead, he had to stop short of his objective and was forced to mount a siege of the city. Grant was not looking forward to another campaign along the lines of Vicksburg, a dull, boring, wearing blockade that would go on and on for months. He had hoped to avoid a siege, but now he had a siege on his hands whether he liked it or not.

Lee, on the other hand, had hoped to keep Grant from getting anywhere near Petersburg. "We must destroy this army of Grant's before he gets to the River James," he told an officer. "If he gets there, it will become a siege, and then it will be a mere question of time." Lee knew that time, as well as men and resources, were on Grant's side.[1]

Petersburg was essential to the Confederacy, as critical as Vicksburg had been in the West. Of the rail lines that came up from the south to supply Richmond, all but one came through Petersburg. "Petersburg was a place the Confederacy had to hold if it meant to hold Richmond," one writer observed.[2] Ulysses S. Grant knew this, and so did Robert E. Lee. Grant's goal was not the capture of Richmond; his main objective was still the destruction of the Army of Northern Virginia. But he knew that Lee would have to defend Petersburg, because losing Petersburg meant losing Richmond. And losing Richmond meant losing the war. Lee would have to tether his army to Petersburg and defend it, no matter what the cost.

Grant managed to get his army away from Cold Harbor and across the James River by pontoon bridge. Cold Harbor, about ten miles northeast of Richmond, was a barren, hostile place. The men could not wait to get away from it. Grant managed to get the army out of the trenches and across the James without arousing the suspicions of Lee, and Robert E. Lee was not an easy man to deceive. Lee finally did find out that the enemy was on the move—the movements of any group of men the size of the Army of the Potomac could not be kept secret for very long—but he still had no real idea exactly where his opponent was heading. Richmond seemed a logical choice, so Lee made the assumption that Grant's objective was the Confederate capital. It was the first time he had ever misjudged Grant's intentions.

Lee found out that the enemy had disappeared on the morning of June 13. The entire Army of the Potomac had vanished, more than 100,000 men, as though someone had rubbed a lamp. Lee was livid. "It was said that General Lee was in a furious passion—one of the few times during the war," a Confederate officer remembered. "When he did get mad, he was mad all over." An artilleryman added that Lee, "who knew everything knowable, did not appear to know just what his old enemy proposed to do."[3]

Grant meant to get to Petersburg before Lee could figure out exactly where the Army of the Potomac was heading. As soon as he reached Petersburg's outskirts, he intended to capture the city, rail lines and all. With any luck, Petersburg would be in Union hands by June 15. But luck was not with Grant.

The commander of his spearhead was General William F. "Baldy" Smith. Smith had graduated from West Point in 1845, where he had acquired the nickname "Baldy" to distinguish him from the other Smiths at the academy. He had been at Chattanooga with Grant and had also been at Cold Harbor. Grant seemed to have a high opinion of him. To Grant, Smith seemed reliable and dependable.

On June 15, Baldy Smith and 10,000 men started toward the fortifications of Petersburg. The city's defenses certainly were frightening—a network of forts, ditches, rifle pits, breastworks, and trenches, all interconnected and all arranged for maximum killing power. Smith knew all about the trenches and the rifle pits. But he did not know that hardly any Confederate soldiers were in them.

Commanding Petersburg's defenses was General Pierre Gustave Toutant Beauregard, who was probably most famous—or, in the North, at least, infamous—for being the man who fired on Fort Sumter. Beauregard may have had an impressive array of ramparts and buttresses, but he had only about 2,200 men, including home guard troops and cavalry. These were spread out in a line so thin—about one man for every 12 or 15 feet—that Baldy Smith could have overwhelmed them and stormed into Petersburg with a minimum of casualties.

Beauregard saw what was coming and sent for help. General Lee immediately saw Beauregard's predicament and promised to send a full division of infantry at once. But these troops would not reach Petersburg for at least 12 hours. Until the reinforcements arrived, Beauregard would just have to hold on as best as he could.

Smith ordered an attack that simply overwhelmed the defenders. The Federals captured 16 cannons and took several hundred prisoners. But he did not follow through with his attack, even though there were many, many more blue uniforms on the field than grey. It was nearly dark by the time Smith's men had taken the Confederate works. But also—and this was probably the most vital reason—he was extremely wary of going up against well-entrenched enemy troops. He had seen what had happened at Cold Harbor and did not want the same thing to happen to him at Petersburg.

Smith had the opportunity to walk through the deserted Confederate lines and move right into the city. Beauregard's men had retreated and left the way wide open to the Federals. Instead, Smith decided to wait until more troops arrived before trying to advance any farther. The 2nd Corps, commanded by General Winfield Scott Hancock, was expected to arrive in the morning. Any sort of renewed offensive would have to wait until then.

Hancock certainly was moving up to join Smith, but he was not exactly driving his men—nobody told him that he was needed at once, or that he would be reinforcing an attack on Petersburg. He did not receive word from Grant's headquarters until about 5:00 p.m., when a courier informed him that he should move forward as quickly as possible. Smith was attacking Petersburg's fortifications, and the 2nd Corps was needed at once. "This seems to be the first information that General Hancock had received of the fact that he was to go to Petersburg, or that anything in particular was expected of him," General Grant later recalled. "Otherwise, he would have been there by four o'clock in the afternoon."[4]

Now that he knew where he was going and what he was supposed to do when he got there, Hancock moved forward with a lot more speed and determination. On the following day, his corps attacked Petersburg along with Baldy Smith's men and Ambrose Burnside's corps. The attack succeeded. More fortifications were taken, and two or three thousand Confederate casualties were inflicted. The next attack should achieve even better results, everyone thought. The way things were going, Petersburg and all its rail connections to Richmond would be in Union hands before long.

But Lee was not sitting still while all this Federal activity was taking place. Now that he was certain that Grant's objective was Petersburg and not Richmond, he was moving south toward Petersburg as well. The entire Army of Northern Virginia was heading south with all the speed its lean and underfed veterans could muster. At best, they would not be able to reach Petersburg until the early hours of June 18. Lee hoped they would not be too late.

Lee received some unwitting help from a few other Federal commanders besides Hancock, who also did not move forward against the Confederate positions with enough aggressiveness to win the day. Baldy Smith's troops took a rebel skirmish line and then stopped. Other generals did pretty much the same thing—moved forward, ran into enemy opposition, and stopped to dig in. Sometimes they sent patrols out to explore the ground and the strength of the enemy. At that stage of the fighting around Petersburg, because the Confederate force defending the city was so small, a little bit of determination and initiative would have gone a long way.

George Gordon Meade tried his best to get his corps commanders to move forward with a bit more alacrity, but nobody seemed to be paying much attention. Meade did not have the sunniest disposition in the world, even when things were going well. Today, he was in a particularly bad mood. Via telegraph, he tried to organize his generals into making a coordinated attack against Petersburg's entrenchments. When this did not work, Meade ordered them to attack individually, without waiting to coordinate movements.

None of his orders seemed to be having any effect—nobody moved and nobody advanced on Petersburg. The "goddamned goggle-eyed old snapping turtle" became angrier and more foulmouthed as the day went on.

By the time anyone was ready to attack, Lee's reinforcements had arrived and were manning the trenches. General David Bell Birney, who had taken over for the ailing Winfield Scott Hancock, formed his main column into four lines and prepared to move forward. The first two lines were made up of veterans who had fought at Chancellorsville as well as at Cold Harbor, and knew what would be in store for them. Green troops, "rookies," made up the last two lines. These men were largely untested and untried, and had not seen what happened when troops ran at Confederate entrenchments.

When the order came to charge the rebel trenches, the veterans simply ignored their officers. The captains and lieutenants could shout and wave their swords all they wanted, but these men were not about to move. One of the new units, the men of the 1st Maine regiment, obeyed the order and began running toward the Confederate works. They had been an artillery unit until recently, when Grant took them out of the forts around Washington and turned them into infantry. They had never been in combat before and did not know what Confederate artillery could do to infantry. They were about to find out.

The Confederates knew exactly how to build their fortifications so that they provided maximum cover while also allowing for greatest killing potential. The men from Maine ran forward—through the veterans, who stayed prone on the ground—and headed for the trenches. By the time the canister fire finished with them, more than 600 of the 900 men had been slaughtered. Some of them had literally been blown apart by the artillery. The fortunate survivors ran back, leaving the ground littered with dead and wounded.

The men of New York's Excelsior Brigade, a veteran infantry unit, had been slated to attack another part of the Petersburg defenses. While they were walking through their own artillery toward the front, one of the gunners asked if they were going to make a charge.

"No, we are not going to charge," came the reply. "We are going to run toward the Confederate earthworks and then we are going to run back. We have had enough of assaulting earthworks."[5] In other words, they were only going to go through the motions of making a charge. The men had seen enough slaughter for one day.

The attacks had been a total failure. General Beauregard had won, just by standing his ground and waiting for reinforcements. At the end of the day General Meade sent Grant a telegram, letting him know that nothing else could be done. The men dug in, making a line of trenches in front of the Confederate works. After the sun went down and the men settled in, they could hear the bells of Petersburg in the distance. They were that close.

"Lee's whole army had now arrived," Grant noted, "and the topography of the country about Petersburg had been well taken advantage of by the enemy in the location of strong works." Although Grant tried his best to resign himself to the situation, he was badly let down. "I will make no more assaults on that portion of the line, but will give the men a rest," he went on, "and then look to extension toward our left, with a strong view of destroying Lee's communications on the south and confining him to a close siege." But Grant knew that he would be confined as well, which was not what he had in mind when he had left the Cold Harbor trenches and set out to cross the James.[6]

One casualty of the failure to capture Petersburg was Baldy Smith. Smith was granted a ten-day furlough at the end of June. When he returned, he was supposed to be given command of the Army of the James—at least that was what Grant told him. But while Smith was away, Grant changed his mind.

The Army of the James was under the not-very-able command of Major General Benjamin Butler. Butler was heartily disliked by Grant. He was also disliked by just about everybody else in the army, including Baldy Smith. Butler seemed to have a special talent for offending people, and for rubbing them the wrong way. He had a very sharp and malicious tongue, which he used to write deliberately insulting orders to subordinates. Following Smith's attack on Petersburg, Butler accused him of "dilatoriness," and also threatened to replace him.

General Grant was becoming increasingly fed up with Ben Butler. He wrote a very diplomatic letter to his chief of staff, General Henry W. Halleck, suggesting that Butler be sent to another theater of operations, possibly Kentucky or Missouri. He probably would have suggested the North Pole if the Union army had an outpost that far off.

General Halleck was sympathetic toward Grant and his desire to rid himself of Butler, "on account of his total unfitness to command in the field and his generally quarrelsome character." But if Grant sent Butler to Kentucky, Halleck warned, he "would probably cause an insurrection in that state." And if he sent Butler off to Missouri, something similar would happen.[7]

Grant was stuck with Ben Butler. But he had an idea: he would retain General Butler to perform administrative duties, while Baldy Smith would carry out all military operations. In other words, Butler was being kicked upstairs.

To everyone's surprise, Butler seemed to be extremely happy with this arrangement. Fat, arrogant, incompetent, mean-spirited General Benjamin F. Butler had no objections to being kicked upstairs. But before Grant put his plan into action, he wanted to have a talk with Smith. It would be a routine interview; Grant just wanted to have a conversation with the officer who was going to replace Ben Butler.

The interview turned out to be anything but routine. Baldy Smith talked and talked and talked, but General Grant was emphatically not impressed by what Smith was saying. He started out by demeaning Ben Butler, wanting to know how Grant could have given the command of two entire army corps to a man "who is as helpless as a child on the field of battle and as visionary as an opium eater in council."[8] Although Grant probably agreed with Smith's assessment, he did not appreciate hearing one of his officers ridicule another.

But Smith was not finished. Next, he went to work on General Meade, blaming Meade for the horrible casualties in the recent campaigns and doing his best to make him look like a blundering, incompetent fool. Smith finally asked Grant how he ever expected to accomplish anything if he had somebody like Meade in command.

By the time Smith left Grant to begin his ten-day furlough, Grant decided that he really did not want Smith to replace Butler. It seemed to Grant that Smith would be as much of a liability and a problem as Butler.

Smith's tirade had offended him, especially his comments about General Meade. Grant was also worried by Smith's performance at Petersburg, "when he captured the Confederate forts and then sent his soldiers to bed instead of into Petersburg."[9]

Grant shared Smith's not-very-high opinion of Ben Butler, but now Butler seemed the lesser of two evils. On the basis of their talk, and of Smith's actions at Petersburg, Grant determined that Smith lacked the judgment for such an important command—he would probably be even more incompetent than Butler. Baldy Smith not only talked himself out of an appointment, but also talked himself right out of the war.

When Baldy Smith returned from his ten-day furlough, he was informed that Grant had revoked his promotion. Butler would stay on as commander of the Army of the James. Smith would be sent to New York to await orders. Like another troublesome general, George B. McClellan, Smith would wait for orders that would never arrive.

Smith would later insist that Butler blackmailed Grant into changing his mind. Grant had started drinking heavily again, Smith said, and Butler had threatened to tell the press that Grant was off on another of his drunken binges unless he was kept on as commander. Butler denied the accusation; Grant simply ignored it. So did Abraham Lincoln.

The men in the ranks heard all about Baldy Smith's dismissal, but they were not satisfied. They really did not care who took the blame for what had happened. All they knew was that they should have been in Petersburg and they were not. Whether Baldy Smith or Ben Butler or Ulysses S. Grant himself was held responsible did not matter to them. They knew that a tremendous opportunity had been missed, possibly a chance to end the war; pointing fingers and delegating blame was beside the point. On the night of June 15, after Smith's men had retired for the night and it had become plainly evident that there would not be any more attacks against Petersburg, one of the men wrote: "The rage of the enlisted men was devilish. The most bloodcurdling blasphemy I ever listened to I heard that night."[10]

Everybody, Union and Confederate, was disappointed over what had happened at Petersburg, and had something to complain about. Lee was sorry that he had not been able to destroy "this army of Grant's," and that he had allowed his enemy to get to Petersburg in the first place. Grant was more resigned than sorry. He knew that he would win in the end, because of sheer manpower and resources if nothing else, but now it would take months instead of days.

Lincoln was probably the most disappointed of all. The capture of Petersburg would have ended the war and also would have assured his re-election. With the war over and behind him, the Democrats would have had to come up with an entirely new campaign—peace without victory would no longer apply. But the failure to take Petersburg gave the Democrats a new supply of ammunition; it meant another stalemate, more dead and wounded, more blood to add to the blood that had already been spent since 1861.

Lincoln's re-election campaign centered on the war, and on winning the war. He went to Philadelphia to speak at the Great Central Fair, to make the public aware of his goals concerning the war. The event was what New Yorkers would call a street fair: stalls filled with all sorts of things to buy, everything from food to works of art to toys. The proceeds of the fair would go to the Sanitary Commission, which had been formed to promote healthy living conditions in Federal army camps. Thousands of people came to the fair, which is why Lincoln decided to attend. He needed an audience; the fairgoers were just what he was looking for.

Lincoln had taken a great deal of time and effort in putting his speech together. He did not want to introduce a wrong note, or say something that might be offensive. It would not be a very long speech, but it might be an important one in his campaign. On the evening of June 16, while the fighting was still going on outside Petersburg, Lincoln spoke to a room full of war-weary but hopeful listeners.

"War, at its best, is terrible and this war of ours, in its magnitude and its duration, is one of the most terrible," he said. He went on to describe the destruction it had caused so far and to express grief over the dead and wounded who had "carried mourning to almost every home." Getting to the main theme of his speech, he told his audience, "We accepted this war for an object, a worthy object, and the war will end when that object is attained. Under God, I hope it never will until that time."

The message was clear: there would be no negotiations with Richmond; there would be no thought of independence for the Confederacy. Regardless of how many more men would be killed or wounded, the war would continue until the Confederacy surrendered. Lincoln ended his address with a well-known paraphrase of General Grant: "I say we are going through on this line if it takes three years more."[11]

Shortly after his speech at the Great Central Fair, Lincoln decided to drop in on General Grant at Petersburg and see the situation there for himself. This was not really a campaign stop; it was more of an inspection trip. But the visit was as much to bolster his own morale as it was to see what Grant was up to. Lincoln wanted to put his mind, and his nerves, at ease. It was not entirely nonpolitical, though—he was fully aware that the Army of the Potomac would be casting its vote in November, along with the rest of the country—but it was more of a fact-finding tour than an election campaign stop.

Lincoln just showed up, unheralded and unannounced. Grant and his staff were sitting in front of the general's tent "when there appeared very suddenly before us a long, lank-looking personage, dressed all in black and looking very much like a boss undertaker," a member of Grant's staff recalled. "It was the President."[12]

Lincoln shook hands with everybody. "I just thought I would jump aboard a boat and come down to see you," he explained to General Grant. "I don't expect I can do any good, and in fact I'm afraid I may do harm, but I'll put myself under your orders and if you find me doing anything wrong just send me right away."[13]

Grant answered that he would do just that, and laughed a hard laugh—this certainly was a case of a true word being spoken in jest. Knowing Grant, he probably would have escorted the president out of camp personally if Lincoln had broken any rules or regulations. But the two of them got along very well and had a congenial lunch together, along with a few of Grant's officers. Grant did not say very much during the meal, as usual, but Lincoln chatted away merrily and even told a few jokes.

After lunch, Grant suggested that they ride off to visit the troops. Lincoln jumped at the chance, announcing that he was ready to start at any time. They set off at about four o'clock in the afternoon, startling every soldier in the area. "Old Abe was here and rode along the Lines with Gen. Grant," an artilleryman scribbled in his diary.[14]

Not everybody was impressed by Lincoln's visit, or by his appearance. One of Grant's staff officers thought he looked like "a country farmer riding into town wearing his Sunday clothes."[15] As Lincoln rode his horse, his trousers gradually rode up his long legs, making him look even more like a country farmer. Captain George Meade, the son of General George Gordon Meade, could not figure out why Lincoln bothered to come in the first place. "No one knows what he came for," he said in a letter. Young Meade was showing that he had the same gift for crabbiness as his father.[16]

Before Lincoln took his leave of Grant and the army, Grant told him something he had been hoping to hear, something that made his entire trip worthwhile. "You will never hear of me further from Richmond than now, 'til I have taken it." His tone of voice had the ring of finality. "I am just as sure of going to Richmond as I am of any future event. It may take a long summer day, but I will go in."[17]

Lincoln seemed impressed by this pronouncement. Grant was a fellow Midwesterner, straightforward and plain spoken, who was not given to boasting and did not make such promises lightly. "I cannot pretend to advise," he said to Grant, but he hoped that whatever Grant went on to accomplish could be done "with as little bloodshed as possible." Grant was in no position to make any promises of that sort.[18]

When Lincoln returned to the White House on June 23, he was in a much better frame of mind than when he left for Petersburg. Even Gideon Welles, Lincoln's dour old secretary of the navy, had to admit that Lincoln's visit had "done him good, physically, and strengthened him mentally in confidence in the General of the army."[19] It also gave him renewed hope that the Union would win the war after all. "We are today further ahead than I thought one year and a half ago we should be, and yet there are plenty of people who believe that the war is about to be substantially closed," he told newspaper correspondent Noah Brooks. "As God is my judge, I shall be satisfied if we are over with the fight in Virginia within a year."[20]

Everyone was glad that Lincoln's morale had taken such a positive turn, and that he was confident that the fighting would be over in 12 months.

The only trouble was that the presidential election would be taking place in a little more than four months.

POLITICAL SUICIDE

The president "couldn't seem to deliver victory on the battlefield or negotiations for peace . . . and the American people were beginning to have second thoughts about him."[21] The predicament being described is the one faced by Lyndon B. Johnson at the height of the Vietnam War in 1967, when both Johnson and the war were becoming increasingly unpopular with the American public. But it might just as well have been said about Abraham Lincoln and his position during the summer of 1864. Both Johnson and Lincoln tried desperately to bring their respective wars to a successful end before their political careers were destroyed.

The war in Vietnam did put an end to Lyndon B. Johnson's career in politics. By the autumn of 1967, his approval rating had dropped to such a low point that he decided not to accept the nomination for another term as president. "My daddy committed political suicide for that war in Vietnam," Johnson's daughter Lucy recalled.[22] In the summer of 1864, Abraham Lincoln faced the same situation. Unless the war took a dramatic turn for the better before the November election, Lincoln would be committing political suicide over the war in Virginia and Georgia.

By the end of June 1864, it must have seemed like a hundred years since General Grant had crossed the Rapidan and began moving against Robert E. Lee. Nearly everyone in the North had their hopes high at the beginning of May, expecting something great to happen—another Vicksburg delivered by Grant, only this time in Virginia, Robert E. Lee's home ground. Instead, the North had seven weeks of hard fighting and a seemingly never-ending procession of dead and dying, with very little to show for it.

The Democrats had originally planned to hold their convention early in July, but decided to postpone it because of fading hopes in the North. The war did not seem to be getting any closer to the victory that the North had been expecting since Grant had taken command of all Union forces.

Leaders of the Democratic Party thought it might be profitable for them to reschedule their convention—by the end of August, morale in the North might be even worse, which meant that the opinion of Lincoln would be a lot lower.

Democratic Party chairman August Belmont called a meeting of party leaders to discuss the changing of the convention date and to talk about campaign tactics. Some of those who attended the meeting wanted to have their convention as soon as possible, arguing that it would be best to begin uniting the party—the Peace Democrats and the War Democrats—at the earliest possible moment. Still others thought that waiting would be their best strategy. With the Union's fortunes declining, the longer they waited, the worse Lincoln and the Republicans would look. The Peace Democrats especially held this point of view. They hoped and prayed that Grant would fail in Virginia and that Sherman would never get anywhere near Atlanta.

After days of arguing and debating, those who had been pushing for a postponement won the day. Backroom politics were no more sanitary in those days than at any other time; men made deals and formed alliances to get what they wanted, and were not above indulging in a little backstabbing. By June 25, all the deals had been made and the word went out: the convention had been pushed back to August 29. Whether anyone liked it or not—and there were very many Democrats who wanted an early convention—the Democratic party would not be nominating its candidate for another ten weeks.

One of the men who had been consulted as to whether or not the convention should be pushed back was General George B. McClellan, who had been in contact with leaders of the Democratic Party since being removed as commander of the Army of the Potomac. He had even been asked to be the Democratic candidate for governor of Ohio. But he decided that he did not want to be governor of Ohio—possibly he had his eyes on a bigger prize. When he rejected the offer, Clement Vallandigham received the nomination instead. Vallandigham came out of exile in Canada to accept the nomination, and was defeated by a landslide—much to Abe Lincoln's undisguised delight.

While he waited for orders that would give him another command,

McClellan allowed himself to become an active member of the Democratic
Party by endorsing Judge George W. Woodward as governor of Pennsylvania.
Some say that this was a reluctant decision. In a letter to the *Philadelphia
Press*, McClellan said that he fully agreed with the judge's views. "I would,
were it in my power, give Judge Woodward my voice and vote," he said.[23]

Although Woodward lost the election to Republican incumbent
Andrew Curtin, McClellan's backing of the Democratic candidate, in what
was considered an important race, made him a committed Democrat. His
name was now being mentioned as a possible presidential contender in 1864.

By midsummer, it had become clear, even to George B. McClellan, that
he was not going to be recalled to active duty—or "to save the Union," as he
would have put it. If he had any chance at all of getting another command—which was very doubtful—his backing of Democrat George
Woodward put an abrupt end to that possibility. So McClellan decided to
leave the army and enter politics as his new career. The only problem was
that giving up his major general's commission would also mean giving up
the $6,000 per year salary that went with it.[24] With this sobering fact in
mind, McClellan reversed his decision and stayed in the army after all. He
was reassured by the fact that General Winfield Scott had been the Whig
Party's candidate in 1852, while he still held his commission—and his
salary—as a major general.

With the encouragement of Democratic chairman August Belmont,
McClellan began to sound and act like a presidential candidate. He went to
West Point on June 15, while Baldy Smith's men were attacking the rebel
trenches at Petersburg, and dedicated a memorial to those who had died in
the war. McClellan's speech was not blatantly political, but it did outline his
views on the war and its objectives. According to McClellan, the war was
being fought for a just cause, "just and righteous, so long as its purpose is to
crush rebellion and save our nation from the infinite evils of dismember-
ment."[25] There was no mention of abolishing slavery, just a call to save the
Union. Since the war had become *the* topic for any political candidate, any
speech regarding the war or war aims was automatically a political speech.
The West Point speech came to be known as "McClellan's Platform." Copies
of it would be distributed to delegates at the Democratic convention.

Another step toward making George B. McClellan a viable presidential candidate was the publication of his *Report*. The *Report*, McClellan's personal account of his term as commander of the Army of the Potomac, put him squarely in the news again. A biographer called it "a work designed to refute his critics and to justify his military conduct to his countrymen and to history."[26]

It was a self-serving and highly controversial account. Among other things, McClellan claimed that his failure on the Virginia Peninsula in 1862 was the fault of Lincoln and his administration. McClellan was not about to admit that he had any part in the Army of the Potomac's humiliation. The fact that McClellan refused to take any offensive action, in spite of Lincoln's repeated efforts to get McClellan moving against the Confederate army, was conveniently overlooked.

The *Report* was widely read; sales certainly supplemented McClellan's major general's salary, and even gave him an income independent of his army pay. Segments of the *Report* were published in several newspapers. The *New York Times* ran a series of articles based on McClellan's account. As campaign literature, it brought McClellan's name to the public's attention better than any paid advertising could have done. Not everyone was impressed, however. Horace Greeley wrote that McClellan "is essentially not a soldier, but a politician, and his fighting and writing have alike been intended to train him for the Presidential race."[27]

Horace Greeley was an outspoken Republican, and his newspaper, the *New York Tribune*, was probably the most widely read and influential newspaper in the country. But there is no such thing as bad publicity, and Greeley's comments about McClellan and his *Report* only helped to further McClellan's political ambitions. People began talking about that man McClellan and began reading his *Report*, which is just what McClellan and the Democrats wanted.

The Democrats were glad that George B. McClellan was a politician, with a politician's knack for making himself look good at his opponent's expense. His *Report*, along with the fact that he had been commander of the Army of the Potomac, made McClellan the leading candidate to oppose Lincoln in November. If what he wrote in his report was controversial, so much the better—a few half-truths and misrepresentations never hurt a candidate's chances of being elected.

The Democrats were not the only ones who were beginning to regard McClellan as presidential material. He was beginning to look like the leading Democratic candidate to the Republicans as well. There would be no official candidate until the convention, of course, but George B. McClellan looked like the best bet for the Democrats. He also looked like an intimidating opponent—a general with the gift of gab and a knack for attracting publicity. The Democrats were looking for someone who could take back the White House in 1864, and who would be able to expand their victory in the 1862 midterm elections. From the Republican point of view, McClellan might very well be that candidate. He was certainly popular enough and, as a soldier himself, would probably receive most of the military vote. "Little Mac" had put the fear into the Republicans.

Things were looking very ominous for Lincoln and his party. The public was looking for a change from the current administration; people were looking for a new government that would either win the war or end it. The war was far from over, everybody could see that, and it did not seem to be going the Union's way. Newspaper reports were not painting a very cheerful or hopeful picture for the North—at least not those that were giving accurate reports, anyway. Some papers were printing outright lies, both to satisfy the War Department and to increase circulation, about Lee and his army being in full retreat. But the truth had a way of getting through, in spite of censorship and unscrupulous editors.

Letters from friends and relatives at the front presented a bleak picture of the war. "It's terrible Mother and I hope for God's sake we will finish this 'job' up pretty quick," wrote Major Peter Vredenburgh Jr. from outside Petersburg. He went on to tell his mother about how much weight he has lost—"I think from 145 lb. weight I have fallen to about 110 lbs. but feel as well as ever"—and warned her about what he called "the public press."

"They lie like thunder and what you have heard about Petersburg being in our possession and our successful assaults is all false," Vredenburgh said. "The rebels got to Petersburg as soon as we got opposite to it and they hold it now." But Major Vredenburgh was not quite finished. "Our army is now half managed—generals trust too much to their subordinates instead of working for themselves and the most astonishing thing is that we get along as well as we do." He closed by cautioning, "Don't show these scraps to anyone"—a warning that his mother probably ignored as soon as she read the letter.[28]

Imagine receiving a letter like this from a soldier in the trenches outside Petersburg—a letter from a major, not from some private in the ranks. According to the letter, the situation in Virginia was anything but hopeful and encouraging. The news reports were "all false," the enemy occupied Petersburg and showed no signs of withdrawing, and the generals were incompetent. Multiply this letter several thousand times and it can be seen why morale in the North was declining, along with faith in Lincoln and his ability to conduct the war. Lincoln and the Republicans had good reason to fear for their chances in the coming election.

A REAL WAR LEADER

"This is the nineteenth day of rain, and the prospect of fair weather is as far off as ever," General Sherman growled. The weather had been filthy for nearly three weeks, with heavy rains that turned roads into swamps and made marching an ordeal. But the weather was not what was bothering Sherman. After griping about the rain, he finally got around to mentioning what was really on his mind: "The enemy still holds Kenesaw, a conical mountain, with Marietta behind it. . . . I am ready to attack the moment the weather and roads will permit the troops and artillery to move with anything like life."[29]

Although Sherman complained, his men did not. They did not really care all that much about the rains, even though they did turn the roads into quagmires. Soldiers know when they are well off, and when they are being well taken care of, and the Federal soldiers in northern Georgia trusted William Tecumseh Sherman. The men called him Uncle Billy, and they liked what he had done so far—he kept pushing the rebels toward Atlanta, but he did it without inflicting wholesale slaughter or murderous casualties on his men. Uncle Billy cared about them. He did not push them into sui-cidal frontal assaults, like they had been told Grant was doing in Virginia. One of them wrote, "If we get to Atlanta in a week, all right; if it takes two months, you won't hear this army grumbling."[30]

Even though his men liked him well enough to give him an affectionate nickname, they still thought Sherman was something of an oddball. For one thing, there was the talk about his mental problems. Nobody men-tioned this extremely touchy subject out in the open, and it was absolutely certain that no one was brave enough to mention it in front of Sherman himself. But word of his "craziness" did get around. Another general once said that Sherman was like "a splendid piece of machinery with all of the screws a little loose." None of the men ever said anything like this; they knew better.[31]

His physical appearance was another topic of conversation. He was any-thing but a spit-and-polish bandbox soldier, which is one of the things that made him so well liked. His uniform usually looked as though he had fallen down in the middle of a dirt road, and he always seemed to be chewing on a cigar—he liked cigars almost as much as his friend General Grant. Overall, his appearance was not very military, although he was probably not as rum-pled looking as Grant. For one thing, his height gave him a sort of ready-made dignity. Sherman was six feet tall in an era when few men were.

He resented being criticized for not being aggressive enough and for not destroying Joseph E. Johnston's army. Sherman had been trying to maneuver Johnston out in the open ever since he left Chattanooga, but Johnston had been too wily and had always fallen back. Even though he was moving closer to Atlanta, Sherman was frustrated—he wanted to force a battle with Johnston so that he could bring his superior numbers to bear. In mid-June 1864, Joe Johnston had moved to Kennesaw Mountain, about 20 miles northwest of Atlanta, and had dug in. Sherman decided that Ken-nesaw Mountain would be the place where he and Johnston would have their full-scale battle. "The points of attack were chosen," Sherman would later write, "and the troops were all prepared with as little demonstration as possible."[32]

On June 27 at 9:00 a.m.—an hour later than scheduled—the order was given to move forward. With a great shout, the men left their positions and started loping toward the rebel works on Kennesaw Mountain. But it did not take very long before they ran into a buttress of rocky cliffs and ridges that were supplemented by man-made trenches. Both the cliffs and the trenches were manned by armed rebels.

General Sherman described the "rifle-trench" used by the Confederates: all trees and brush were cleared for about 100 yards in front of the trenches; the parapets sheltering the riflemen were from four to six feet high and made from the earth that had been taken from the ditches. A "head log," a tree trunk, was placed on top of the earthworks, which acted as a beam to reinforce the whole system and provide added protection. "The men of both armies became extremely skilful [*sic*] in the construction of these works," Sherman dryly remarked, "because each man realized their value and importance to himself."[33]

Although the Confederates were well protected by their rifle-trenches, they had no trouble seeing above the solid earthworks or spotting the Federals as they approached. The rebels had a clear view of the advancing enemy and shot at the men in blue from many places along their lines. A major with an Ohio regiment remarked that the bullets buzzing past him were so thick that "if I should hold out my hand I could catch several of them—a handful—immediately." He was surrounded by the "sickening sound" made by the "thud of a minie ball through human flesh."[34]

The fight was not entirely one sided. A Federal brigade commanded by Colonel Dan McCook—who had been Sherman's law partner when they were both living in Kansas—reached a section of entrenchments that the Confederates called the "Dead Angle." Colonel McCook was fatally wounded in the attack on the angle, but his brigade planted its flag on the parapet. Defending rebels fired at McCook's men until their rifles seized up from overheating—the barrels became so hot that they were clogged with molten lead from their own bullets.

McCook's brigade did manage to secure the Dead Angle, in spite of the defending fire that was truly murderous, but most units had no success at all. Federal troops caught in the open by rebel riflemen and artillery were either annihilated or forced to turn and run for their lives. "I tell you the men were mowed down like grass," a soldier in McCook's brigade wrote to his parents. Some fell flat and pretended to be dead, waiting until dark before escaping to their own lines.[35]

Sherman's attempt at storming the fortified enemy positions at Kennesaw Mountain had the same disastrous results as General Grant's attack at Cold Harbor. "By 11.30 the assault was in fact over, and had failed," Sherman admitted.[36] In about two and a half hours, he had lost about 2,500 men, according to his own estimation. Johnston lost about 800. One of Sherman's commanders, General George H. Thomas, told him that "one or two more such assaults would use up this army." Sherman already knew this.[37]

Sherman never actually admitted that he had made a mistake at Kennesaw Mountain, but he never tried another direct frontal assault, either. He would continue his flanking movements, trying to go around Joe Johnston—dancing him to death instead of beating him to death.

On the evening of June 27, General Johnston informed his superiors that the enemy had advanced upon his entire line that day and had been repulsed. This news was certainly well received in Richmond. In Atlanta, the reaction to Johnston's report was joy mixed with relief—maybe Old Joe would chase Sherman and his Yankees out of Georgia after all! It was the first time that Johnston had faced Sherman in a pitched battle. Not only did he beat him back, but he also gave Sherman a bloody nose that would be felt all the way back in Washington. "Their loss is supposed to be great," Johnston said, "ours known to be small."[38]

But Johnston's position had not improved any, in spite of Kennesaw Mountain, and he knew it. While the Federals and the Confederates agreed to an unofficial cease-fire to bury their dead—the swollen corpses were quickly rotting in the 100-degree Georgia heat—Sherman was already planning to resume his attempts to outflank Johnston. At the same time, General Johnston had already begun pulling out of his Kennesaw fortifications. At 10:00 p.m. on July 2, men of the 52nd Ohio regiment discovered that the rebel troops had left their trenches. When Sherman made his next advance toward Atlanta, Johnston wanted to be in place to block him. He knew what Sherman was going to do and hoped that he would be able to stop him again.

Newspapers in the North tried to make the best of a bad situation in their reports of what had happened at Kennesaw. The *New York Times* concentrated on Sherman's flanking movements after the battle, reporting that Sherman forced the rebels to abandon Kennesaw by moving southward around Johnston's lines. But no matter how encouraging the newspapers tried to make the situation, most Northerners only saw another Federal setback: Sherman had lost the battle, and had been thrown back at Kennesaw Mountain. The war was not going the way everyone had hoped when the spring campaigns began.

The country was becoming sickened by the loss of life and the endless bloodshed. Horace Greeley spoke for many of his countrymen when he wrote about "our bleeding, bankrupt, almost dying country." He wrote to President Lincoln of the apprehension he felt concerning "the prospect of fresh conscripts, of further devastations, and of new rivers of human blood."[39]

Lincoln was all too aware of the mounting dead and wounded from the battles in both Virginia and Georgia, but he also realized that he was not able to do anything about it. "Doesn't it seem strange to you that I should be here?" he asked a congressman. "Doesn't it strike you as queer that I, who couldn't cut the head off a chicken, and who was sick at the sight of blood, should be caught in the middle of a great war, with blood flowing all around me?"[40]

Throughout the North, more and more people tended to agree with Lincoln, and were also finding it strange that he should be in the White House. Abraham Lincoln was showing himself to be something less than successful as a war president. The public wanted someone like Andrew Jackson, a soldier who had proven himself as a leader in war. If old Andy Jackson had been facing those rebels, he would have had Robert E. Lee and Jeff Davis hanged by now! People were thinking that the country needed a real war president, a soldier with a war record. Maybe the country needed George B. McClellan.

Chapter Four

SUMMER OF
DISAPPOINTMENTS

SO DAMN FAR

Small things, items that seem insignificant or unimportant at the time, often decide turning points in history. Major battles, like Midway or Saratoga, usually turn the momentum of wars and decide the eventual winners and losers. But the minutiae of life can sometimes turn events around as completely as any full-scale battle. In the summer of 1864, events were about to be reversed, and the course of a war and an election were to be changed, because of a personality clash between two men.

Joseph E. Johnston and Jefferson Davis detested each other. For as long as they had known each other, the president of the Confederacy and one of the Confederacy's leading generals had never seen eye to eye. It is probably safe to say that the feeling between them bordered on hatred. By the summer of 1864, the two men had become irreconcilable foes. Until the time of the Atlanta campaign, however, their hostility had been largely personal. But their loathing for one another was about to take an ominous turn in the northern approaches to Atlanta, and would have far-reaching and permanent repercussions.

The bad blood between Davis and Johnston apparently began when they were both at West Point. Joseph E. Johnston was a member of the class of 1829—along with fellow Virginian Robert E. Lee. Davis was one year ahead of Johnston, a member of the class of 1828. According to some accounts, Cadet Davis and Cadet Johnston had a disagreement over the so-called Egg Nog Riot of Christmas Eve 1826, when 22 cadets were arrested for being drunk and disorderly after drinking eggnog that had been forti-fied by two half-gallon jugs of "grog."

Davis was arrested for taking part in the riot but was later released. Johnston had not been involved in the incident at all. Even so, the two pos-sibly had a disagreement over the riot itself, or its aftermath—no solid evi-dence exists that gives any definitive answers.

Another, more entertaining, story involves a girl. According to this romantic account, both Davis and Johnston became involved with a certain young lady who used to visit the academy on regular occasions, and each possibly fell in love with her. The two of them had a fistfight over the girl, the story goes, and held a grudge over the incident for the rest of their lives. No actual evidence exists to support this story, either. Also, no one knows who won the fight, or the girl.

Whatever happened, and whichever story is believed, Jefferson Davis and Joseph E. Johnston were anything but friends during their time at West Point. A biographer of Johnston had this to say: "When Davis graduated with his class in July 1828, he and Johnston appear to have parted on less than amicable terms."[1] This is putting it politely—the two parted with a hostility that would outlive their West Point years.

This hostility never went away, in spite of the passage of time. In 1855, while he was secretary of war under President Franklin Pierce, Davis blocked Johnston's request to be ranked on the army list as a brevet colonel. (Brevet rank is a battlefield promotion, usually awarded for gallantry in the field, and usually without a corresponding increase in pay.) Johnston had been made a brevet colonel for gallantry at the battle of Sierra Gordo, during the Mexican War. Because Johnston's previous promotion had been from captain to brevet major, Davis decided that Johnston should only be advanced to lieutenant colonel, which was one rank below full colonel. Davis's ruling insulted and infuriated Johnston, as Davis knew it would.

Five years later, when Davis was a US senator from Mississippi, he opposed Johnston's appointment as quartermaster general, which included a promotion to brigadier general. This time, Davis did not get his way; in spite of his opposition, Johnston received his appointment on June 28, 1860. But Davis's antagonism only served to intensify the bad feeling between the two.

When Jefferson Davis became president of the Confederacy, Johnston's wife, Lydia, had a word of warning for her husband. She said that Davis "hates you, he has the power & he will ruin you."[2] But Davis actually ended up advancing Johnston and his career, although he did it unwillingly and against his better judgment.

At the end of 1863, Davis needed a new commanding general for the Army of Tennessee. The most recent commander, General Braxton Bragg, had shown that he was not up to the job, and the acting commander, General William J. Hardee, turned down Davis's offer to take permanent command of the army, which meant that the main Confederate army operating between the Appalachian Mountains and the Mississippi River was without a commanding general. This left Jefferson Davis with a dilemma of major proportions.

Davis only had three generals who had both the rank and the qualifications for such a command, an uncomfortably short list. First and foremost on the list was Robert E. Lee. Davis would have loved to have appointed Lee to command the Army of Tennessee. But Lee had become so closely identified with the Army of Northern Virginia that assigning him to another command was unthinkable. And even if he were to remove Lee, Davis would have to find another general to replace him in Virginia. So Lee could not even be considered for the job.

Next on the list was Pierre Gustave Toutant Beauregard. Beauregard had given the order to fire on Fort Sumter and had an excellent reputation as an officer and a commander throughout the army. But he was not very well liked by Davis, either—both men were vain and tended to be arrogant. In other words, they had too much in common to get along with each other. Also, Beauregard had commanded the Army of Tennessee once before, in 1862, and had been removed from command by Davis's order. There was every reason to believe that Beauregard would do something to get himself fired a second time, and there was no point in going through that all over again.

The third candidate was Joseph E. Johnston, and Davis would rather have appointed anyone else in the world. But there simply was no one else available. "Naming Johnston commander of the Army of Tennessee was wormwood and gall to Davis," one writer said. "If he could have avoided doing it, he would have." But Davis could not avoid it, in spite of his loathing for Johnston. He had no other general, and no other choice. On December 16, 1863, he telegraphed General Johnston to report to Dalton, Georgia, and take command of the Army of Tennessee.[3]

President Davis watched Johnston's withdrawal through northern Georgia, just ahead of Sherman's armies, with mounting anxiety and irritation—through Dalton, Resaca, Calhoun, Adairsville, Cassville, and Alatoona. After Kennesaw Mountain, he expected that Johnston would change his tactics and attack Sherman. Davis wanted him to go after the Yankees, to charge at Sherman and chase him out of Georgia. But Johnston's main concern was keeping his army intact, which was much more important to him than protecting territory.

In short, Johnston refused to comply with Davis or his wishes. Instead of attacking Sherman, he continued with his strategy of withdrawal. After Kennesaw Mountain, Johnston pulled back again. Fearing that Sherman would outflank him, Johnston ordered his army to retire across the Chattahoochee River, northwest of Atlanta. From his new position on the other side of the river, he intended to work out a plan to stop Sherman from getting any closer to Atlanta.

Jefferson Davis was not going to wait for Joe Johnston to mount an offensive that was probably never going to take place. He was tired of Johnston, tired of hearing about Johnston's constantly retreating from the enemy, and exasperated with Johnston's refusal to fight. "Everybody has at last come to the conclusion that Johnston has retreated far enough," another general complained. "I fully expect to hear of his retreat behind Atlanta."[4]

Jefferson Davis fully agreed. If anybody but Joseph E. Johnston had been in command of the Army of Tennessee, Davis might have given him a bit more leeway. He might have sent a messenger to tell the general that it would be in his own best interests to mount some sort of offensive against Sherman immediately or be replaced, a communiqué more in the way of a plea than an ultimatum. Maybe Johnston would have paid attention to this sort of directive. But there had been too much injury and bad feeling between the two of them, and Davis could not bring himself to make the gesture. He had had enough, and decided that Johnston had to go.

For his own part, Joe Johnston was no more cordial toward Jefferson

Davis than Davis had been toward him. His replies to any communiqués from Davis had always been formal and correct, at best, but Johnston never gave away very much information or told Davis any more than he absolutely had to. It was as though he did not want to share any news or information with his longtime enemy.

When Davis telegraphed Johnston to ask about his "plan of operation" against Sherman, Johnston acted as though the question was totally impertinent. "As the enemy has double our numbers, we must be on the defensive," he responded. "My plan of operations must therefore depend on that of the enemy. It is mainly to wait for an opportunity to fight to advantage."[5] Johnston certainly was not giving away any secret intelligence, or even telling Davis anything that he did not already know. But he was letting Davis know that he was not going to tell him anything that he did want him to know, even if Davis was the president of the Confederacy.

If Davis had been looking for an excuse to get rid of Johnston, he now had the perfect excuse. Not only had Johnston failed to keep Sherman from advancing on Atlanta, but he was also reticent about sharing his plans to the point of insubordination. "General Johnston has failed, and there are strong indications he will abandon Atlanta," Davis telegraphed Robert E. Lee at Petersburg. "It seems necessary to remove him at once. Who should succeed him? What do you think of Hood for the post?"[6]

General Lee seemed taken aback by Davis's question. "It is a bad time to relieve the commander of an army situated as that of Tennessee," he replied. "We may lose Atlanta and the army too." Lee's opinion of General Hood was even less positive than his opinion of Davis's plan to relieve Johnston. "Hood is a bold fighter. I am doubtful as to the other qualities necessary."[7]

Lee wrote Davis an even more apprehensive letter later that day. "Hood is a good fighter, very industrious on the battlefield, careless off, & I have had no opportunity of judging his action when the whole responsibility rested upon him," Lee said, trying his best to be diplomatic. "I have a very high opinion of his gallantry, earnestness & zeal," he went on, but "General Hardee has more experience in managing an army."[8] Hood may have been a good fighter and all that, but Lee preferred General Hardee. The only problem was that Hardee had already turned down the job.

Davis read Lee's communiqués, both of them, and was grateful for the advice. But he had already made up his mind: he was going to relieve General Johnston of command of the Army of Tennessee and replace him with General Hood. On July 17, Johnston was informed by telegram that the secretary of war had no confidence in his ability to stop or defeat the enemy and that he should turn his command over to Hood.

After he fired Joe Johnston, Davis was as relieved as he was pleased with himself. Not only had he rid himself of someone he detested, but he had also replaced him with a general who would fight, a general who would attack Sherman and begin to reverse Johnston's habit of retreating. If he was lucky, he would never have to see or hear from Joe Johnston ever again.

Johnston gave up his command with characteristic graciousness, although being fired by his old antagonist bothered him more than he let on. He sent a congratulatory letter to General Hood, shot off a snippy telegram to Jefferson Davis, and set out to join his wife in Macon. As far as he was concerned, he was well rid of Jeff Davis, and reciprocated Davis's feelings completely.

With Joe Johnston's departure from the Atlanta campaign, an entirely new phase of the war began. The mutual hatred that existed between Johnston and Davis would not only have an immediate impact on the fight for Atlanta, but it would also begin to reverse public opinion in the North and give Abraham Lincoln's re-election campaign a new burst of hope. No one knew it at the time, but Lincoln had just been given a priceless gift from a totally unexpected source.

Abraham Lincoln had certainly heard of General John Bell Hood. Even if he did not know all that much about Hood, he would have recognized his name. Hood, a lieutenant general, had been wounded at Gettysburg and at Chickamauga, where he'd had a leg amputated. Lincoln haunted the telegraph office, where he read every dispatch from every battlefront as soon at it was decoded. Hood's name was regularly mentioned in these telegrams. If Lincoln had known what impact Hood would have on the outcome of the war, and on the November election, he probably would have taken the time to get better acquainted.

William T. Sherman lost no time in getting better acquainted with Hood. On July 18, a Yankee spy from Atlanta came into camp with a newspaper account of Hood assuming command of all Confederate forces around Atlanta. As soon as Sherman read the report, he sent for Major General John M. Schofield, who had been in the same class as Hood at West Point. He wanted Schofield to tell him everything he could remember about his former classmate.

General Schofield certainly gave Sherman the lowdown on John Bell Hood. From what Schofield had to say, Hood was no Einstein. He was also no Robert E. Lee. Hood very nearly flunked out of West Point, and probably would have if not for Schofield's own efforts to help him with his studies.

Hood had a very hard time with mathematics. Schofield, who had been assigned as his math tutor, had just as hard a time with Hood. From what Schofield had to say, it would have been hard to tell who was having the worst of it, Cadet Hood or Cadet Schofield. At one point during one of their tutorials, Hood had had just about enough—enough of mathematics, enough of West Point, and more than enough of Cadet Schofield. "Which would you rather be," he shouted in frustration, "an officer in the army or a farmer in Kentucky?" It was clear that he would rather be a farmer in Kentucky or in any place other than West Point.[9]

Hood managed to survive his mathematics course, thanks in large measure to the pains of John Schofield. He graduated with Schofield in 1853, forty-fourth in a class of 52 cadets. If Hood had failed in mathematics, he would have been dismissed from the corps of cadets. Schofield wondered if he had made a mistake by coaching Hood through his math course.

John Bell Hood was a tall, sad-eyed individual, with the countenance of a basset hound. He may not have been the brightest person in the world, or even the best officer, but there was one thing about him that brought him to the attention of his superiors—he would give anybody a fight, any time, any place. If Hood was no Robert E. Lee, he was also no Joseph E. Johnston. Outmaneuvering the enemy was not his style, or in his character. He was more like Ulysses S. Grant: his objective was to attack the enemy, to go right after him and beat him to death, not to play chess with him. As John Schofield put it, "He'll hit you like hell, now, before you know it."[10]

If Jefferson Davis was glad that John Bell Hood was now in command of the Army of Tennessee instead of Joe Johnston, Sherman was absolutely ecstatic. When Schofield told him what he could expect from the new commander, Sherman was relieved to hear it. "This was just what we wanted, viz., to fight in open ground, on any thing like equal terms, instead of being forced to run up against prepared intrenchments."[11]

The news was also telegraphed to General Grant, outside Petersburg—the telegraph was the perfect medium for transmitting such vital information, and for keeping Grant, and President Lincoln, informed of what was happening down in deepest Georgia. Grant and Lincoln knew of Johnston's replacement almost as quickly as Sherman.

"My satisfaction at Hood's being placed in command was this," Grant wrote in response to Sherman's telegram. "[Johnston] was a most careful, brave, wise soldier. But Hood would dash out and fight every time we raised a flag before him, and that was just what we wanted."[12] Sherman agreed. "Notice of this important change was at once sent to all parts of the army," he said, "and every division commander was cautioned to be always prepared for battle in any shape."[13] The word went out via telegraph to all commanders—watch out for Hood, and get ready for a fight. General Schofield predicted that Hood would attack within 48 hours. His prediction would turn out to be almost eerily accurate.

John Bell Hood took over the Army of Tennessee on July 18. He spent the next two days taking stock of his army and trying to size up the enemy. When he discovered that Sherman had divided his army and that one of these armies was occupied with crossing Peachtree Creek, Hood did what General Schofield said he would do: he attacked.

Peachtree Creek should properly have been called Pine Tree Creek, since the name comes from the pines, known as "pitch trees" because of their pitchy sap, that covered the area. But General Hood was not concerned with the etymology of north Georgia place-names. His mind was set on going after Sherman and his Yankee army; more specifically, on launching an attack against one of Sherman's commanders, Major General George H. Thomas and his Army of the Cumberland.

General Thomas managed to get his army across Peachtree Creek before Hood threw two of his three corps at it. "The enemy attacked me in full force at about 4 P.M.," Thomas reported to Sherman, "and has persisted until now, attacking very fiercely, but was repulsed handsomely by the troops all along my line."[14]

By 6:00 p.m., the attack had run its course, and John Bell Hood got the worst of it. "The leading companies, or what was left of them, swayed backward upon those in the rear," a soldier in an Ohio regiment wrote. "They, in turn, broke, and then all went in wild disorder back to the friendly cover of the timber."[15] Hood's attack did not gain any advantage at all against Sherman. Before his men retreated, Hood sustained between 2,500 and 4,769 casualties, depending upon which source is consulted. Sherman's casualties came to an estimated 1,700.

Where Johnston had been careful and sensible in his management of the Army of Tennessee, as well as in his defense of Atlanta, Hood had thrown his men at the enemy recklessly, just as General Schofield had predicted. He certainly was a bold fighter, and he had made a daring attack, but that was just what Sherman wanted, and the battle had ended just as Sherman hoped it would. Hood blamed the failure at Peachtree Creek on Lieutenant General William J. Hardee, known as "Old Reliable," complaining that Hardee did nothing more than skirmish with the enemy. The army was commanded by Hood, all six foot two of him, and the responsibility for the loss at Peachtree Creek rested squarely upon his broad shoulders, whether he liked it or not.

A few days before Peachtree Creek, Sherman received telegrams from both General Grant and General Halleck. The message to Sherman was that, from then on, the Atlanta campaign would take precedence over what was happening in Virginia. The war was not being won in the battleground south of Richmond—the siege of Petersburg looked to be a very long and drawn-out affair—and it was fervently hoped that Sherman might be able to provide some good news from Georgia. If the war were going to be won, a lot more responsibility for winning the war would now rest upon William Tecumseh Sherman.

President Lincoln read all the telegrams that came into the War Office, including everything that was sent between Grant and Sherman. He knew all about the dispatches to Sherman from both Grant and Halleck, and he also read about what had happened at Peachtree Creek. Even though Sherman's defeat of Hood was hardly a Gettysburg, it certainly was encouraging news in that summer of disappointments. But if he were to have any chance of winning in November, Lincoln was going to need a lot more Peachtree Creeks.

Hood seemed more than willing to comply with Lincoln's needs. He saw an opportunity to outflank Major General James B. McPherson's Army of the Tennessee and, on July 22, sent General Hardee's corps to attack the Federal flank. Nobody had to wave a flag at him, as Grant famously said; Hood did not need an excuse to fight.

Sherman was surprised by Hardee's attack; so was General McPherson. McPherson did not even know that Hardee's corps was in the area until about 12:15 p.m., when he heard rifle fire about a mile and a half to the southeast. But his corps commanders reacted quickly. General Grenville Dodge promptly formed 5,000 soldiers into a line of battle to block the oncoming rebels. One of Dodge's officers wrote that the Confederates "came tearing wildly through the woods with the yells of demons."[16] But the men were not intimidated by the rebel yell or by the charging rebels themselves, and managed to beat back the attack.

General McPherson watched while Dodge held the line against the charging Confederates, well satisfied that General Dodge had been in the right place at the right time. But another fight had broken out on McPherson's right flank. McPherson had received several reports that one of his divisions was under attack and that the enemy was trying to force its way through a gap between two other divisions. He decided that it would be best if he rode over to see the situation for himself.

He mounted his horse and galloped off toward the fighting with two other men. Confederate skirmishers were on the move on the same road, advancing toward the Federal lines; McPherson stumbled right into them. The Confederate captain ordered McPherson to surrender. Instead, he tipped his hat, turned his horse around, and galloped at full speed away from the skirmishers. The captain ordered his men to open fire; they shot and mortally wounded McPherson.

General James McPherson was well known and well liked by both Grant and Sherman. When his body was brought to headquarters, Sherman acted as though he had lost a son. Tears ran down his face while he continued issuing orders and reading dispatches. He "paced back and forth in a headquarters room," according to one account, "barking orders, barking his grief, tears running down his cheeks into the red beard."[17] Grant also cried from grief when he heard that McPherson had been killed. And he started drinking again, although McPherson's death may or may not have been the cause of his taking to the bottle.

General McPherson would be greatly missed, but there was still a battle to be fought. General John A. Logan succeeded McPherson as commander of the Army of the Tennessee, inheriting the problem of how to stop Hood's attacks. General Logan was well liked by his men. He was a flamboyant and flashy officer with long black hair and an enormous, flowing black moustache, and his personality had been described as easygoing.

There was nothing easygoing about Logan on July 22. He rode along the lines of blue-uniformed men, holding his hat so that his hair would blow in the breeze, and shouted to his men to hold the line for him. The men responded by chanting his nickname, "Black Jack! Black Jack! Black Jack!" and by ramming .57 caliber minie balls down the muzzles of their rifled muskets. And they held the line, "beating off assaults that seemed to come from all directions."[18]

The attacking and counterattacking went on all afternoon. Late in the day, after 6:00 p.m., General Hardee threw his men at the Federal lines one last time. This was probably the most furious attack of all. The two sides went at each other with bayonets, clubbed rifles, and fists; officers used their swords as weapons for the first time—they had never considered them to be anything more than ceremonial ornaments. The clubbing and the stabbing went on until it was too dark to see. When the rebel soldiers withdrew into the woods, the Battle of Atlanta—also known as the Battle of Decatur—was over.

After the battle, General Hood did his best to make the best of a bad situation. He telegraphed Richmond that Hardee's corps had attacked the enemy and driven them from their works, and also reported that General

McPherson had been killed. According to Hood, the battle was a great success. His men had captured several thousand enemy prisoners, he said, along with some artillery pieces and several of the enemy's battle flags. Although all these things were true, Hood failed to mention the fact that he had not dislodged Sherman at all and that the enemy was as much of a threat to Atlanta as ever. For all the gallantry shown by the Confederate troops that day, which was mentioned prominently in his report, Hood and his army lost the Battle of Atlanta.

Confederate casualties came to about 8,000. (General Logan gave his estimate as 10,000.) Sherman's casualties at Atlanta were about 3,600. At Peachtree Creek and Atlanta, Hood lost nearly as many men as Joseph E. Johnston had lost in ten weeks. And he had nothing to show for it. Sherman was still as dangerous as before, in spite of Hood's aggressiveness.

In the North, reports of the fighting around Atlanta were confusing and contradictory. Nobody was quite sure what had happened. The first communiqués stated that Sherman had occupied Atlanta "beyond a doubt," but later reports admitted, "Atlanta is not ours yet."[19]

Most of the dispatches were encouraging. After Peachtree Creek, an official communiqué quoted a Union general as saying, "I have buried four hundred dead rebels, and four thousand wounded lay at my front." Another dispatch, this one regarding the fighting of July 22, reported that "a great battle was fought in Atlanta on Friday, resulting in a horrible slaughter and a complete repulse of the enemy at every point."[20]

The word from Georgia sounded bright and hopeful, with lots of talk about rebel casualties and of Sherman closing in on Atlanta. "GENERAL SHERMAN CONFIDENT OF SUCCESS," read one particularly optimistic report.[21] But General Sherman always seemed to be on the brink of success, and he had won several terrible battles. The North had read about the Battle of Atlanta and about Peachtree Creek, but readers still wondered if Sherman would ever be able to capture Atlanta. That was the question on everyone's mind. Would Sherman ever win a decisive victory, occupy Atlanta, and bring the war one step closer to being won?

General Sherman himself had no doubts at all that he would capture Atlanta, although he had no idea when. "My plan of action was to move the

Army of the Tennessee to the right rapidly and boldly against the railroad below Atlanta," he wrote. "All the orders were given, and the morning of the 27th was fixed for the movement."[22]

John Bell Hood was still full of fight, in spite of the losses he had suffered in two battles with Sherman. He was not about to let the enemy make any move against Atlanta's railway without another battle. Hood anticipated Sherman's movements and sent four divisions to stop him. Even though he knew he would be outnumbered, Hood was hoping that he would be able to surprise the Federal army, like Stonewall Jackson had at Chancellorsville. But this was not 1863, he was not Stonewall Jackson, and he would not be fighting Joe Hooker.

Hood would be up against the Army of the Tennessee again, only now it was under the command of General Oliver Otis Howard. Sherman had decided to remove John Logan from command and replace him with Howard, even though General Logan had helped to save the day on July 22 after James McPherson had been killed. Sherman's main criticism of Logan was that he was a politician, not a professional soldier. Logan had been an Illinois congressman before the war, while Howard was a West Point graduate. Sherman preferred career soldiers. Logan stepped down gracefully and went back to his old command, the Army of the Tennessee's 15th Corps.

Oliver Howard was the polar opposite of John Logan when it came to personality and temperament. Where Logan was flamboyant and outgoing, Howard displayed all the flamboyance of a New England pastor at a funeral. In fact, he had considered becoming a pastor after graduating from West Point. His men called him "Old Prayer Book"; he did not smoke, drink, or use foul language. Whenever he heard anyone damning or blasting, Howard would blush like a first-year divinity student, a trait that made other generals go out of their way to use particularly vivid language whenever Howard was within earshot.

Howard may have been prim and proper, but he was also one of Sherman's most reliable generals as well as a veteran of many campaigns— he had lost his right arm at Fair Oaks, Virginia, in 1862. Now he was in position for another battle. Howard put three corps, including John A. Logan's 15th Corps, in a good defensive position to block Hood. Near a small Methodist chapel called Ezra Church, Howard's men dug in and waited.

They did not have a very long wait. The first attacks came at about 12:30 on the afternoon of July 28, when three Confederate brigades came boiling out of the woods. Screaming and howling, they headed straight for Logan on the Federal right flank. The rebels were beaten back, but they regrouped, charged again, and were beaten back again. When Sherman heard the sound of gunfire, he was surprised that Hood was so keen to force yet another battle—this would be the third in just over a week. The thought occurred that maybe the 15th Corps had run into one of Hood's units. "Logan is feeling for them," he remarked, "and I guess he has found them."23

A short while later, one of General Howard's aides came galloping in to report that Logan had come under heavy attack. When he heard the news, Sherman almost jumped up and down with delight. It was as though he had just received the best Christmas present in the world. "Just what I wanted," he shouted. He was so excited that he repeated himself, and his words tumbled over one another. "Tell Howard to invite them to attack, it will save us the trouble, save us the trouble," Sherman rattled on. "They'll only beat their own brains out, beat their own brains out."24

Sherman was right—Hood's men were beating their own brains out. All throughout the afternoon of the 28th, the rebels came howling and screaming at the Federal lines. Every time, they ran up against murderous musket fire. One of the attacking brigades lost three commanding officers, one after the other. On the Federal right, where the attacks were the heaviest and most frequent, pools of blood formed in front of the entrenchments. A solder in an Ohio regiment stated that he "never saw the [rebel] dead lying so thick in [his] life—they are almost in piles—looking as though they had been swept down whole ranks at a time."25

The slaughter went on far longer than anyone on either side thought it would and finally died down at about 5:00 p.m. "During that time, six successive charges were made," General Logan would later report, "which were six times gallantly repulsed, each time with fearful loss to the enemy."26

The Battle of Ezra Church was another disaster for General Hood. Confederate losses are usually given as 5,000 killed, wounded, and missing, though General Logan's own estimate was that the enemy's loss could not have been less than six or seven thousand men. Sherman's losses were between 500 and 600. And Ezra Church was less than three miles from the heart of Atlanta.

When Jefferson Davis replaced Joseph E. Johnston with John Bell Hood, he got exactly what he expected: an aggressive general who would challenge Sherman and fight him at every opening. Hood certainly turned out to be aggressive. He had hit Sherman "like hell," just as John Schofield had predicted. But the results of his aggressiveness did not turn out the way Davis expected.

In the three battles Hood fought against Sherman, he lost more than 18,000 men out of a total force of about 60,000. Every one of his offensives had ended in failure and, as one writer put it, "Hood's army was very nearly fought out."[27] Hood's celebrated aggressiveness had turned out to be a liability instead of the asset Jefferson Davis had expected. President Davis probably wished that he had listened to Robert E. Lee's doubts concerning Hood, swallowed his West Point grudge, and retained Joe Johnston as commander of the Army of Tennessee.

In spite of Sherman's battering of Hood, however, there were no celebrations in the North, even though news headlines reported that Sherman and his army were rapidly closing around Atlanta. By the end of July, Sherman had been advancing toward Atlanta for nearly three months, and the Confederate Stars and Bars still flew defiantly over all the city's public buildings. Sherman was always moving closer to Atlanta, at least according to the newspapers, but he never seemed to get there.

Sherman's army really was closer to Atlanta than ever before. Federal troops were even close enough to see smoke from the factories within the city, but that made little difference to readers of the *New York Times* and other newspapers. A soldier from an Illinois regiment called across to the rebel lines, "Hello, Johnny, how far is it to Atlanta?"

"So damn far you'll never get there," came the mocking reply.[28]

That was the way it seemed to an increasing number of people in the North—Atlanta was so damn far that Sherman would never get there, no matter how many battles he fought. Everyone north of the Mason-Dixon

Line wanted a decisive victory. They wanted Sherman to capture Atlanta, to march into the city and give the rebels a conclusive and final whipping from which they would never recover. Instead, all they were getting was encouraging news reports, with no clear-cut victory anywhere in sight.

Nobody could quite figure out what was wrong—was incompetence the problem, or stupidity, or just a lack of the will to win? But more and more people were inclined to blame Lincoln for not ending the war. As commander in chief, it was Lincoln's job to obtain the final victory over the Confederacy. If he did not, he would be replaced in November.

WITHERED HOPES

One of the primary causes of war weariness in the North—a combination of low morale and diminishing faith in the war—was Ulysses S. Grant's inability to gain any ground against Robert E. Lee. "Who shall revive the withered hopes that bloomed at the opening of Grant's campaign?" moaned the *New York World* on July 12.[29] The siege of Petersburg was a humiliation and a disgrace, the article continued, and was symptomatic of the failure of the entire war effort.

The *New York World* tilted heavily toward the side of the Democratic Party, so such an editorial opinion did not come as much of a surprise. But a great many people were coming to agree with this point of view, and not all of them were Democrats. It began to look as though Grant's campaign, which started off as the bright hope of the Union cause, had come to nothing, and that Grant was well on his way toward losing both the campaign and, very possibly, the war.

Actually, nothing could have been farther from the truth. Grant had Lee right where he wanted him. The Army of Northern Virginia was tightly bottled up in Petersburg, which meant that General Lee no longer had the open ground for turning and maneuvering, as he had had at Chancellorsville and at other battles. Petersburg was not really under siege; it was still connected to the rest of the Confederacy by two rail links and at least one road. Grant did not need to surround Petersburg. He needed to keep

Lee and his army confined there while he brought his superior numbers in men and resources to bear. If he could do that, Grant knew that he would win. As Lee himself had pointed out, it would be only a matter of time.

But people in the North did not see it that way. It looked as though Lee had the Army of the Potomac trapped at Petersburg, not the other way around. As far as most Northerners were concerned, Grant had fought his way south to Petersburg, suffering horrible casualties all along the way, and now he was stuck. He might never get to Richmond because Lee would not let him.

Even reports that did their best to sound encouraging somehow managed to add to the general despair. "Passengers by the mail-boat report that on Thursday afternoon, the rebels in front of Petersburg opened a fire upon our forces from their batteries," the *New York Times* said.[30] The article went on to say that Federal artillery returned fire, but that was beside the point. Grant and his army had been outside Petersburg for well over a month, shelling the city every day. But in spite of everything, the rebels were as defiant and full of fight as ever.

The morale of the troops at Petersburg was a lot higher than the morale of their friends and relatives back home. "The siege goes on, and tons of iron are poured into the city," wrote Elisha Hunt Rhodes of the 2nd Rhode Island Volunteers. "Rebel prisoners say we can never take the city, but we think differently."[31] Not many civilians had that much optimism. The war went on, and the North was becoming more frightened and anxious with time.

At the beginning of July, something happened that made Northerners even more frightened and anxious. General Lee sent about 14,000 men, commanded by General Jubal A. Early, northward through the Shenandoah Valley and across the Potomac into Maryland. Lee could not take his army away from Petersburg, so he sent Jubal Early instead. Maybe Early could capture the Federal prisoner of war camp at Lookout Point and release the Confederate prisoners being held there. Maybe he could even capture Washington. At the very least, he would frighten the hell out of everybody and lower the North's already-shaky morale. Early was to commit mischief and mayhem for Lee by proxy.

Early's instructions were fairly vague. He was to cross the Potomac and raise as much hell as possible—burn houses and seize property and create any other kind of trouble that might present itself. Grant would have to detach part of his army from Petersburg to protect Washington, which could only help Lee's position. In addition, invading the North again, even with only 14,000 men, would help to diminish Lincoln's image as a war president and would also decrease his chances for re-election. Anything that might help the Democrats win in November was well worth the effort. The Confederacy was as pro-Democrat as the *New York World* and Clement Vallandigham combined.

Jubal Early was not especially loved by his fellow officers. He was too profane, sarcastic, and just plain nasty to command affection, and he was too hard-bitten to care. Old Jube was another West Point graduate—class of 1837—who had gone over to the Confederacy after Fort Sumter. Bearded, balding, foul-mouthed, and tobacco-spitting, Early seems to have gone out of his way to turn himself into a caricature—a combination of old soldier and Old Testament prophet.

He may not have been the most popular officer in the Confederate States Army, but Jubal Early was a more-than-capable soldier and a veteran officer who had led men into battle at First and Second Manassas, Antietam, Fredericksburg, Gettysburg, and Chancellorsville. General Lee had enough confidence in him to give him the assignment of going north to threaten the enemy's capital. If everything went well, Old Jube might be able to do considerable damage to the Union's war effort and also inflict a psychological defeat on the North.

First reports of Early's advance were sent on June 29 by employees of the Baltimore and Ohio Railroad. General Lew Wallace, in command of the Middle Atlantic Department, was given the job of confronting Early's Confederates and turning them back. General Grant was also informed that Early was coming north, and he detached about 17,000 men to reinforce General Wallace.

"Wallace moved with commendable promptitude," as General Grant put it. The only trouble was that General Wallace's troops were not the best in the world, to put it mildly—they were usually described as being ragtag, raw, and inexperienced. Grant himself admitted that they were "very much inferior" to the veteran units within the Army of the Potomac.[32] The troops that Wallace's men would be facing over the barrels of their muskets were the lean, battle-hardened veterans of the Army of Northern Virginia. Jubal Early had taken over Stonewall Jackson's old unit, his "foot cavalry." There was no tougher, leaner, or more experienced unit in the Confederate army. Lew Wallace and his ragtag army would have to do their best against Early's veterans until Grant's reinforcements arrived.

Early's and Wallace's mismatched forces met on July 9, just outside Frederick, Maryland, at the Battle of Monocacy. The results were predictable. Another very different American army faced a similar situation 79 years later with almost identical results. In February 1943, at the Kasserine Pass in Tunisia, the untried US 2nd Corps encountered Erwin Rommel's veteran Afrika Korps and were completely routed. Lew Wallace's men did not fare much better. By late afternoon, the Federals were in full retreat. Their losses totaled almost 1,300 dead, wounded, and missing. Confederate losses are usually given as between 700 and 900.

With Wallace's paltry force out of the way, Early pushed forward. His foot cavalry was slowed by fatigue and by the withering July heat, but Early drove and coaxed and blasphemed the men to keep on moving. By noon on July 11, the rebels had reached Silver Springs, Maryland, a few miles northeast of Washington. Early sat upright on his horse and stared off into the distance through his telescope, where he could see the dome of the United States capitol shimmering through the heat waves like a mirage.

Washington, DC, was ringed by an impressive system of fortresses and trenches, which fairly bristled with heavy artillery and guns of all sizes and calibers. But General Grant had taken the 18,000 or so artillerymen out of the fortifications and sent them to Virginia with the Army of the Potomac—they were not doing any good in Washington, Grant thought, and he needed as many men as he could get against Robert E. Lee. All the grand forts and emplacements were now manned by reservists—clerks, hospital staff, office workers, and frightened militia who had been pressed into service for the emergency. Early knew all about how undermanned Washington's forts actually were; captured Federal troops had told him. As he looked at Washington through the heat waves, Old Jube licked his chops and grinned.

Grant knew all about Washington's pitifully undermanned fortifications as well. The 17,000 troops he rushed north were to reinforce the
beleaguered and puny garrison. Captain Elisha Hunt Rhodes of the 2nd
Rhode Island Volunteers was told that the "Rebel General Early" was
moving toward the Washington suburb of Brightwood, and that an attack
was expected at any time. He and his regiment had just arrived on July 12.
In a diary entry made at "Brightwood near Washington, D. C.," he wrote
that he marched through the city, up Pennsylvania Avenue, and through to
Brightwood. "The people in Washington seemed to be very happy to see us,
and were much frightened," Captain Rhodes commented.[33]

The residents of Washington certainly were frightened. Everyone in
the city heard talk that a rebel army of 50,000 had sacked Maryland and was
now coming after them. Civilians milled about in the streets, listening to
lurid gossip concerning the approaching rebels and spreading some of their
own. They probably would have left town, many of them, except that they
were more afraid of running into the Confederates outside of the city than
of waiting for them to come in. It was much safer just to stay put.

But by this time, Early had decided not to attack Washington after all.
While he was making his way toward the capital, moving as quickly as the
July heat and the fatigue of his army would allow, the Union troops of the
veteran 6th Corps had relieved the clerks and the mild-mannered office
workers and the 100-day militia. The 2nd Rhode Island Volunteers were
part of the 6th Corps. When rebel skirmishers began exchanging fire with
the new arrivals, they quickly discovered that the men on the other side of
the line were anything but an untrained bunch of amateurs.

General Early saw the same things as his skirmishers and reached the
same conclusions. The troops in the Federal trenches did not wear the
brand-new blue uniforms of state militia volunteers. These men had blue
uniforms, but they were faded and sun-bleached—the soldiers who were
facing Early's men had spent many long hours in the hot Virginia sun,
walking south through places like Spotsylvania and the Wilderness and
Cold Harbor. If he needed any further proof, Early could also see battle
flags when he looked across at the enemy lines—the flags all had the Greek
cross of the 6th Corps. The Army of the Potomac had arrived, and Early's

chances of capturing Washington had disappeared with the arrival of the Yankee veterans. Early knew that his chance had gone and that there was nothing he could do about it.

Old Jube was not about to give up without some sort of a fight. But it was a half-hearted fight. The men were exhausted and knew that they were in a position that was not to their advantage. It was a brisk skirmish while it lasted, but it did not last very long. "The Rebels first supposing us to be Penn. Militia stood their ground, but prisoners told me that when they saw our lines advance without a break they knew we were veterans," Elisha Hunt Rhodes recalled. "The Greek cross of our Corps told the story, and the Rebels broke and fled."[34]

President Lincoln decided to pay an unannounced visit to one of the Washington forts, Fort Stevens. He arrived in a carriage with his wife. He would visit the soldiers, hopefully raise their morale, see the situation for himself and, quite possibly, acquire a few soldier votes for the November election. The commander of the 6th Corps, General Horatio Wright, met the president and asked him if he would like to see some of the fighting for himself. To General Wright's surprise, Lincoln said yes and climbed up on one of the ramparts where he could get a good view.

Rebel sharpshooters could see the president a lot better than he could see them. Lincoln was six feet four inches tall in his bare feet; his boots and his stovepipe hat added another couple inches. Towering over everybody else, Lincoln stood on the wall and looked out over the field, completely oblivious to the sniper fire zinging all around him. He certainly made a splendid target for the rebel marksmen, a fact that was pointed out to him by General Wright. An officer standing not three feet away from Lincoln was hit by a sniper's bullet. But in spite of everything, the president continued to stand his ground.

Not everybody at Fort Stevens even knew that Lincoln was on the premises. A twenty-three-year-old from Massachusetts named Oliver Wendell Holmes did not recognize the president; he saw only a very tall civilian inviting some rebel sniper to put a bullet in him. Holmes would go on to become a US Supreme Court justice, but in 1864 he was just a captain. "Get down, you damn fool, before you get shot!" he shouted in exasperation.[35]

Lincoln finally got the message. He climbed down from the parapet and sat with his back to it—chastened, but at least he could claim to be the only president to have come under fire in combat.

Jubal Early regretted that he would never get inside Washington. He might have gotten there if he had not been held up at Monocacy, which would have allowed him to attack early in the morning. But as Elisha Hunt Rhodes dryly pointed out, "Early was late."[36] Now the only thing for him to do was to go back to Virginia. At dusk, he ordered a retreat. He and his men began walking back to the Shenandoah Valley.

He had certainly put a scare into the North, just as he had planned, and he had also raised a fair amount of hell. Among other things, he tried to extort $500,000 from the residents of Chambersburg, Pennsylvania, and he burned the town when they would not or could not pay. He actually did extract about $220,000 from two other towns—which would buy a lot of arms and ammunition in the Confederacy—and also sacked the country house of Francis P. Blair, a journalist who had been an adviser to presidents since Andrew Jackson.

But Early wished that he had done a lot more. If he had been able to take Washington, he would have thrown the entire North into a cold panic. He very nearly accomplished this just by marching toward the city. Also, there were so many glittering prizes within the city that were just out of his reach. There was the United States Treasury with all those Yankee greenbacks and all that gold. And there were the arsenals—it would have been a pleasure to take all those rifles and cannons and turn them against the Yankees. They might also have taken a few congressmen prisoner—that would have made for a few lurid headlines in the New York press. They might even have captured the president himself. Of course, there were any number of Northerners who would have loved to see Abe Lincoln taken prisoner by the Confederates, especially the Democrats and the Radical Republicans. But how much of a ransom might have been demanded for Honest Abe?

But the opportunity was gone, and there was no use brooding over it. The rebels retreated in good order and were across the Potomac on July 14. "The retreat to the Potomac went smoothly, free of pursuit or even effective harassment by any major Federal force," according to one of Jubal Early's biographers.[37]

General Grant was glad that the emergency was over and that Early had gone back to Virginia. But he was angry that Early had been able to escape to the Shenandoah. The Shenandoah Valley had been a thorn in the Union's side—more like a knife at its throat—since the beginning of the war. Grant began to think of a way to remove the knife, using tactics that would be typical of him—brutal and direct.

In the meantime, General Grant still had the problem of how to break the stalemate at Petersburg. A colonel in a Pennsylvania regiment, which was made up predominantly of coal miners, came up with a unique way of destroying one of the rebel fortresses in the Petersburg line. If it worked, it might just break the line and lead to the capture of Petersburg.

Lieutenant Colonel Henry Pleasants of the 48th Pennsylvania was a mining engineer by profession. "That God-damned fort is the only thing between us and Petersburg," he observed, "and I have an idea we can blow it up."[38] His idea was to dig a tunnel under the fort, fill it with explosives, and touch the whole thing off. The resulting explosion would obliterate the rebel fortification and blow a hole in the trenches in front of Petersburg. If troops moved fast enough, an attack through the gap would overwhelm the city and its defenses before the rebels had time to react.

Colonel Pleasants turned his idea into a formal proposal, cleaning up the language and presenting it to his commander. The proposal was then passed up the chain of command to the 9th Corps' commander, General Ambrose E. Burnside—the same Ambrose Burnside of Fredericksburg and the Mud March. Burnside liked the idea and sent it along to generals Grant and Meade.

Neither Grant nor Meade was wild about the proposal. It was probably too unconventional for Meade, who would have preferred a more straightforward method of attack. As for Grant, the levelheaded Midwesterner, the whole concept of blowing up a fort by planting a charge of explosives underneath it seemed a bit far-fetched. But both of them approved the idea anyway. "Burnside had submitted the scheme to Meade and myself, and we both approved it," Grant said, "as a means of keeping the men occupied." Even if the plan failed, Grant reasoned, at least it would keep the men busy and out of trouble.[39]

The project got under way on June 25. Colonel Pleasants recruited men who had been coal miners before the war and divided his crew of diggers into shifts. He had everything organized, with each shift working eight hours, and was determined to go ahead with his design. Army engineers did not think that the tunnel was a practical idea—for one thing, they thought a 500-foot tunnel would be impossible to ventilate—and refused to help.

In spite of all the obstacles, both physical and bureaucratic, Colonel Pleasants managed to complete his tunnel, which eventually measured 511 feet. Next came the job of loading the explosives into the shaft. Pleasants did not get any help with this, either. "I called for twelve thousand pounds of explosives," he complained; "they gave me eight thousand." He was also given the wrong type of fuses, in the wrong length.[40]

But mainly because of Colonel Pleasants's persistence, the explosives were loaded into position and everything was made ready. On the morning of July 30, the fuse was lit; at 16 minutes before five o'clock, the three-hundred-odd kegs of gunpowder went off all at once. A soldier from Michigan described the detonation as a deep tremor, like an earthquake, "then a heaving and lifting of the fort and of the hill on which it stood; then a monstrous tongue of flame shot fully two hundred feet in the air."[41]

Bits of masonry and other wreckage also shot hundreds of feet in the air, "mingled with men and guns, timbers and planks, and every kind of debris."[42] It seemed as though the entire fort had gone straight up in the air and never came down again. Almost 300 men in the fortifications above the explosion were either killed outright or injured.

The blast made a crater 30 feet deep and 60 feet wide. A gap had been blown in the Petersburg defenses, just as Colonel Pleasants had anticipated. "Burnside's mine," as Grant called the explosive-packed tunnel, had worked. Now it was up to 9th Corps to rush through the gap and into Petersburg.

General Burnside planned on having 15,000 infantrymen charge into the breach in four waves. A division of black troops was originally supposed to have led the first wave. They had not seen much fighting and would be fresher than most other units. They had also received special training for this particular operation. But General Meade rescinded this order and had white troops lead the first wave instead. Grant approved Meade's change in orders. He was afraid that it would look as though the black troops were being shoved in front so that they would be killed "because we did not care anything about them."[43]

General Burnside now had to find someone else to go in first. He called his three division commanders to draw straws for the privilege. The long straw was drawn by General James H. Ledlie, which would prove disastrous for Burnside and the troops that would make the charge that day. A brigadier who knew Ledlie said that he was "a drunkard and an arrant coward . . . it was wicked to risk the lives of men in such a man's hands."[44]

With General Ledlie in command, the operation had no chance at all. At the order to advance, Ledlie's men left their trenches and ran toward the gigantic hole that had been blown in the ground. But instead of running around the crater, they ran into it. Once inside the crater, they stayed there—it seemed safe and nobody told them to keep moving. Hundreds of men piled into the deep pit and waited for something to happen or for somebody to tell them what do to.

General Ledlie was supposed to have been with his men, and to have led them out the other side of the pit and into Petersburg. But Ledlie was 400 yards to the rear of the Federal lines, sitting in a safe dugout and drinking medicinal rum that he had promoted from one of the surgeons. When he received word that his division had crammed itself in a hole in front of the rebel lines, he issued orders that the men should move forward. Then he resumed his drinking. General Burnside was just as useless. He had taken cover in a 14-gun artillery position behind the lines and had no idea that the attack had gone wrong. At least he was not getting drunk.

For well over an hour, no attempt was made to move Ledlie's division out of the crater. During this time, while the Federals should have been pressing their advantage of surprise, the stunned Confederates began to react. They brought up reinforcements; they brought up artillery. Mortars began dropping shells into the crater, which did horrible damage to the densely packed Federal troops. The Battle of the Crater, as it came to be known, was already lost.

But Burnside had no idea what was going on. He ordered more men forward into what was now a slaughterhouse, including the black division that was supposed to have led the attack. They actually made a run toward the enemy defenses, but the rebels waiting for them counterattacked. The black troops turned and ran. Others became caught up in the panic and began to run as well.

For the men who had not been shot or blown to pieces by artillery shells, the only goal now was to survive. By midmorning, the attack was finally over. Nearly 4,000 men had been killed, wounded, or herded off to Confederate prisoner of war camps. Nothing at all had been gained by the attack.

Colonel Henry Pleasants was absolutely livid by what he had seen that morning. His part of the plan had worked—he had placed his explosives directly under the rebel fort, which was nothing short of an amazing piece of calculating, and the resulting blast had done exactly what he had said it would do. But the officers in charge of the attack on Petersburg had made a bloody, hideous mess of everything. Pleasants told Burnside that he had nothing but fools and cowards for brigade commanders, and meant every word he said. Pleasants had a temper, along with a vocabulary that had been seasoned by working with Pennsylvania coal miners. Burnside probably had not heard that kind of language in his entire life, or at least not since he had been wearing general's stars. But by that time, it really did not matter what anyone said. The damage had already been done.

"The effort was a stupendous failure," in General Grant's opinion.[45] Nobody on either side would have disagreed. A student at Virginia Military Institute commented, "In the whole history of war, no enterprise so auspiciously begun ever resulted in a conclusion so lame and impotent."[46]

The two generals largely responsible for the disaster, Major General Burnside and Brigadier General Ledlie, both left the army because of their conduct on July 30. General Burnside was given a 20-day furlough and was never recalled to active service. General Ledlie was granted a 20-day "sick leave" that went on for four months. When he returned to the army in December, Ledlie was sent home to await further orders. He resigned his commission a month later.

Jubal Early's raid on Washington and the failure at the Crater combined to lower morale throughout the North to a new depth, especially since the two shocks to the national psyche followed so closely one after another. First, Grant had not been able to stop a rebel force from approaching the very outskirts of Washington, or from burning Chambersburg, Pennsylvania, about 25 miles from Gettysburg. Next, an attempt to break through the enemy's line at Petersburg resulted in what the *New York Times* described as a shameful slaughter of Union troops.

The North was desperate for some good news, for any Union victory, no matter how small. Instead, all the newspapers seemed to be reporting that the war was turning into a fiasco and that all the dead and wounded in all the battles since early May had brought nothing but failure and humiliation. Jubal Early had done more damage to the Union war effort than he realized, even though it would turn out to be only temporary. Burnside had done his fair share of damage, as well, although his had been unintentional. "Many in the North saw [Early's] raid as evidence of northern mismanagement and the impossibility of ever winning the war," one writer stated.[47]

Reports from Petersburg were even more alarming. According to most newspapers, Grant's army had suffered a disastrous defeat at the Battle of the Crater. The *New York World* tried to turn the battle into a full-fledged catastrophe, with panic-stricken and demoralized troops in full retreat before victorious Confederates. The *World* was unapologetically anti-Lincoln, and it always slanted its news to make the Union war effort seem like a lost cause. But other papers ran articles that were just as pessimistic.

The *New York Times* was staunchly pro-Lincoln. Its editors did their best to publish stories that put Lincoln and the Union cause in the best possible light. In its August 2 edition, underneath a line about "the failure in the late attack at Petersburgh [*sic*]," the editors made a point of declaring: "It is understood that Gen. GRANT still expresses the utmost confidence in his ability to take Richmond."[48]

General Grant really did have confidence, both in his ability to take Richmond and in the outcome of the war. Grant knew, positively, that the South had no chance at all of winning the war—barring some unforeseen Union catastrophe or some miracle on behalf of Robert E. Lee and the Confederacy. And the longer the war went on, the more certain Grant became regarding the South's ultimate defeat.

By the summer of 1864, Richmond might be seen as a symbol of the Confederacy and its plight. Even though both the Confederacy and its capital city seemed vital and active, both were actually on the brink of disaster. Both were certainly defiant—government buildings in Richmond flew the Confederate flag and carried on as if the city, and the rest of the country, had all the time in the world on its side—but the truth was that neither Richmond nor the Confederacy had nearly as much time as many people thought. To use the theatrical phrase, they were both doomed.

But the North could not see this. Northerners saw only the defiance and the vitality and had no idea that the Confederacy was running on its last reserves—nerve and courage. The war had already been going on for over three years, and it seemed as if it could go on for another three years—three more years of fighting and killing and boatloads of maimed and wounded soldiers landing at the Union's sprawling base at City Point, Virginia.

It was good to know that General Grant was confident about capturing Richmond, but his confidence was shared by fewer and fewer people with each day that his army stayed at Petersburg. It did not mean anything during the summer of 1864, but Petersburg is only about 80 miles from Appomattox.

BEATEN OUT OF SIGHT

Abraham Lincoln was absolutely certain of one thing: he had absolutely no chance of being re-elected.

Lincoln had been reading the same reports as everyone else, and he knew the nation's mood. He also was fully aware that the Democratic Party was growing in strength, and that his own popularity was declining in direct proportion. The Democrats were preaching that the war was a total failure, and the public listened and believed. Ever since Jubal Early's raid on Washington and the Battle of the Crater, the North seemed more convinced than ever that the South was going to win the war.

"You think I don't know I am going to be beaten," Lincoln remarked to a friend, "*but I do* and unless some great change takes place *badly beaten*."[49] He also knew that if he lost, the war would be lost. If the Democrats took control, they would end the war and let the Confederate states secede permanently.

General Grant agreed with the president—if the Democrats were to win the election, the war would be as good as lost. When he was asked about the possibility of Lincoln not being re-elected, Grant answered in his usual frank and straight-from-the-shoulder manner. "I consider it as important to the cause that he should be elected," he said, "as that the army should be successful in the field."[50] Eighty years later, a British general would calculate that General Dwight D. Eisenhower's grin was worth an army corps. Grant went several steps farther. He thought that Abraham Lincoln's presence in the White House was worth an Antietam or a Shiloh.

The Confederates also held the opinion that Lincoln was indispensable to the Union's war effort, and that a defeat in November would mean Confederate independence. And it was beginning to look as though Lincoln would not be re-elected—at least it was a distinct possibility. Word was filtering down across the Mason-Dixon Line—from men who had been up north recently or from newspapers that had found their way to Virginia and parts south—that George B. McClellan would be the Democratic candidate, and that he stood an excellent chance of unseating Lincoln. The North was tired of the war, people were saying, and was also tired of Lincoln. If McClellan won the election, he would end the war and allow the South to form its own sovereign state.

Southern newspapers had been running stories about Northern opposition to the war for over a year. In July 1863, just three weeks after Gettysburg, the *Richmond Examiner* had this to say: "the people of the North are tired of the war and will no longer furnish army after army to be slaughtered, for the fruitless purpose of destroying the Southern States and driving its people into exile."[51]

The Confederacy did not have to win the war. It just had to keep from losing it—keep fighting the Yankees and continue the stalemate at Petersburg and Atlanta. Keep killing the blue invaders, the thinking went, and the Yankees will get tired of the slaughter and give up. That was the best hope for the South in the summer of 1864.

That was also Abraham Lincoln's deepest dread—that the rebels would continue the killing just long enough to cost him the election. The probable Democratic candidate was George B. McClellan, who had been an advocate of a "soft war" even when he was still commander of the Army of the Potomac. In July 1862, he had handed Lincoln a listing of his ideas on how the war should be fought: "It should not be a war looking to the subjugation of the southern people," McClellan wrote, "and it should be conducted upon the highest principles known to Christian civilization.... Neither confiscation of property ... nor forcible abolition of slavery should be contemplated for a moment. Military power should not be allowed to interfere with the relations of servitude.... A declaration of radical views, especially upon slavery, will rapidly disintegrate our present armies."[52]

If McClellan became president, it looked as though he and the Democrats would lose no time in putting those suggestions into action: do not offend the rebels, do not treat them too harshly, do not confiscate their property, and do not interfere with their keeping of slaves. Everything Lincoln had been trying to accomplish since the war began would be completely canceled out unless he won the election. And all the political bosses were saying that he had no chance of winning.

Lincoln was given to melancholy by nature. Knowing that he was almost certain to go down in defeat in the most important election of his life and that he would drag his party down with him made him even more depressed than usual. A year earlier, in the summer of 1863, his wife's dressmaker noticed how unhappy and dejected Lincoln appeared to be. "His step was slow and heavy, and his face sad," she remembered. "Like a tired child he threw himself upon a sofa, and shaded his eyes with his hands. He was a complete picture of dejection." He had just returned from reading telegraphs in the War Department, and said that the news was "dark, dark everywhere."[53]

This happened only a short time after Gettysburg and Vicksburg, when the news had been hopeful and everything looked promising for the Union. If Lincoln was feeling down and dejected at that time, in the days just following two important Union victories, it can well be imagined what his state of mind must have been in July 1864 when absolutely nothing seemed to be going right.

At the beginning of August, something happened that made Lincoln's spirits sink even lower than before. An election was being held in Kentucky, a county election to select a few local officials and an appellate judge. Even though the election itself was hardly of national importance, a great deal of significance was being placed on how the voting would turn out—this could possibly be a harbinger for November. If the Republicans did not do well in Kentucky, their chances in the upcoming national election would look anything but optimistic.

Lincoln had been in politics long enough to recognize the importance of the contest, and he decided to do everything in his considerable power to make certain that the Democrats did not win it. He had leading Democrats arrested on charges of disloyalty and suspended habeas corpus until after Election Day. He also had the candidate for the judgeship dropped from the ballot for the same offense. This meant that the Democrats had to come up with a last-minute substitute, which put their candidate at a distinct disadvantage against his Republican rival.

The election was held on August 1. In spite of everything Lincoln had done to influence the outcome, and even though Lincoln himself had been born in Kentucky and should have held an advantage as a native son, the Democrats won every seat, including the judgeship.

Four days after the Kentucky drubbing, Horace Greeley told Lincoln, "We shall be beaten out of sight next November."[54] Lincoln did not need to be told. Unless Grant or Sherman managed some sort of victory within the next three months, something that even the *New York World* would not be able to turn into a propaganda victory for the Democrats and the Confederates, he would have absolutely no chance against any candidate the Democrats chose to run against him.

Chapter Five

NATURAL MILITARY CONSEQUENCES

DAMN THE TORPEDOES!

J ust a few days after the Republican loss in Kentucky, an election that Abraham Lincoln wanted desperately to win, events took a definite and perceptible turn for the better for Lincoln and the Union cause. This turning of events did not take place in Georgia or in Virginia, where everyone expected it, but in the Gulf of Mexico port city of Mobile, Alabama.

Mobile was the Confederacy's last major port on the Gulf coast for blockade-runners, which made it strategically vital for the South—and made holding it essential for Southern morale. A writer described Mobile as a "charming old Alabama gulf city protected by more than fifty forts and redoubts in concentric circles."[1] The largest of these were Fort Morgan and Fort Gaines, which flanked the entry into Mobile Bay.

Because of its value to the Confederacy, Rear Admiral David Glasgow Farragut was intent on capturing Mobile, along with any Confederate ships that happened to be there at the time. In January 1864, he wrote, "I am satisfied that if I had one ironclad at this time, I could destroy their whole force in the bay."[2] Farragut had about 80 ships at his disposal, but most of them were either in dry dock, undergoing repairs, or on blockade duty. Before he could do anything about the rebel fleet at Mobile, the admiral would have to wait for his warships to return to the fleet. He also lobbied Washington to send him a few ironclads, the new twin-turreted monitors, which would prove to be essential when he went up against the rebel force at Mobile.

Admiral Farragut was as aggressive as Grant and Sherman, as he would demonstrate when his fleet was finally assembled. He had as much vigor and energy onshore as he had when he was aboard ship. In the summer of 1864, Farragut had just turned 63 years old, although he refused to act his age. Even though he suffered terribly from gout, he insisted upon staying out late and drinking too much red wine. As a birthday stunt he would turn handstands, along with other acrobatic stunts, and he often went horseback riding even when the weather would have convinced a more moderate soul to stay indoors. Virtually his entire life had been spent in the navy—he became a midshipman at the age of nine, and his first sea fight had come against the British navy during the War of 1812. By 1844, he had been promoted to lieutenant, and he reached the rank of captain by 1855. Farragut was born in Tennessee, near Knoxville, but he determined to remain with the US Navy instead of transferring to the Confederate fleet when the war began, as many of his fellow officers from the South had done.

Farragut made a name for himself at New Orleans in April 1862, when his fleet pounded the Confederate forts defending the city and also sank several rebel warships. New Orleans surrendered at the end of April, and Farragut became a national hero. His fleet also bombarded shore batteries at Vicksburg while General Grant held the city under siege. Congress created the rank of rear admiral in July 1862 in recognition of his energy and aggression. By the beginning of 1864, when most naval officers his age were looking forward to retirement, Admiral Farragut was planning how to destroy the force of rebel warships inside Mobile Bay.

The admiral would have a sizable and formidable war fleet under his command by the time he was ready to go after the enemy's fleet at Mobile. Fourteen of his ships were either screw sloops—wooden ships powered by steam engines and screw propellers, but also having masts and yardarms for sails—or gunboats. And he had also been given the four monitors he had requested: the single-turret *Tecumseh* and *Manhattan*, which were each armed with two 15-inch cannons and were protected by ten inches of armor on their turrets, and the twin-turreted *Winnebago* and *Chickasaw*, also well-armored and with twin 11-inch guns in each turret.

These four monitors were vital to Farragut because the rebels had an ironclad of their own—CSS *Tennessee*. Just the sight of the hulking *Tennessee* was enough to panic the sailors aboard any of Farragut's wooden ships. She was over 200 feet long and about 50 feet in the beam. Her armament, a battery of 7-inch and 6.4-inch guns, was formidable enough, but her real power was in her protective iron plating. The *Tennessee* had six inches of armor on her forward section and five inches on her sides, backed by 24 inches of solid oak and pine. Her sides sloped at a 33-degree angle, which would deflect both solid shot and explosive shells. When Admiral Farragut first saw the ironclad, he said that the ship reminded him of a huge turtle—he was too much of an old curmudgeon to admit that he was afraid.

Although CSS *Tennessee* was certainly a fearsome warship, even if dour old Farragut would not admit it, she had her share of weak points, most of which stemmed from the Confederacy's lack of industry and industrial resources. Her engines, salvaged from a river steamboat, were totally inadequate for powering a warship the size of the *Tennessee*. But that was the best that the builder could do—there simply was nothing else except second-hand engines available to shipyards in the South.

Another glaring weak point was a failure in the ironclad's design. The *Tennessee*'s steering chains stretched over her deck, on the outside of the ship, instead of being inside the hull. This defect made her extremely vulnerable to enemy fire in spite of all her armor, and could also be attributed to the South's lacking of resources—most naval engineers and designers lived north of the Mason-Dixon Line.

The *Tennessee* would have only three escorts at Mobile Bay, and these were side-wheel gunboats—another inadequacy imposed by the South's insufficiencies. But in spite of all the drawbacks, the big rebel ironclad was an ominous and frightening force. The admiral in command of the *Tennessee* and her small escort group, Franklin Buchannan, complained that everyone expected the ironclad ram to sink a dozen of the enemy all by herself. The way things turned out, Admiral Buchannan would try to do exactly that—take on Farragut and his fleet single-handedly.

Farragut referred to Buchannan as "Old Buck," a friendly enough sounding nickname. But Buchannan was the kind of officer that Farragut despised—he had transferred his allegiance to the Confederacy, which made him a traitor in Farragut's eyes. Farragut refused to change sides in 1861, and he had expected all his fellow officers to follow his example, including Buchannan.

Franklin Buchannan served in the United States Navy for more than 45 years. He'd joined as a midshipman at the age of 15—although he was nearly a year older than Farragut, he had six fewer years of service in the navy. During his career, Buchannan had taken part in Admiral Perry's expedition to Japan in 1853 as captain of the steam sloop *Susquehanna*. He had also served as the US Naval Academy's first superintendent from 1845 to 1847, but had resigned his post to return to active duty during the Mexican War, which ended the following year.

Buchannan's distinguished career continued after he joined the Confederate navy. Among other duties, he had commanded CSS *Virginia* (*Merrimac*) during her fight with USS *Monitor* at Hampton Roads, Virginia, in 1862—the first-ever battle between ironclad ships. Although the *Tennessee* was not as large as the *Virginia*, Buchannan was certainly familiar with the handling of ironclads. He would be as aggressive at Mobile Bay as he had been at Hampton Roads, when he had sunk the warships USS *Cumberland* and USS *Congress*.

On August 4, the night before he planned to take his flotilla against Old Buck's force, Admiral Farragut wrote to his wife. "My dearest Wife, I write and leave this letter for you. I am going into Mobile Bay in the morning, if God is my leader, and I hope He is, and in Him I place my trust."[3]

The morning turned out to be gorgeous, with a clear blue sky. "Morning came at last, after so busy a night that only an hour could be given to sleep," a surgeon aboard the sloop USS *Lackawanna* wrote.[4] The wind was blowing from the west, which was an advantage for Farragut. The wind would blow all the cannon smoke from the fleet toward Fort Morgan, interfering with the rebel gunners' view of the Union ships.

At about 4:00 a.m., the fleet began making final preparations for the coming day's fighting. Each sloop had to have a gunboat tied to its port side, and the day's activities started with this task. The gunboat *Seminole* steamed alongside the sloop *Lackawanna* and was securely lashed to her port side by a team of sailors in the predawn darkness. According to Farragut's Order No. 10, this was being done so that if one of the ships happened to be disabled by gunfire, "their partners must carry them through, if possible."[5] Farragut was getting ready for a tough, knockdown fight.

The wooden ships made their way from the Gulf of Mexico into Mobile Bay in this slightly awkward way, two by two. The sloop *Brooklyn*, tied to the *Octorara*, steamed at the head of the column because she had been fitted with a mine-clearing device that was called a "cowcatcher" because of its resemblance to the devices of the same name that were affixed to the front end of railway locomotives. The flagship *Hartford*, which carried Farragut and had been tied to the gunboat *Metacomet*, fell in behind the *Brooklyn*. The four monitors, with the *Tecumseh* in the lead, chugged along just ahead of the wooden ships.

The entrance into the bay was treacherous—it placed the advancing flotilla squarely between Fort Gaines (26 guns) and Fort Morgan (23 heavy guns and 46 smaller guns). But the forts were only part of the problem facing Farragut. Two-thirds of the three-mile-wide channel were blocked by obstructions, placed there by the Confederates to force any approaching Union ships under the guns of Fort Morgan. The passageway that remained open had been sown with about 200 "torpedoes"—which, in another era, would be known as sea mines.

In spite of the torpedoes and the guns of Fort Morgan, Farragut's plan was to push his way through the narrow passage into Mobile Bay. He knew that the mines were not in top condition and that many of them probably would not explode either because they were defective or because their firing mechanisms were corroded. Confederate deserters and prisoners had assured Farragut and his officers that "from their having been some time in the water, they were probably innocuous."[6]

When Admiral Buchannan was told that the enemy fleet was approaching, he had only been awake for a short time and had not yet dressed. The admiral went up on deck in his underwear to look for himself. After seeing what he wanted of Farragut's ships, Buchannan went below to dress and to prepare his officers for what he knew was to come. Do your duty, he told them, because he intended to meet the Yankees and fight them at close quarters.

The first shot of the battle was fired by the monitor *Tecumseh* at about 6:20 a.m. Her target was Fort Morgan. The gunners inside the fort did not reply until Farragut's ships were well within range of their cannons, which was about 7:00 a.m. By that time, USS *Hartford* was only about a mile away, which was much too close for comfort for Admiral Farragut.

"It is a curious sight to watch a single shot from so heavy a piece of ordinance," the same surgeon aboard the sloop *Lackawanna* noted. "First you see the puff of smoke . . . and then you see the shot coming, looking exactly as if some gigantic hand had thrown a play ball toward you." The shell went overhead with "a shriek like a thousand devils." The sloops and the forts kept blasting away at each other, as fast as the gunners could fire and reload. "Shell, grape and canister from the great cannon went hissing through the air, until it seemed as if hell itself had broken loose."[7]

Not all the shells missed. The *Hartford* was hit several times; a solid shot struck the mainmast and lodged there. Farragut was thankful that it had not been an explosive shell. Farther back in the battle line, the *Monongahela* was also taking a beating; she was hit any number of times. Her executive officer had his right leg torn off by an unexploded shell. But Fort Morgan was also absorbing its share of punishment. Farragut's gunners were blowing chunks of brick and masonry from the walls and battlements, literally knocking the place to pieces. But in spite of all the damage and destruction, the two sides kept up their withering barrage.

While the fleet was making its way past the guns of Fort Morgan at a speed that was much too slow to suit the men on board the ships, the captain of the monitor *Tecumseh* made a turn to port. The turn was against orders, and the reasons behind the maneuver remain unclear. Very shortly after turning out of line, the thing that was feared most by every sailor aboard every ship actually happened—the monitor hit a torpedo. The massive explosion that immediately followed shook the ironclad and sent her to the bottom, bow first, along with all but eight of her crew. It was a sudden and stunning loss—one moment, the little ship was steaming along, exchanging gunfire with Fort Morgan; the next moment, she was gone.

Aboard the *Tennessee*, an officer watched as the monitor went down; "she 'laid to' for a moment, seemed to reel, then slowly disappeared into the gulf." All the men who saw the *Tecumseh* go under were both shaken and sobered by what they had just seen. "The men peered through the portholes at the awful catastrophe, and we spoke to each other in low whispers, for they knew that the same fate was probably awaiting us."[8]

The officers and men aboard the Union ships had also seen what had happened to the *Tecumseh*, and the sinking put fear into them as well. The lead ship, the *Brooklyn*, slowed to a stop and began backing up, stern first, toward the *Hartford*. Farragut's confident advance into Mobile Bay had degenerated into fear and confusion. The admiral saw what was happening and was not happy—he had climbed the rigging to get a better view, and was tied there by a line to keep from falling. He called across to the *Brooklyn*, "What's the trouble?"

"Torpedoes," came the quick answer. This was just what Farragut did not want to hear. His lead sloop was backing up, holding up the rest of the column and giving the gunners in Fort Morgan the most inviting target they could ever ask for. Farragut did not care about the torpedoes. Unless the flotilla started moving again, Farragut would not have to worry about torpedoes or about Frank Buchanan and the *Tennessee*. Fort Morgan's gunners would sink his entire force without any help from Buchannan or the torpedoes.

"Damn the torpedoes!" Farragut exploded in exasperation. "Four bells! Captain Drayton, go ahead. Jouett, full speed." David Jouett was captain of the *Hartford*'s companion gunboat the *Metacomet*. The flagship *Hartford* made her way around the *Brooklyn* and took the lead, where Farragut wanted to be, where he could lead from the front.[9]

The captains of the other ships followed the admiral, but not with very much enthusiasm—if torpedoes could sink the ironclad *Tecumseh*, what chance did a wooden screw sloop have? But the Confederate prisoners and deserters who had said that the mines were "innocuous" had not been lying, as some Union officers had feared. Apart from causing severe anxiety, the mines did no damage. None of the torpedoes in the channel exploded, although some of the men heard detonators go off as the mines scraped along the bottom of their ships.

As soon as the *Hartford* cleared the minefield and was inside Mobile

Bay, the *Metacomet*, her escort, was cut loose from the flagship. The gunboat went after the Confederate gunboat CSS *Selma*, hitting her with her forward gun and forcing her to surrender. Farragut's gunboats also knocked out CSS *Gaines*; her crew scuttled her to avoid capture. The third Confederate gunboat, CSS *Morgan*, took cover under the protective fire of Fort Morgan; that night, the *Morgan* escaped Farragut's warships under cover of darkness.

So far, Admiral Farragut had done everything he had set out to do. He had taken his fleet past Fort Morgan into Mobile Bay and had also steamed through the dreaded minefield that barred the way. Also, his gunboats had disposed of all three of the *Tennessee*'s escorts. Now he would have to face Franklin Buchannan and the *Tennessee* herself. If he could not sink or at least neutralize the Confederate ironclad, everything else he and his fleet had accomplished would not count.

Farragut had planned to allow his men time for breakfast before turning his attention to the *Tennessee*. His flotilla was about four miles inside Mobile Bay; he expected Buchannan to stay under the protection of Fort Morgan's guns and force the Union fleet to come after him. But at about 8:45 a.m., a sailor aboard the *Hartford*, looking out from the top of the mainmast, pointed off into the distance and began shouting—here comes the ram!

All hands, including Farragut, turned to see what all the shouting was about. They saw the *Tennessee* heading straight for them, black smoke pouring out of her funnel, looking like some sort of prehistoric creature bent on destroying the entire Union fleet. Everybody on board knew immediately that breakfast had been postponed indefinitely. "I perceived the ram *Tennessee* standing up for this ship," Farragut recalled. "I was not long in comprehending his intention to be the destruction of this flagship."[10]

Farragut thought Old Buck was coming after *him*—his admiral's flag was certainly visible to everybody aboard the ironclad. Actually, Buchannan was intent on fighting the entire Union fleet; he planned to ram or shell every Yankee ship that came within range and withdraw under the guns of Fort Morgan when he ran out of ammunition. He had done it a year and a half before; at Hampton Roads, aboard CSS *Virginia*, he had rammed and sunk the *Cumberland* and set fire to the *Congress* before coming back on the following day to fight USS *Monitor* to a standstill. He was going to do his damndest to do it all over again in Mobile Bay.

But Mobile Bay was not Hampton Roads. This time, Buchannan was up against three monitors, along with 14 other ships. He intended to use his ship's ram against the wooden ships in the bay, but the sloops easily evaded the clumsy ironclad. Instead, the Union sloops turned the tables and attacked the *Tennessee*. The first to charge the grim iron ship was the *Monongahela*, which had been fitted with her own iron ram. She plowed into the *Tennessee* at full speed, but did more damage to herself than to the enemy—the force of the collision opened her seams and started leaks, and her iron prow broke off on impact. The *Monongahela's* gunners also fired a full broadside at point-blank range, but were treated to the sight of their shot bouncing off the iron plating and splashing into the water.

The *Lackawanna* also rammed the Confederate ironclad, with the same results—no damage to the *Tennessee* but the collision crushed her own bow, which opened her seams and let several tons of water into her forward section. The *Hartford* was next in line. She struck the *Tennessee* a glancing blow, which did no damage to either ship. Her gunners also fired a broadside at the ram, but had no better luck than the *Monongahela's* crew—they also watched their shot hit the ironclad and bounce into the bay.

Farragut's three monitors were also coming into the fight. They could do battle with the *Tennessee* on equal terms, and their presence would have a telling effect. The twin-turreted *Chickasaw* took up a position just astern of the *Tennessee*. Her crew fired the two 11-inch guns of her forward turret as quickly as they could be reloaded. The *Manhattan* and the *Winnebago* also kept peppering the enemy, but it was the *Chickasaw* that did the most damage. The solid shot from her forward guns hammered the *Tennessee's* armor plating, seriously denting the iron casemate and splintering the heavy wooden backing underneath. A metal splinter hit Admiral Buchannan, breaking his left leg below the knee.

Even though none of the hits managed to penetrate the *Tennessee's* casemate, the effects of being struck more than 100 times began to tell. Her funnel had been shot away, giving the ironclad an even more sinister appearance and reducing the draft to her boilers. The *Chickasaw's* relentless pounding destroyed the *Tennessee*'s exposed steering chains. When a system of "relieving tackles" was set up to replace the chains, these were also smashed by the *Chickasaw*'s gunners. Several of the ironclad's gunport shutters were jammed shut by hits from solid shot, which effectively put her guns out of action, one by one.

When the shutter covering the stern gun was disabled, which prevented the *Tennessee*'s gunners from firing back at the *Chickasaw*, a machinist's mate was called in to repair it. While the machinist was at work, a shot from the monitor killed him outright, literally ripping him to pieces. What was left of him was scraped up with a shovel, loaded into a bucket, and thrown overboard.

The *Tennessee* had been "rendered utterly helpless," as summed up by her captain, James D. Johnston. She could not steer; she could not bring any guns to bear on the enemy. When he informed Admiral Buchannan of his ship's condition, he was told, "Well, Johnston, if you cannot do them any further damage you had better surrender."[11]

"I concluded that no good object could be accomplished by sacrificing the lives of the officers and men in such a one-sided contest," Johnston wrote.[12] He ordered the white flag hoisted on one of the gunner's ramrods. The flagstaff had been shot off during the battle.

The battle had lasted just over three hours. Farragut thought that it had been the most desperate fight of his long career. "The almighty has smiled upon me once more," he wrote to his wife after the battle. "I am in Mobile Bay."[13] He had disposed of Old Buck and his war fleet, and the surrender of the forts surrounding the bay, including Fort Morgan, was now just a matter of time.

This was the best news that the North—as well as Abraham Lincoln and the Republicans—had heard all year. Mobile had been permanently closed to the Confederacy. Admiral Farragut had become a national hero all over again and had won a clear victory against the rebels without the horrible casualties of Grant in Virginia.

Newspapers fairly crowed with excitement. Reports went on and on about how Farragut and his fleet had subdued the Confederates in Mobile Bay and ravaged the rebel fleet that came out to stop them. "Our Fleet

Passed Fort Morgan and Close to Mobile," the *New York Times* reported. "Dreadful Havoc Among the Rebel Gunboats. The Iron-Clad Tennessee Surrendered. . . . The Rebel Admiral Buchannan Maimed and Captured." For many readers, the most significant—and encouraging—news was: "Only One Union Monitor Reported Lost."[14]

Not every paper got its facts straight, of course. Some reported that the *Tecumseh* had been sunk by gunfire from Fort Morgan and that Admiral Buchannan had lost a leg and that Farragut's entire fleet had been ironclads. But even the most muddled accounts told the public what it wanted most desperately to hear—Union forces had won a decisive victory without losing thousands of men.

What Admiral Farragut had done at Mobile Bay certainly was welcome news in the summer of 1864, coming after the Crater and Cold Harbor and the raid on Washington. Members of the public ate up the news, devouring every account of the battle and everything they could find about Admiral Farragut. "Damn the torpedoes!" entered the American lexicon. Public opinion brightened instantly. Maybe Mobile Bay was a sign of better things to come, people thought. Maybe the battle showed that the tables really were beginning to turn to the Union's advantage after all. But Grant was still stalled south of Petersburg, and Sherman was not getting any closer to Atlanta.

LITTLE PHIL

President Abraham Lincoln welcomed the news of Mobile Bay as much as anybody else in the North—if not more so, since his political career was riding on the shoulders of the likes of Farragut, Grant, and Sherman. But in August 1864, Lincoln was preoccupied with events that were much closer to home.

Lincoln had a small confrontation of his own to settle, between his secretary of war, Edwin M. Stanton, and Ulysses S. Grant. Their disagreement was fairly straightforward—Grant wanted to put Major General Philip H. Sheridan in command of all the troops in the Shenandoah Valley but

Stanton disagreed. Stanton thought that General Sheridan was much too young and that he should not be trusted with such an independent and important command.

Sheridan was a short, aggressive, driving commander in the mode of Grant himself, but he was only 33 years old. Secretary Stanton, a humorless and unimaginative sort, could not see the merits of having a young, forceful commander in charge of an army that desperately needed just such an officer. He held the obstinate belief that someone older should be appointed commander. Grant thought otherwise. On August 1, he telegraphed General Halleck, "I want Sheridan put in command of all the troops in the field, with instructions to put himself south of the enemy and follow him to the death. Wherever the enemy goes let our troops also go."[15]

Lincoln intercepted Grant's telegram at the War Office and completely sided with him. Stanton and his War Department cronies were too timid and exasperatingly nonbelligerent to suit him. If Grant wanted Sheridan— it seemed to Lincoln that Sheridan was the sort of general who would latch onto the enemy and follow him to the death—then Grant would have Sheridan. If the war were ever going to be won, it would be by generals with iron in them, like Grant and Sherman and Sheridan, men who were not afraid to fight. Stanton and his objections were overruled.

Actually, Lincoln's first reaction was to agree with Stanton. He thought that Sheridan was too young as well. But two days after Lincoln read Grant's telegram to Halleck, he endorsed the appointment of Sheridan as commander of what would henceforth be known as the Army of the Shenandoah.

Lincoln was struck by the phrase "follow him to the death." Grant had said exactly what the president wanted to hear. "This, I think, is exactly right, as to how our forces should move," Lincoln telegraphed Grant. But he also warned, "I repeat to you it will neither be done nor attempted unless you watch every day, and hour, and force it." He was glad that Grant had enough faith in Sheridan to appoint him commander of the Army of the Shenandoah, but he also wanted to make certain that Grant kept an eye on his new young commander to make sure that Sheridan really did follow the enemy to the death.[16]

Immediately after reading Lincoln's telegram, Grant traveled to Monocacy, Maryland, to have a talk with General David Hunter, the present commander of the 30,000 men Sheridan was about to inherit. Grant did not think that Hunter had either the ability or the nerve to destroy Early's army. He was planning to offer General Hunter a mainly administrative post with the newly named army, while Sheridan would lead the troops in the field. But Hunter wanted no part of that arrangement. Instead, he asked Grant to remove him entirely, rather than leave him as nominal commander. Grant was only too happy to comply with General Hunter's request. And so on August 7, 1864, in spite of the misgivings of some, General Sheridan took command of the Army of the Shenandoah.

Grant knew all too well just how vital the Shenandoah Valley was to the Confederacy, "because it was the principal storehouse they now had for feeding their armies around Richmond."[17] It had also been a principal source of trouble for the Union armies since the beginning of the war, during Stonewall Jackson's campaigning, even before it became the staging ground for Jubal Early's raid on Washington. Grant set out to close this sanctuary for rebel armies once and for all. And he was convinced that Phil Sheridan was just the man to do it.

Sheridan had been chronically underestimated all his life—for his youth and, even more, for his short stature. At five feet five inches in height, he was three inches shorter than Grant. Lincoln thought that Sheridan was "a brown, chunky little chap, with a long body, short legs, not enough neck to hang him, and such long arms that if his ankles itch he can scratch them without stooping." When someone mentioned to Grant, for probably the ten thousandth time, that Sheridan was not very tall, Grant very patiently explained, "You will find him big enough for the purpose before we get through with him." His men usually called him "Little Phil" and meant it affectionately, although they never called him that to his face.[18]

Before taking a train to Monocacy Junction to assume his new command, Sheridan was summoned to Washington to confer with the president. He was probably expecting nothing more than a formal send-off and maybe some words of advice from Stanton and Halleck. Instead, Sheridan got an eye-opener from Lincoln, along with a lesson in practical politics.

Sheridan came to town wearing his best uniform, which made him feel uncomfortable enough. He would have preferred wearing his mud-spattered field uniform, but he was in Washington and knew that he had to keep up appearances. What Lincoln had to say made him even more ill at ease.

Lincoln told Sheridan, point-blank, that he must not be beaten, under any circumstances or for any reason. Because Grant was making no headway at all against Lee at Petersburg, and because Sherman did not seem to be getting any closer to Atlanta, and also because Early's raid was still on everyone's mind, the Lincoln administration could not afford a setback. Any kind of defeat or reversal involving the Army of the Shenandoah would bring about a disaster for Lincoln, Sheridan was told, since "the defeat of [his] army might be followed by the overthrow of the party in power." In other words, if Sheridan lost in the Shenandoah Valley, it would be tantamount to costing Lincoln the election and losing the war, since the Democrats were certain to abandon the entire war effort if they won the White House. That was quite a load of responsibility for a thirty-three-year-old general to carry off to his new command.[19]

But Grant had a lot more faith and confidence in Phil Sheridan than Lincoln or Stanton or anyone in the War Department, and that was all that really mattered. When Sheridan finally arrived at Monocacy Junction on August 6, after the upsetting and demoralizing business in Washington, he found Grant waiting for him with a copy of orders that had originally been written for General Hunter. Now Sheridan would be carrying them out.

Sheridan's instructions were twofold: he was to go after the rebel troops in the Shenandoah Valley until all of them were either dispersed or dead, and he was also to turn the valley's rich farmland into a fire-ravaged desert. The first part of his instructions was fairly clear-cut and simple—he was to destroy the enemy. The Confederate forces in the valley were commanded by Jubal Early. No one knew exactly what Early had in mind—if he would try another attack on Washington, which was unlikely, or if he had decided upon some other kind of mischief. Whatever Old Jube had in mind, Sheridan was to either drive him out of the valley or destroy him.

The second part of Sheridan's orders instructed him to carry out a completely different kind of warfare. The farmers of the Shenandoah Valley had become as vital to the Confederate war effort as any army, including Robert E. Lee's fabled Army of Northern Virginia. The valley was usually described as the breadbasket of the Confederacy—its farmers supplied the soldiers with the provisions and supplies they needed to carry on with the rebellion. General Grant decided to treat the good farmers of the valley in the same way that he would have dealt with Lee and his army—he determined to destroy them. Destroy the valley and its ability to supply Lee's army, and Grant would be halfway to destroying Lee's army. This was exactly the task Grant had in mind for Phil Sheridan.

The orders that Sheridan received were direct and to the point. "Take all provisions, forage, and stock wanted for the use of your command. Such as cannot be consumed, destroy." Grant was specific abut what he meant by "destroy"—Sheridan "should make all the Valley south of the Baltimore and Ohio railroad a desert as high up as possible," and his army was "to eat out Virginia clear and clean as far as they go, so that crows flying over it will have to carry their provender with them." Sheridan would do his best to see that Grant's orders were carried out to the letter.[20]

Not very many of Sheridan's men had ever seen the valley before—many had not even heard of it—and were struck by its lushness. "All you have ever heard of the beauties and fertility of the Shenandoah Valley have been true— for it really is lovely beyond description," wrote Major Peter Vredenburgh, of the 14th New Jersey Volunteers, in a letter back home. "Tell Henry that it beats all places for game that either he or I ever saw," he continued, and went on to rhapsodize over "the rich, rolling fields profuse with golden crops and luxuriant verdense and other natural concomitants as handsome horses, large barns, rich fields, etc."[21] Elisha Hunt Rhodes of the 2nd Rhode Island Volunteers said simply, "This valley is very beautiful, a perfect garden."[22]

But the Shenandoah Valley's beauty and perfection could not withstand the methodical destruction carried out by Sheridan and his men. First, Sheridan pushed Jubal Early's army out of the way by ordering a general advance on August 9. Early's outnumbered force withdrew south to Winchester and then farther south to Fisher's Hill. This left Sheridan free to carry out his campaign against the farmers of the Shenandoah, which they would refer to as "the burning."

"We have been down the Valley as far as Strasburg, some eighty miles, and burned all the grain and stole all the horses, cattle, sheep and the like that we could find," a New Jersey lieutenant said in a letter, "living meanwhile splendidly on everything good in the shape of apples, green corn, peaches and honey."[23] Columns of smoke from blazing barns could be seen for miles. Not all the men enjoyed their jobs; they hated the expressions on the faces of the farmers as they watched their crops being burned and their horses and livestock either confiscated or driven off. But they carried out their orders just the same, regardless of how distasteful they found them.

One estimate gave the total destruction of "the burning" as "about 2,000 barns and 70 mills, along with other property."[24] A Southern observer of the destruction described "glowing spots of still-burning buildings . . . tongues of flame still licking about heavy beams and sills—flames sometimes of many colors from burning grain and forage." It seemed like the end of the world to the farmers, who had no choice but to stand by and watch as everything they owned—the result of a lifetime's work—was destroyed. It was the end of their world. "Until this day, no such desolation had been witnessed since the war began. What were we coming to? What would all this end in?"[25]

Throughout the North, no one seemed to know, either, but people were more concerned over when it all would end rather than what they were coming to. As far as most people were concerned, "it"—the endless and endlessly frustrating war, which, so far, had produced nothing but horrendous casualties—was not ending soon enough to suit them. Philip Sheridan's campaign in the Shenandoah Valley seemed to be just one more exercise in frustration.

Grant was well satisfied with Sherman's progress in the valley. Sheridan had not followed the enemy to the death—not yet, at least—but he was systematically turning the valley into a desert. That was just as important to Grant. But Grant was not a civilian residing in New York or Pennsylvania or Maryland, and he had a great deal more insight into the war and its intricate workings than anyone who depended upon the Northern press for his information. The general population did not know that torching the Shenandoah meant starvation for Lee's army. They could only see that the war against the rebel army in the Shenandoah was not being prosecuted with enough force and strength to suit them.

Jubal Early's army was still out there somewhere, still armed and dangerous, and might very well attack Washington again. The North—especially residents of Maryland and Pennsylvania—wanted this army destroyed. Burning crops and barns and farms was all very well—the damned rebels had it coming to them—but it did not seem to be bringing the end of the war any nearer. Sheridan ought to be fighting the rebel army instead of harassing Southern civilians. Sheridan's doings in the Shenandoah looked like just one more failure, alongside Sherman's stalled campaign outside Atlanta and Grant's poor efforts to destroy Lee and his army.

If Mr. Lincoln could not choose better generals than Grant, Sherman, and Sheridan, maybe it would be a good idea to choose another president in November.

WITH A BULLDOG GRIP

The management of the *Express*, a newspaper in Buffalo, New York, displayed a large sign outside of its building: "GOD – GRANT – VICTORY."[26] This was a very nice gesture by the owners of the paper, and was probably much appreciated by the patriotic citizens of Buffalo, but nobody knew exactly what it meant—was it a plea for God to grant victory, or did it mean that God plus Grant equaled victory?

Throughout the North, an increasing number of the population would not have seen any meaning in either interpretation. If God had any intention of granting victory to the North, in this increasingly discouraging summer, he certainly had a strange way of going about it. And if God plus Grant was supposed to equal victory, more and more people were wishing that Grant would be left out of the equation. The *Express*'s sign maker made no mention of Abraham Lincoln, which was probably just as well. The general opinion of Lincoln was even lower than the opinion of Grant.

General Grant's reputation was probably at its lowest point in those late-summer weeks. He had not destroyed Lee's army; he had not captured Richmond; he could not seem to extract himself from Petersburg; and everything he had done up to this point, all his failures put together, had resulted in nothing but thousands of dead and wounded. The Democrats were calling him a butcher—"Butcher Grant." Sometimes he was called a drunken butcher. Even the president's wife, Mary Todd Lincoln, said that Grant was a butcher and that she could do a better job of running the army herself.

Actually, Grant was no more of a butcher than many other generals on both sides, including Robert E. Lee. In fact, Lee had a higher rate of casualties, dead and wounded, than Grant. "Lee was more reckless with men's lives," a biographer of Grant noted, "yet got away with it."[27] The most pointed example of Lee's disregard for casualties is Pickett's Charge, at Gettysburg, which resulted in many more casualties than Grant's attack at Cold Harbor. Another historian grumbled, "If any general deserved the label 'butcher,' it was Lee."[28] But Grant had been called "butcher" too many times in the Northern press, especially by anti-Lincoln papers, and the name stuck.

But General Grant was not about to let this break his stride or change his style. His objective was still the same as it had been since May—the destruction of Lee's army. He was well on his way to attaining this goal, and he knew it. At this point in time, Robert E. Lee also knew it. Grant had the men and the resources and the determination to keep on grinding Lee and wearing him down until he had no option but to surrender. Maybe the majority of voters in the North did not see this in August 1864, but both Grant and Lee did.

In mid-August, Grant decided to make an advance toward Richmond to distract Lee from reinforcing Jubal Early in the Shenandoah. "To prevent these reinforcements from being sent out from Richmond," Grant wrote, "I had to do something to compel Lee to retain his forces about the capital."[29] If everything went the way Grant wanted, his plan to make Lee fight would accomplish two things at the same time. Lee's forces around Petersburg would be further decreased and cut down, which was Grant's long-term strategy, and Early's army would be deprived of receiving fresh troops.

Three battles were fought in mid- to late-August, all meant to divert Lee and force him to defend Petersburg and the city's rail link with the outside world. The first was at Deep Bottom, which was given its quirky name because of the depth of the James River at that point. General Winfield

Scott Hancock commanded the Federal troops at Deep Bottom, which is about ten miles northeast of Petersburg. He sent about 10,000 men against the rebel defenses on the morning of August 14, but the attacks did not turn out to be nearly as successful as Hancock had hoped. "As was characteristic of the Federal generals of that day," an infantryman complained, "those in command lost the advantage of their superior numbers by excess caution and slowness of advance."[30] Private soldiers of every war have never been at a loss for words when criticizing their superior officers.

Even though the Confederates were more than holding their own against the Federal attack, Lee had convinced himself that Hancock was posing a serious threat to Richmond. He wired the cavalry divisions of Wade Hampton and W. H. F. "Rooney" Lee, the second son of Robert E. Lee, to return to Richmond. Grant had already accomplished one of his goals. From Confederate prisoners, Grant learned that at least four different brigades that were supposed to have gone to strengthen Jubal Early had been recalled by General Lee.

One of Hancock's corps commanders, General David Birney, spent most of the following day scouting the Confederate positions. Fighting resumed on August 16, when Birney's men attacked rebel entrenchments. After suffering early losses—a regimental commander observed, "the first division went down like so many tenpins"—the Federals pressed their attack and chased the rebels out of their trenches.[31] But the Confederates counterattacked and drove the Federals back at bayonet point. The day ended with the rebels back in their own rifle pits and with Hancock's men having gained no ground.

No fighting took place on August 17, while both sides removed their dead and wounded from the previous day. But on the 18th, Lee tried to overwhelm the Federals with a combined cavalry and infantry attack. In spite of all the coordinating and planning between the units that were supposed to do the attacking, nothing started until the cavalry began moving at about 5:00 p.m.—six hours late. Confederate officers were just as likely to misinterpret orders and miss communications as their Union counterparts, although most Yankee soldiers would have found this hard to believe. Because the offensive began at such a late hour, it was dusk before any real gains could be carried out. Lee's offensive faded away with the daylight.

But the implacable Grant was not about to change his plans or allow himself to be sidetracked, in spite of the fact that he had lost twice as many men as Lee at Deep Bottom. His next move would be against the Weldon Railroad, a vital rail connection with Wilmington, North Carolina. Wilmington was one of the Confederacy's last remaining Atlantic seaports. Cargoes of cotton and tobacco were shipped out of Wilmington and vitally needed supplies—everything from shoes and medical supplies to rifles and ammunition—were unloaded at its wharves and sent throughout the South. The Weldon Railroad, also known as the Wilmington and Weldon Railroad, was a direct link between Wilmington and Petersburg. Grant knew that Lee had no choice but to defend the Weldon Railroad with as much determination as he would defend the approaches to Richmond.

Major General Gouverneur K. Warren was given the assignment of destroying as large a section of the Weldon Railroad as possible and as fast as his men could smash and demolish, but on August 19 his orders were changed. He was sent an additional 6,000 men and told to hold the rail line, not just rip it up. Warren thought that he was well suited to the job and responded that he could be relied upon both to capture and to hold the railroad. General Meade liked Warren's spirit, but some of his aides did not have as much confidence—holding the line was not going to be as easy as Warren supposed.

Warren had already captured a section of the rail line at Globe Tavern, a few miles south of Petersburg, when the Confederates struck back. The resulting Battle of Globe Tavern turned out to be just as rough-and-tumble as Deep Bottom, and as hard and taxing as General Meade's staff had thought. Troops commanded by P. G. T. Beauregard and two divisions under A. P. Hill did their best to dislodge Warren's men, but the Federals managed to beat them off. After four days of attacks and counterattacks and pounding by Union artillery, the Confederates finally gave up and let Warren have his section of track. The price had proved to be much too high, higher than anyone expected to pay.

But Lee still had to get supplies into Petersburg, railroad or no railroad. His only option was to use supply wagons, hundreds of them, to carry the necessary goods and provisions northward. The nearest railhead to Petersburg was now Stony Creek, about 20 miles to the south. Moving everything by wagon instead of by rail would be slow, much too slow to suit the citizens of Petersburg, but Lee realized that there was nothing he could do about it.

Capturing a section of the Weldon Railroad was a major accomplishment for Ulysses S. Grant. Not only had he severed the rail link into Petersburg, he had also extended his lines westward to Globe Tavern. Lee now had no choice but to stretch his own lines farther to the west, as well, and run a line of parallel trenches to keep pace with Grant's new entrenchments. But Lee's lines would be much weaker, and they would be undermanned compared with Grant's—the Confederates could dig trenches as well as the Yankees, but they did not have nearly as many men to put in them.

Warren's stand at Globe Tavern made the Union position at Petersburg much stronger, while Lee's position had become weaker and more tenuous. Grant knew that he had taken a decisive step toward trapping Lee's army. Lee was also all too aware of what had happened, and that sooner or later Grant would use his superior numbers and his determination to force him out of Petersburg. And when Grant captured Petersburg, Richmond would very soon follow.

But Grant was not satisfied with thoughts of future glories. He wanted the Weldon Railroad completely torn up between Globe Tavern and Stony Creek, or at least as far south as his men could manage. His attempt to accomplish this resulted in the third battle around Petersburg in less than two weeks, which would be known as the Battle of Ream's Station.

General Hancock arrived at Ream's Station, about four miles south of Globe Tavern, on August 24. He set his men to work destroying railroad track; by sundown, they had demolished about three miles of Weldon Railroad south of the station. But, as Grant had reckoned, Lee was not about to allow Warren or any other Yankee to do any more damage—Warren had already cut one of his supply lines and was threatening to outmaneuver him and force him out of his trenches. He sent about 8,000 men, including several cavalry detachments and an artillery unit, to attack the Union position around Ream's Station.

Skirmishing between Confederate and Union cavalry started at around noon on August 25. The real fighting began at about 2:00 p.m., when three rebel infantry brigades were driven back by a Federal division at the northern section of their fortifications. But Confederate reinforcements arrived late in the afternoon and, screaming their nerve-tingling rebel yell, six brigades threw themselves at the Union trenches again at about 5:30 p.m. This time, supported by artillery fire, the Confederates managed to break through the Federal lines. Two Union regiments dissolved under the pressure, with "men running in panic from [the] Rebel counterattack."[32] The men of one regiment stayed prone on the ground and refused to fire their rifles.

General Hancock was on hand and saw what was happening. He tried his best to rally his troops, riding among them with his sword in one hand and his hat in the other and shouting at them not to run. "Come on," he yelled. "We can beat them yet! Don't leave me, for God's sake!"[33] But his shouting and coaxing did no good—his men had had enough and continued to head for the rear as fast as they could go.

The Confederates won the Battle of Ream's Station spectacularly and overwhelmingly. Union casualties numbered over 2,700; Confederate losses totaled less than 900. Casualties for all three battles were just as one-sided: more than 9,000 Federal troops were killed, wounded, or captured (mostly captured), while Confederate losses came to under 4,000. But even though Lee had won a decisive tactical victory, he had lost more than he had gained. Grant had broken the Weldon Railroad, Warren's troops still held the ground they had captured at Globe Tavern, and the flow of supplies to Petersburg and Richmond had been permanently reduced. Grant had done exactly what he had set out to do in these three battles—he had undermined Lee's position and had begun to isolate Petersburg, even though he had lost more men. He would continue this winning strategy until he had driven Lee and his Army of Northern Virginia out of their trenches and captured Richmond.

Lee knew the predicament he was in, and especially realized how undermanned he was compared with Grant and Meade. "Unless some measures can be devised to replace our losses, the consequences may be devastating," he told Confederate secretary of war James A. Seddon on August 24. "Without some increase in our strength I cannot see how we are to escape the natural military consequences of the enemy's numerical superiority."[34] He could already see that the road ahead would not lead to victory and Southern independence. Instead, the remainder of the war would be a long, slow journey that would end in Wilmer McLean's sitting room in Appomattox Court House.

Deep Bottom, Globe Tavern, and Ream's Station will never go down in history alongside Shiloh, Antietam, and Gettysburg. But they were just as influential in their own way. These three battles were the start of Grant's reaching out and strangling the Army of Northern Virginia. Beginning with these seemingly minor combats, Grant would press his advantage, coming always closer to the rail lines that Lee needed to keep intact if he were to keep his army intact. They also showed Lee that no matter how many times he won tactical victories in the field, he was going to lose in the end.

Abraham Lincoln also saw what Lee and Grant could see. He realized that as long as Grant kept applying pressure, Lee was bound to surrender and the war would be over. Not very many people in the North saw this, but Lincoln did.

Not every general could see what Grant was accomplishing, either. Henry Halleck, "Old Brains," should have had a better grasp of the situation around Petersburg, but he had a habit of missing major details. He was, as he had pointed out, only an adviser. Halleck warned Grant that draft riots would break out in the North unless troops were withdrawn from Petersburg to put down any uprisings. Grant did not agree with Halleck at all. He telegraphed his chief of staff that any draft riots would have to be dealt with by the militias of the individual states because he had no intention of withdrawing any troops from Petersburg. Taking combat troops away from the fighting in Virginia was tantamount to a retreat, at least in Grant's eyes, and Grant was not about to retreat.

President Lincoln intercepted Grant's reply to Halleck and liked what he read. "I have seen your despatch expressing your unwillingness to break your hold where you are," he replied to Grant. "Neither am I willing. Hold on with a bulldog grip and chew and choke as much as possible."[35]

When Grant read the telegram, he began laughing out loud. This was a highly unusual thing for Grant to do—he typically wore an expression that could be best described as grim and determined. Sometimes he would indulge in a quiet chuckle, but it was usually a wry, humorless chuckle. But on this occasion, he stood holding Lincoln's telegram and laughing for everyone to hear. It was such an unusual occurrence that a few of his staff officers came over to find out what would possibly make their commanding general break out laughing.

Grant obligingly handed them Lincoln's message and said, "The President has more nerve than any of his advisors."[36]

One thing was certain: the president had more faith in Ulysses S. Grant than any of his advisers. Even through debacles like Cold Harbor and the Crater, Lincoln stood by his general in chief. With this telegram, Lincoln was indicating that he would continue to stand by Grant. As far as the president was concerned, the Buffalo *Express*'s sign meant nothing less than God + Grant = Victory.

Grant could only hope that the registered voters in the North had as much nerve as Lincoln, and that they would not panic and lose faith in Lincoln or the war before November. If the voters kept the faith and voted for Lincoln, Grant knew that the war would be as good as won.

TOO IMPATIENT FOR A SIEGE

At the beginning of August 1864, General William T. Sherman received an unexpected letter from his younger brother, Senator John Sherman. A letter from home was always welcome, even for a major general, but this particular letter left its recipient more anxious than cheerful.

In his letter, Senator Sherman told his brother, in effect, that the outcome of the entire war depended upon him and what he did in Georgia. He also implied that the result of the November election was also his brother's responsibility. "We all feel that upon General Grant and you, and the armies under your command, the fate of this country depends," General Sherman read. "If you are successful, it is ardently hoped that peace may follow with a restored union." But "if you fail, the wisest can hope for nothing but a long train of disasters and the strife of factions." The letter said essentially the same thing that Lincoln had told Phil Sheridan, only in kinder words.

It was clear to the senator that Grant could not be counted upon. "Grant has not had much success," Senator Sherman went on. Even though he was doing his best, "he has not taken Richmond, and I fear will not this campaign." Because General Grant was not getting anywhere in Virginia, the entire war effort now rested entirely upon brother Cump.[37]

This was an alarming letter for General Sherman to receive, especially in the middle of such a long and drawn-out campaign. And especially since Senator Sherman did not know what he was talking about. Grant *was* having success against Lee. He was slowly choking the Army of Northern Virginia to death and was isolating both Petersburg and Richmond. If Grant continued with his present strategy, Lee would have to give up sooner or later.

But Senator Sherman was only repeating what everyone in the North was saying: Grant had failed in his campaign against Lee and was stuck in a deadlock south of Richmond. If the war were to be won and the Union restored, it would be up to Sherman. Sherman was the Union's last hope. If Atlanta were to be captured, he knew that he would have to follow the same basic strategy his friend Grant was using in Virginia—attack the enemy's rail lines and cut off all supplies. He also knew that destroying the city's rail connections would be only the first step.

Sherman planned to make a counterclockwise sweep from Ezra Church around the Confederate entrenchments, which would be his first move against the Macon and Western Railroad. "On the 4th of August I ordered General Schofield to make a bold attack on the railroad anywhere about East Point," he wrote.[38] General Schofield and his Army of the Ohio made their attack at Utoy Creek, a few miles east of Atlanta. Although the battle went on for two days, the Battle of Utoy Creek did not accomplish what Sherman had hoped. Federal troops forced a full Confederate division out of its trenches, but the rebels only retreated to another line of entrenchments. Sherman later commented that it had been "a noisy but not a bloody battle." He would have to try again.[39]

Even though Schofield did not succeed, Sherman was not about to give up. He would keep at it, trying to cut the railroad, always trying to destroy the line that was keeping Atlanta alive. Sherman also kept his artillery fully occupied by shelling Atlanta. His aim was to demoralize the city's population and to wreck its already-depleted industry by bombarding the city with withering cannon fire each and every day. If he could not isolate the city, he would destroy it.

"We keep hammering away all the time, and there is no peace inside or outside of Atlanta," he wired General Halleck. "I am too impatient for a siege, and don't know how but this is as good a place to fight it out as further inland." As a parting thought, he told Halleck, "One thing is certain, whether we get inside of Atlanta or not, it will be a used-up community when we are done with it."[40]

Sherman might have been too impatient for a siege, but he was too smart just to sit back and try to shell Atlanta into submission. His gunners fired thousands of shells into the city every day, but at the same time Sherman kept trying to cut the Macon and Western Railroad. What he really wanted to do was draw John Bell Hood into an open fight. But Hood had changed his tactics—the general who would charge any time someone waved a flag at him had suddenly become restrained and conservative. "Since July 28th, Hood has not attempted to meet us outside his parapets," Sherman complained in a telegraph to General Grant.[41]

Although Sherman could not compel John Bell Hood to come out from behind his fortifications, he did manage to get him to send an official, and somewhat indignant, protest regarding the bombardment of Atlanta. There was no military purpose behind the shelling, Hood objected. He went on to point out that thousands of civilians were still living in the city, and he also mentioned that his own lines were a mile and more from its outskirts.

Sherman probably got a grim chuckle out of Hood's message. He emphatically disagreed with it, and said so. Atlanta was very much a military target, Sherman responded. The city was not only a manufacturing center, it was also one of the main suppliers of the Confederate war machine. Atlanta's civilians provided the Confederate soldiers with their weapons, their ammunition, their rations, and everything else they needed to carry on with the war. Destroy the enemy's ability to keep the army armed and provisioned, and you destroy the army's ability to fight. Sherman noted Hood's protest and kept up the barrage. On August 24, he telegraphed General Halleck, "Heavy fires in Atlanta all day, caused by our artillery."[42]

But apart from the artillery barrage, Sherman's offensive had stagnated into a stalemate. There was always skirmishing, along with the occasional hapless victim of sniper fire, but the two armies basically just stood by and kept a wary eye on each other. Sherman was not happy about the situation, and he became even more short-tempered and irritable than usual. "The enemy hold us by an inferior force," he said to General Schofield; "we are more besieged than they."[43] He might have been too impatient for a siege, but he had one on his hands just the same.

Sherman was also troubled by the fact that the stalemate was not helping to relieve the despair in the North. The fighting around Atlanta had become the primary theater of operations. To his chagrin, Sherman knew that his brother had been right after all about one thing—the outcome of both the war and the November election now depended upon him and what he did in Georgia.

But Sherman had come up with an idea to break the stalemate. On August 25, he abruptly stopped shelling Atlanta, ordered his men out of their trenches, and sent his troops on a sweeping movement to the south around the Confederate lines—Sherman called it a general left-wheel. All three armies under his command—the Army of the Cumberland, the Army of the Tennessee, and the Army of the Ohio—moved out of their works in almost complete secrecy and started walking in a semicircle that would take them well beyond Hood's entrenchments, which extended only as far as East Point.

If General Hood suspected that Sherman was up to something, he did not do anything about it. When his patrols reported that the Federals had abandoned their trenches, Hood made the assumption that Sherman had retreated. His intelligence network had been saying that the enemy was low on rations, information that was based partially on reports from interrogated Federal prisoners. Hood came to the conclusion that the Yankees were in full retreat, half-starved and heading toward Tennessee.

As soon as word began to spread that the Federal camps had been evacuated, the citizens of Atlanta also persuaded themselves that the hated

Yankees had gone. The shelling had stopped and the enemy had miracu-
lously disappeared. This momentous news was telegraphed throughout the
South and was met with outpourings of relief and euphoria. Victory parties
were given in Atlanta to celebrate the defeat and withdrawal of the enemy.
Several trains came up from Macon and points south, filled with patriotic
Confederates looking to join in the celebration.

While Atlanta was basking in its festivities, generals ~~Henry~~ George Thomas
and Oliver Howard, commanders of the Army of the Cumberland and the
Army of the Tennessee respectively, were busily tearing up the West Point
Railroad, south of Atlanta. This line intersected with the Macon and
Western Railroad at East Point; Thomas's and Howard's men were doing
everything physically possible to put it permanently out of commission. In
Sherman's words, they were breaking it up thoroughly.

Sherman seemed to take a particular delight in wrecking the rail lines,
as well as in describing the methods used to wreck them. "The track was
heaved up in sections the length of a regiment, then separated rail by rail,"
he later recounted in detail. "Bonfires were made of the ties and of fence
rails on which the rails were heated, carried to trees or telegraph-poles,
wrapped around and left to cool."[44] The rails were looped around in a complete circle, making certain that they would never be used again. The results
of this looping and bending were known as "Sherman's neckties," or
"Sherman's hairpins." The general seemed genuinely tickled by the dubious
honor of having these objects of destruction named after him.

On August 28, while the West Point Railroad was still being methodi-
cally demolished, rebel scouts discovered that Sherman had not retreated
after all. The remains of the Yankee bonfires were plainly evident; bent and
twisted rails were found wrapped around trees in a trail that went on for
miles. The Yankees who had done the job were obviously still nearby. John
Bell Hood was as surprised by this bit of news as everyone else, but he did
not seem to be particularly unnerved by it. He thought that the Federals
were nothing but a diversionary force, given the task of destroying the West
Point Railroad while the rest of the army made its way northward.

Hood was under the impression that only two or three Federal corps
were attacking the rail system, but actually Sherman had six full corps south

of Atlanta. To confront the Yankee army operating between East Point and Jonesborough, which was about 12 miles to the south, Hood ordered two corps under the command of General William J. Hardee to attack the Federals and push them west beyond the rail lines. With any luck, he might even be able to destroy the Yankees, or at least give them such a beating that they would no longer pose any threat.

Poor old Hood was operating completely in the dark, and he had no idea how to go about defending Atlanta. Sherman, on the other hand, knew exactly what he wanted to do and how to do it. He had enough confidence in himself and his strategy to tell General Thomas, "I have Atlanta as certainly as if it were in my hand."[45]

He was right. On the same day that he made his prediction to General Thomas, all three armies under his command moved straight for the Macon and Western Railroad. General Thomas and the Army of the Tennessee reached the railroad at Jonesborough and found that General Hardee and his corps had dug in and were ready for a fight. Sherman was more than willing to oblige; he sent generals Schofield and Thomas south to bolster General Howard, ripping up more rail line as they advanced. On the afternoon of August 31, the climactic battle for Atlanta was about to begin.

THIS ADMINISTRATION WILL NOT BE RE-ELECTED

As the days began growing shorter, and with September and the cooler days of autumn just around the corner, Abraham Lincoln could see the November election slipping away from him. Election Day was still over two months away, but he knew that his chances of being re-elected were nonexistent. No one, not even Republican Party leaders, gave him any chance at all. It would take a miracle for Lincoln to pull off a win at the polls. Either a miracle or a Union victory, which, in the minds of the Northern public, amounted to the same thing.

The North was winning the war, but nobody in the North knew it. Newspapers from Chicago to Boston to New York had been so full of gloom and doom for so long that gloom and doom had become their official editorial position. Anti-Lincoln papers, including the *New York World*, published nothing but scathing denunciations of the war, declaring that it was already as good as lost. More moderate papers, or at least papers that had a less anti-Lincoln bias, tended to be less prejudiced in their war reporting, but still did not offer very much encouragement concerning a Union victory. Even the *New York Times*, which was unapologetically pro-Lincoln, had become lukewarm regarding the military fortunes of the Northern armies. At the end of August, an editorial offered an opinion that Sherman would probably capture Atlanta, although there could be no guarantee that he actually would. At that point in the war, such an outlook counted as a ringing endorsement of the Atlanta campaign.

Lincoln knew that his three leading generals, Grant, Sherman, and now Sheridan, were strangling the Confederacy, and that a final Union victory was now only a matter of time. The trouble was that the public at large throughout the North did not know it, or at least did not believe it. And if Northerners did not believe that the Federal armies were winning the war, or had the chance of winning it, they certainly were not about to cast their vote for a presidential candidate committed to continuing the war.

Republican Party executives seriously considered replacing Lincoln with another candidate and held a meeting in New York City for the purpose of requesting Lincoln to withdraw as the Republican presidential candidate. As a replacement, a military officer was preferred; the leading names were Grant or Sherman, and maybe Admiral Farragut for vice president. It looked as though the Democrats were going to nominate a general as their candidate, George B. McClellan, so the Republicans wanted a general of their own. With Lincoln out of the way and a general on the ballot, maybe they could win in November in spite of everything that had happened so far.

Americans seem to have a peculiar affinity for electing generals to the presidency. George Washington, Andrew Jackson (War of 1812), and William Henry "Old Tippecanoe" Harrison (Battle of Tippecanoe in Tecumseh's Rebellion, 1811) all became chief executive because of their war records, not because of any gift for statesmanship. In years to come, Ulysses S. Grant and Dwight D. Eisenhower would be elected for the same reason.

Having a general as their candidate would also assure the Republicans of a larger percentage of the soldier vote. The way things stood in late August, it looked as though the army would vote overwhelmingly for McClellan over Lincoln. A nurse stationed at City Point, Virginia, noted that "if . . . left to the soldiers, his election is sure."[46] The army, especially the Army of the Potomac, loved George B. McClellan. It almost went without saying that the veterans would cast their ballots for McClellan en masse. Having Grant or Sherman or any other general with a war record would help to counter the McClellan threat, and would represent a vast improvement over Lincoln.

It seemed to Abe Lincoln that everything had turned against him, but he refused to step down as his party's presidential candidate. He believed that he was the best man for the job, Democrat or Republican, and he was not about to quit. Lincoln decided that he would stay in the race until the bitter end, whether the party leaders liked it or not.

But Lincoln was realistic enough to know that the future did not look very encouraging. He had written a strange sort of memo, not addressed to anyone in particular, that perfectly expressed his state of mind regarding the war as well as his own political fortunes. At a cabinet meeting on August 23, Lincoln presented a copy of the memo to his cabinet members, with an odd request: he did not want anyone to read it, but asked all present to sign the back of the folded and sealed document, sight unseen. The memo read:

> This morning, as for some days past, it seems exceedingly probable that this Administration will not be re-elected. Then it will be my duty to so co-operate with the President elect, as to save the Union between the election and the inauguration; as he will have secured his election on such grounds that he can not possibly save it afterwards.
>
> A. Lincoln[47]

Lincoln at this time was frequently described as looking tired, haggard, and careworn, as though he did not have a friend in the world. He must have seemed even more tired and depressed than usual during this particular meeting, and with good reason. His memo showed that Lincoln believed everything was lost: the war, the election, and any hope of restoring the Union. It was a memo for the future. At the end of August, the future looked hopeless and depressing.

Abraham Lincoln was absolutely convinced that he would not be re-elected in 1864. Ulysses S. Grant's campaign against Robert E. Lee in Virginia had resulted in horrible casualties and William T. Sherman was stalled in his drive to capture Atlanta. The Democrats were telling voters throughout the North that the war could not be won, and the public was ready to vote Lincoln out of office. *Courtesy of the National Archives.*

Lincoln's choice for general in chief was Ulysses S. Grant, the hero of Fort Donelson, Shiloh, and Vicksburg. Lincoln was confident that Grant would destroy Robert E. Lee's Army of Northern Virginia, but the task turned out to be a lot grimmer than either Lincoln or Grant guessed. *Courtesy of the National Archives.*

General William Tecumseh Sherman was given the assignment of destroying the army of Confederate general Joseph E. Johnston. His campaign in Georgia and capture of Atlanta turned out to be a turning point in the war, as well as in Abraham Lincoln's prospects for re-election. *Courtesy of the National Archives.*

During the summer of 1864, General Robert E. Lee and his Army of Northern Virginia posed as much of a threat to Abraham Lincoln's re-election as the Democrats. *Courtesy of the Library of Congress.*

Andrew Johnson, Lincoln's running mate, was a Democrat. The Lincoln/Johnson ticket was called the National Union Party. Adding Johnson to the ticket was an attempt to persuade War Democrats to vote for Lincoln. *Courtesy of the Library of Congress.*

George B. McClellan, in the uniform of a major general in the United States Army. As a presidential candidate, McClellan was a War Democrat running on a peace platform. This put him in an awkward position: he wanted to win the election but did not want the North to lose the war. *Courtesy of the National Archives.*

Clement Vallandigham, at the center of the photo, was an outspoken Peace Democrat. The Peace Democrats, also known as "Copperheads," advocated an immediate end to the war, full independence for the Confederacy, and allowing Southerners to keep their slaves. *Courtesy of the Library of Congress.*

General Joseph E. Johnston's tactical retreats north of Atlanta made him unpopular in the South and gave Jefferson Davis an excuse to dismiss him. *Courtesy of the Library of Congress.*

Confederate president Jefferson Davis allowed his personal feelings to affect his decision to dismiss General Joseph E. Johnston as commander of the Army of Tennessee. *Courtesy of the National Archives.*

General John Bell Hood had a well-deserved reputation for aggressiveness. But after replacing Joseph E. Johnston, Hood's aggressiveness turned out to be a liability for the Confederacy. *Courtesy of the Library of Congress.*

The remains of some of the dead of Cold Harbor being reburied in 1865. The North began to lose faith in President Lincoln and in the war because of the appalling casualties suffered by the Union army in the summer of 1864. *Courtesy of the Library of Congress.*

A pro-McClellan cartoon. While Abraham Lincoln and Jefferson Davis tear the country apart, McClellan admonishes, "The Union must be preserved at all hazards." In the summer of 1864, McClellan looked as though he would defeat Lincoln in the November election. *Courtesy of the National Archives.*

At the Battle of Mobile Bay in August 1864, Admiral David G. Farragut gave the North a decisive victory that did not cost the lives of thousands of men. Mobile Bay was the first encouraging news that Lincoln heard all summer. *Courtesy of the Library of Congress.*

General Sherman's men destroying railroad track outside Atlanta. The capture of Atlanta and the message "Atlanta is ours, and fairly won" electrified the North and turned public opinion firmly in favor of Lincoln and his re-election. *Courtesy of the Library of Congress.*

General Philip Sheridan's successful campaign against Jubal Early in the Shenandoah Valley gave Lincoln's re-election hopes an additional boost in the autumn of 1864. Sherman's capture of Atlanta, followed by Sheridan's victories in the Shenandoah, virtually ensured Lincoln's re-election. *Courtesy of the National Archives.*

Decided on the battlefield. Men of a Pennsylvania regiment vote in the field in the autumn of 1864. Lincoln feared that the soldier vote would lean heavily toward Democrat George B. McClellan, a fellow soldier and former commander of the Army of the Potomac. *Courtesy of the Library of Congress.*

After capturing Atlanta, General Sherman began his march to the sea. In this illustration, Sherman looks through his telescope at a particularly lurid landscape, while his men destroy everything in their path. Lincoln had confidence that Sherman would succeed in his march through Georgia. *Courtesy of the Library of Congress.*

On election night, November 8, 1864, Lincoln haunted the War Department's telegraph office for election returns from throughout the North. *Courtesy of the Library of Congress.*

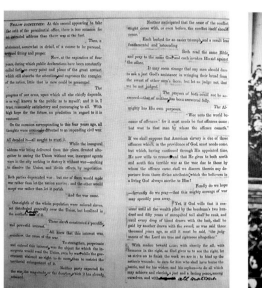

Abraham Lincoln's Second Inaugural Address, the copy from which he addressed the public on March 4, 1865. *Courtesy of the Library of Congress.*

"To bind up the nation's wounds." Abraham Lincoln reads his inaugural address from the Capitol on March 4, 1865.

Chapter Six

TURNING THE TIDE

FOUR YEARS OF MISRULE

Even before their convention began, the Democrats had a major problem with their projected presidential candidate. The problem with George B. McClellan was that he could not decide exactly what he was or what he wanted. Although he had become a politician, he claimed that he detested politicians. He wanted the Democrats to win the election, but he did not want the North to lose the war. His fellow Democrats wanted peace without victory, but McClellan adamantly declared that the Union must be preserved—at all hazards, as he would later write.

Abraham Lincoln famously insisted that the Democrats would have to nominate either a Peace Democrat on a war platform or a War Democrat on a peace platform. George McClellan could not make up his mind what kind of Democrat he wanted to be. He did not want to declare himself a Peace Democrat, which would have meant endorsing Confederate independence and the dissolution of the Union—he was still a major general in the United States Army, even though he did not have a command, and was also Lincoln's former general in chief. But, on the other hand, he did not want to be a War Democrat, either, since this would alienate the party's peace faction. McClellan's little quandary had also become a dilemma for the Democratic Party.

Their preferred candidate might have been a cause for some concern, but the Democrats opened their convention in Chicago filled with confidence. At noon on August 29, 1864, while General Sherman's armies were moving toward Jonesborough, Georgia, Democratic National Committee chairman August Belmont rapped his gavel and brought the gathering to order. The boisterous assembly was being held in the Wigwam, at Lake Street and Market. The Wigwam was not a tent—loosely translated from the Algonquin language, *wigwam* means something like "temporary shelter"—but was a huge, rambling wooden building said to be able to accommodate 15,000 people. On this particular August afternoon, all 15,000 seemed determined to make as much racket and commotion as humanly possible.

Chairman Belmont's gavel brought the bedlam to a stop, at least temporarily. His opening speech tore into Lincoln and the Republicans, as was expected. "Four years of misrule by a sectional, fanatical and corrupt party have brought our country to the verge of ruin," he told his fellow Democrats, enjoying himself hugely. "The past and present are sufficient warnings of the disastrous consequences which would befall us if Mr. Lincoln's re-election should be made possible by our want of patriotism and unity."[1]

It was a rousing and partisan speech and, best of all, a fairly short one. But before stepping down from the podium, Belmont put in a good word for the party's front-running candidate, predicting that the "American people" will "rush to the support of your candidate and platform, provided you will offer to their suffrage a tried patriot, who has proved his devotion to the Union and the convention." He did not mention George B. McClellan by name, but everybody knew whom he was talking about.[2]

Belmont then turned the proceedings over to William Bigler, the former governor of Pennsylvania. Bigler gave the party's slant on the war: it had been a three-year bloodbath that had accomplished absolutely nothing. "And now, at the end of more than three years of a war unparalleled in modern times for its magnitude and for its barbarous desolations . . . the hopes of the Union, our cherished object, [have] in nowise improved."[3]

"The men now in authority," Bigler went on about Lincoln and his party, "because of their blind fanaticism about an institution of some of the States . . . are rendered incapable of adopting the proper means to rescue our country—our whole country—from its present lamentable condition." Having summarized his party's position on slavery, Bigler next gave its views on the outcome of the war. When Lincoln and his administration were finally overthrown "by the ballot," the first duty of the new administration would be to "wield all the influence and power of the government to bring about on terms honorable and just to all sections, North and South, East and West... the consummation of permanent peace amongst the States and renewed fraternity amongst the people."[4]

The speech showed the general tendency of the convention to lean toward the point of view of the Peace Democrats. "It was noticeable that peace men and measures and sentiments were applauded to the echo," one observer reported, "while patriotic utterances, what few there were, received no response from the crowd." The crowd cheered when the band played "Dixie," but songs from the North, especially songs like "Glory! Glory Hallelujah!" and "Rally Round the Flag," were met by dead silence.[5]

After William Bigler finished, a brief prayer was said to bless the convention and to ask "O Father of Mercies" to forgive "the sins and transgressions that have brought upon us the desolation of civil war."[6] Exactly which sins and transgressions were not mentioned. Following the prayer, the business of the day began. The selecting of committees and the seating of delegates would be the main activities of the afternoon.

The most controversial activity was the naming of Clement Vallandigham to the Committee on Resolutions. This was the same Clement Vallandigham who had been arrested by an overzealous Ambrose Burnside for treasonable activities in 1863. After being deported to the Confederacy and doing a stint in Canada, Vallandigham was back in the North and as outspoken as ever. He was also as much of a Copperhead as before, and had one thought on his mind as the convention began—stop the war and allow the Confederate states to secede and take their slaves with them.

The Committee on Resolutions was responsible for writing the Democratic Party's official platform, including its position on the war. No one at the convention had any doubts at all about what Vallandigham's contribution to the committee would be. He would push for an immediate armistice with Richmond and the complete withdrawal of all Federal troops from all Southern states—the War Democrats and everybody else be damned!

The seating of delegates ran its course, taking up most of the convention's first day. "The Convention then adjourned until ten o'clock on Tuesday morning," according to the official proceedings.[7]

The second day of the convention, August 30, would turn out to be just as noisy as the first, with every square inch of the Wigwam jammed with shouting delegates, onlookers, and gawkers. The opening prayers—five of them, including the Lord's Prayer—gave the proceedings a measure of serenity for a short time. But the calm did not last long. Immediately following the prayers, a list of recommendations from the Conservative Union, an independent political organization that had held its own convention a few days before, was read to the gathering. The proposal that made the greatest impact, and caused the most noise, concerned George B. McClellan. The Conservative Union, which was anti-Lincoln and pro-Democrat, recommended McClellan's immediate nomination as the party's presidential candidate on the grounds "that his triumphant election is certain."[8]

The assembled delegates could not have agreed more. "When the name of Gen. McClellan was mentioned in reading these resolutions, it was greeted with such a demonstration of applause as must have satisfied . . . the deep hold he has on the public heart." Everyone kept on cheering and applauding for the next several minutes. Just hearing McClellan's name made the delegates ecstatic. He was the man of the hour and seemed unbeatable. There was no question in anyone's mind that he would be the next president of the United States.[9]

The next speaker was Governor Horatio Seymour of New York, who had just been made president of the convention. After spending a minute or so thanking the delegates for the tribute, he began another blustery tirade against the Republicans. The Republicans had destroyed the country, he said, and could not save the Union even if they tried; they were too preoccupied with emancipating the slaves and invading the South. "The bigotry of fanatics and the intrigues of placemen have made the bloody pages of the history of the past three years," Seymour declared. The Windy City was never windier.[10]

"Enthusiastic and long-continued cheering followed the conclusion of Gov. Seymour's remarks," noted the proceedings' official chronicler. When the cheering finally died down, Seymour asked if the Committee on Resolutions was ready to make its report.[11]

James Guthrie of Kentucky had been selected as chairman of the Resolutions Committee. Clement Vallandigham wanted to be chairman, very badly, but during a late-night meeting he had been outvoted by a margin of 12 to 8. Although he was not chairman, Vallandigham was still the committee's guiding light; he had a lot to say about what went on within the group and how it should be run. Being outvoted was not about to stop him from exercising his considerable influence on Chairman Guthrie and everybody else on the committee.

Guthrie informed the convention that the Committee on Resolutions was not yet ready, but expected to have its presentation prepared by four o'clock that afternoon. After some debate, the convention adjourned until 4:00 p.m. Guthrie, Vallandigham, and the other 18 members of the Committee on Resolutions left the convention floor to get ready for the afternoon session.

Everyone looked forward to hearing what the committee would have to say. Even though James Guthrie may have been chairman, every delegate present knew that its voice was Clement Vallandigham. No matter what the committee produced, Vallandigham was certain to leave his mark all over it.

When the convention reconvened at four o'clock, the Committee on Resolutions was ready. It had prepared six resolutions—actually, a six-plank platform—for presentation to the convention. These resolutions were to represent the Democratic Party's official position on the running of the war. As everyone had thought, Clement Vallandigham's influence was glaringly evident in the creation of the Democratic platform.

James Guthrie handed the six resolutions to the secretary of the convention, William Wallace, who proceeded to read them to the rapt audience. Everyone inside the Wigwam hung on his every word, as though Wallace were delivering the most moving speech in all of dramatic literature.

The first resolution, or plank, was straightforward enough. It pledged to "adhere with unswerving fidelity to the Union under the Constitution." The delegates listened with "deep, almost breathless attention," according to the proceedings. But it was as though they had been expecting something else, something a lot more controversial, and were let down by what they had just heard.[12]

If the convention's delegates were disappointed by the absence of gunpowder in the first plank, they certainly got what they were hoping for when Wallace spoke again. The second plank was the peace plank, Clement Vallandigham's plank, and it certainly sounded like Vallandigham—obstinate, outspoken, and vehemently anti-Lincoln. The delegates heard "that after four years of failure to restore the Union . . . justice, humanity, liberty and the public welfare demand that immediate efforts be made for a cessation of hostilities, with a view to an ultimate convention of the States or other peaceable means, to the end that at the earliest practicable moment peace may be restored on the basis of the Federal union of the United States."

The effect of Vallandigham's peace plank on the convention was electric. Delegates cheered and shouted with so much enthusiasm that Wallace had to stop halfway through. After everyone had cheered themselves out, Wallace resumed. He read the resolution again, from the beginning, and managed to get all the way through before the audience began cheering again—or, as the author of the official proceedings put it, "the audience again surrendered itself to the wildest enthusiasm."[13]

Eventually, the delegates ran out of breath. "When the vast audience was hoarse and exhausted, order was restored and the business of the convention was proceeded with."[14]

The remaining four planks were not nearly as inflammatory as the second, but they were just as anti-administration. The third resolution chastised Lincoln and his government for interfering in local elections. The fourth insisted that the rights of individual states must remain unimpaired, along with the rights of individual citizens—states' rights was one of the leading banners of the Confederacy, and the mention of the suppression of individual rights was a swipe at Lincoln's suspension of the writ of habeas corpus. Next on Wallace's list, the fifth resolution reprimanded the Lincoln administration for its "shameful disregard" of Federal prisoners of war captive in Confederate prison camps. Both Lincoln and General Grant had refused to exchange prisoners unless the Confederates agreed that no distinction would be made between black and white prisoners. The sixth and final resolution expressed the sympathy of the Democratic Party for the nation's soldiers and sailors and promised to give them the care and protection they had earned.

Following another wave of cheering and applauding, all six resolutions were adopted by the convention with almost no opposition. "One or two voices arose with negative votes from the body of the hall."[15] There were actually more than one or two War Democrats who did not agree with the Democratic platform. August Belmont was one dissenter; he thought that his party's position on the war was a mistake, and he said so.

But the overwhelming majority agreed with Clement Vallandigham. They might not have thought that the war was an unwinnable fiasco, as Vallandigham did, but a majority of the delegates agreed that the South should be allowed to secede from the Union and that an armistice should be declared as soon as possible. In the summer of 1864, war weariness was good politics, and the convention did not want to go against the majority's point of view. And the majority went along with the Peace Democrats' point of view, which was that whatever helped the Confederate cause and hindered Lincoln and the Union also helped the Democratic Party. "So the resolutions were adopted, when applause rose, cheer upon cheer, oft repeated from the floor and galleries alike."[16] Jefferson Davis himself could not have written a platform more sympathetic to the Confederacy.

After the party's platform was approved, the next item of business was to nominate a candidate for president. The preferred nominee was George B. McClellan, as everyone in the country had known for some time. But getting McClellan approved as the Democratic candidate turned out to be a lot more difficult than anyone supposed, in spite of the fact that he was the front-runner.

McClellan was nominated by John P. Stockton of New Jersey, which was seconded by Samuel S. Cox of Ohio. Most McClellan backers thought that would close the nominations. But no sooner had this been done than Lazarus W. Powell of Kentucky was also nominated. This apparently took Mr. Powell by surprise as much as everybody else. In response, he said that he was flattered by the offer but that he would like his name withdrawn from consideration. The reason he gave was that, in his opinion, the Democratic candidate should come from a nonslaveholding state. His actual reason was apparently that he had no desire to become president, at least not at that point in time. It looked as though any candidate the Democrats might run against Lincoln would be unbeatable, and Powell did not want to be the next president of the United States in the middle of a civil war.

Following Mr. Powell's rapid withdrawal from consideration, the name of Thomas H. Seymour of Connecticut, a Peace Democrat, was entered. Benjamin Harris seconded the nomination, but he also had a lot more to say. Harris, a Peace Democrat from Maryland, had no use at all for George B. McClellan. As far as Harris was concerned, McClellan was nothing but a damned War Democrat, and he was not bashful about letting his fellow delegates know exactly how he felt or why he was so furiously anti-McClellan.

"Gen. McClellan was the very first man who inaugurated the system of usurping State rights," Harris shouted at the convention. "Maryland has been cruelly trampled upon by this man," he continued indignantly. "Now you propose to reward in the shape of Presidential honors the man who first set the iron heel of despotism upon my State."[17]

To back up what he had just said, Harris proceeded to read a letter from Major General McClellan, dated September 12, 1861. McClellan commanded the Army of the Potomac at the time and had agreed with the Lincoln administration to arrest the entire Maryland legislature. In the letter, McClellan said that the arrests "will go far towards breaking the back-bone of the rebellion," and that steps should be taken to make certain that none of the legislators escaped.[18] Harris considered the mass arrests an act of barbarism, and considered McClellan not only a tyrant and an oppressor but also a crony of Lincoln and the Republicans. The Democrats had no business nominating anyone like George B. McClellan as their presidential candidate, Harris told the convention.

McClellan had a great many friends and backers among the delegates who did not appreciate hearing their candidate slandered. Harris had to shout over the hisses and catcalls of the pro-McClellan faction just to make himself heard. But Harris took it all in his stride and kept on with his criticism. Among other things, Harris charged that McClellan was nothing but a tool of Abraham Lincoln. He added that he could never bring himself to vote for McClellan's nomination.

After turning the Wigwam into a madhouse, Harris calmly left the platform and began walking toward his seat. But he did not stay very calm for very long. Delegates stood up—some say they "sprang to their feet"— and let Benjamin Harris know exactly what they thought of him. He was shouted at, blasted, and threatened. According to one account, a delegate called him a damned traitor. Harris responded by punching his tormentor and knocking him to the floor. Harris managed to make it back to his seat without being killed.

By this time, the sun was setting and it was becoming too dark to see— the Wigwam was too cavernous for any sort of effective lighting. Several delegates moved that the convention adjourn until next morning, a motion that was finally carried. Further skirmishing and name-calling would have to be postponed.

By ten o'clock the next morning, August 31, the atmosphere inside the Wigwam had changed completely. The delegates were still determined to choose their candidates for president and vice president, but they had something just as important in mind: they wanted to get the nominating process over so everyone could go home. The screaming and shouting of the previous day was conveniently forgotten. Following the opening prayer, a motion was made that the reading of the minutes of the preceding day's proceedings be dispensed with. That particular motion was passed with no opposition. It had been bad enough just sitting through all the commotion of the day before; nobody wanted to hear about it all over again.

Before the business of nominating the party's candidates began, Charles A. "Old Kentucky" Wickliffe made an unusual, almost bizarre, motion. Wickliffe was the Peace Democrats' answer to the Radical Republicans' Thaddeus Stevens, except that Wickliffe was even older and nastier. He had been crippled by rheumatism for many years, a condition that gave him a permanently sour disposition. (There were those who would argue that he was born with a sour disposition and that his rheumatism just made it worse.)

Wickliffe moved that "the dissolution of this convention shall not be affected by its adjournment after it finishes its labors today, but to leave it to the Executive Committee . . . to convene us at such time and place as the National Executive Committee shall designate."[19] In other words, he requested that the convention never be formally dissolved at the end of the day, just temporarily adjourned. This was in case there might be a need to reconvene in future.

The reasoning behind this motion was simple enough: Wickliffe was afraid that George B. McClellan might reject Clement Vallandigham's peace plank after he was nominated. Charles Wickliffe did not trust any War Democrat, including McClellan. If McClellan did what Wickliffe feared and rejected the peace plank, Wickliffe's motion would allow the convention to reconvene at a later date to replace McClellan with a Peace Democrat. "Old Kentucky" may have been old and crotchety, but he was also tricky and devious.

Wickliffe's motion was referred to the Committee on Resolutions, where it was approved. Immediately after this, one of the delegates moved that the day's main order be addressed: the nomination of a candidate for president of the United States. The motion was carried unanimously, and the state-by-state roll call vote began.

There was never any real question of who would be the Democratic nominee. George B. McClellan received 174 votes on the first ballot. This was more than twice the number of votes received by the runner-up, Thomas H. Seymour. When the results of the voting were announced, the delegates could see that McClellan was going to win by a landslide and lost no time in changing their votes—no one wanted to be caught on the losing side. Illinois cast all 16 of its votes for McClellan, stating that its delegates would "stand firm for George B. McClellan."[20] Even Charles Wickliffe himself said that his state's delegates "surrender to George B. McClellan, and cast our vote for him."[21] He might not have liked or trusted McClellan, but as a consummate politician, he knew the importance of throwing in his lot with the winner. Clement Vallandigham spoke up and moved that the voting for McClellan be made unanimous, a motion that was carried. It galled him to do it, but Vallandigham could also see that opposing McClellan at that stage would be a losing cause.

With the nomination of McClellan having been declared unanimous, the delegates used the occasion as an excuse to go insane. For 15 minutes, the delegates shouted, whooped, bellowed, applauded, and generally carried on like children who had just been let out of school. "Gentlemen upon chairs swung their hats," said one observer. "Ladies waved their handkerchiefs." When the noise began to die down, members of the McClellan Executive Committee of New York carried a pro-McClellan banner forward. This started another wave of pandemonium. The banner featured a portrait of the "Hero of Antietam," along with a slogan: "McClellan, our Country's Hope and Pride."[22]

In spite of all the noise and chaos, the nomination of McClellan went more quickly, and with a lot less infighting and name-calling, than anyone could have hoped for. The next item of business was the nomination of a candidate for vice president. Everyone present hoped that the naming of the vice president would be just as quick and incident-free. When McClellan's running mate was officially chosen, everybody would be able to go home.

George H. Pendleton of Ohio and James Guthrie of Kentucky were the two front-runners. Guthrie was a War Democrat and was the choice of the conservative bloc, including Chairman August Belmont. The Peace Democrats wanted Pendleton. Pendleton was as anti-war and pro-Confederate as Clement Vallandigham. It looked as though another noisy fight between the war and peace factions might be in store.

Guthrie won the first ballot by ten votes—65½ votes for Guthrie and 55½ for Pendleton, with the remaining votes scattered among a half dozen other candidates. Such a close vote might have triggered a fight for delegates among the Guthrie followers and the Pendleton supporters. But after the results were announced, something surprising happened—delegates began switching their votes to Pendleton without any sort of persuasion from the Pendleton backers. Illinois, New York, Kentucky, Missouri, and the other states all changed their votes to George H. Pendleton. The switch was as quick as it was unexpected. When the delegates had changed their votes, the secretary of the convention declared that the voting for Pendleton was unanimous and that he would be George B. McClellan's running mate. It had been quicker and easier than anyone had expected.

Not everybody was happy with the outcome, of course. August Belmont and the other War Democrats did not like the idea of having anyone as rabidly anti-war as George H. Pendleton on the same ticket as George B. McClellan. The convention might just as well have nominated Clement Vallandigham himself. Belmont and his fellow conservatives were convinced that having Pendleton as the country's vice president would be disastrous, both for the country and for the Democratic Party.

But the decision had been made, in spite of any objections or misgivings. The Democrats had decided upon their platform and had also chosen their candidates, for better or worse. For all intents and purposes, the Democratic National Convention was now over. There were still a few last-minute details to be taken care of before all the delegates could go back to their home states. The citizens of Chicago were thanked for their hospitality toward the delegates and a motion was passed that 50,000 copies of the proceedings of the convention should be printed and distributed.

When all the loose ends had been tidied up, nine cheers were given for George B. McClellan, "the next president of the United States." The convention was then formally adjourned—subject to George B. McClellan's reaction to the peace plank and possible recall by the National Committee.[23]

Nobody knew exactly what McClellan's reaction would be. And McClellan did not seem to know, either. He was at home in Orange, New Jersey, when he received word of his nomination, but he could not quite make up his mind on what to say to his fellow Democrats in response. For a solid week after the convention ended, McClellan worked on his letter of acceptance. He wrote six drafts of the letter, always tinkering with the language and fine-tuning his phrasing.

Everybody in the country waited to hear from McClellan, including Abraham Lincoln. Lincoln seemed to be highly amused by the sluggishness of his former general in chief—it probably reminded him of old times. When he was asked about McClellan's failure to respond, Lincoln suggested that he was probably digging in for a siege, just like he had done in Virginia in 1862. He had become known as "Mac the Unready" and the "Virginia Creeper" during those days, and he had obviously not changed very much. Maybe he intended to wait for the Republicans to attack.

Lincoln and McClellan did not have very much use for each other.

McClellan referred to the president as a gorilla, and always seemed to imply that he himself would make a much better president than the gangling oaf in the White House. Lincoln's opinion of McClellan was not nearly as angry or bad-tempered. Lincoln's dislike seemed to have been based mainly upon McClellan's inability to take the bull by the horns and make up his own mind. When he was asked if McClellan might turn down the Democratic nomination, Lincoln said that McClellan did not have the ability to make that decision for himself. Somebody else would have to make it for him. "For, of all the men I have had to deal with in my life, indecision is most strongly marked in General McClellan."[24]

On September 8, eight days after the convention adjourned, George B. McClellan finally submitted his letter of acceptance. He told his wife that he was satisfied with what he had written and that he was "not afraid to go down to posterity on it." Whether or not the letter was worthy of posterity, every newspaper in the country copied it and spread McClellan's words to every city and town.[25]

The document certainly was George B. McClellan—full of pomp and pomposity on one hand, but straightforward and dignified on the other. The first point McClellan wanted to make was that "this nomination comes to me unsought." He wanted the Democrats to know, in no uncertain terms, that the Hero of Antietam could very easily do without the Democratic Party. They needed him a lot more than he needed them.

From that point on, the letter concentrated on McClellan's view concerning the war and why it was being fought: "The preservation of our Union was the sole avowed object for which the war was commenced." This was emphasized again and again throughout the letter: the war was being fought to save the Union—not to abolish slavery. McClellan did not mention slavery at all, not even in passing.

As far as any sort of agreement with the Confederacy was concerned, McClellan stated that "the reestablishment of the Union in all its integrity, is, and must continue to be, the indispensable condition in any settlement." If "our present adversaries" should state that they are "ready for peace," everything possible should be done "to secure such peace, re-establish the Union and guarantee for the future the constitutional rights of every State."

There could be no hope of peace unless the Confederate states rejoined the Union. "The Union is the one condition of peace—we ask no more." In McClellan's view, the elimination of slavery should not be a condition for readmitting the Southern states.

McClellan wanted nothing to do with the idea of peace without victory, as he also made clear to the Democratic Party. "I could not look in the face of my gallant comrades of the army and navy, who have survived so many bloody battles, and tell them that their labors and the sacrifices of so many of our slain and wounded brethren had been in vain; that we had abandoned the Union for which we have so often periled our lives." Peace without victory, without restoring the Union, was out of the question. No peace could be permanent without union, McClellan wrote, and the Union "must be preserved at all hazards."

In summing up, McClellan wrote, "Believing that the views here expressed are those of the convention and the people you represent, I accept the nomination."[26] George B. McClellan has never been famous for having much of a sense of humor, but this sentence sounds like it was meant as some sort of underhanded joke. First he demolishes the peace without victory plank, the central plank of the Democratic platform, and then he says that he believes that his views are the same as the convention. If it was supposed to be funny, nobody was laughing.

The War Democrats, including August Belmont, were relieved to hear that McClellan would not support the peace plank. Somebody, at long last, had the gumption to go against the pro-Confederate mood of the convention. But Peace Democrats were anything but relieved or happy. When Clement Vallandigham heard about McClellan's rejection of his peace platform, he refused to go on campaigning for McClellan or the Democratic ticket.

Although their convention was now over, the Democrats were still in a predicament. They had their candidate of choice, the man they wanted to lead their party to victory in November, but they did not know what to do with him. McClellan was certainly a War Democrat—he had finally made that clear enough—but he had a Peace Democrat for a running mate. Some local wit said that the McClellan-Pendleton ticket represented the joining of a warhorse and a peace jackass. The combination certainly was awkward.

At least "Old Kentucky" Wickliffe did not petition to have the convention reconvene so that a replacement for McClellan could be nominated. That would have thrown the party into total confusion.

The Democrats knew that they had to rise above name-calling and partisan infighting. Their first priority was to get George B. McClellan elected. After the inauguration in March 1865, when McClellan was safely installed in the White House, pressures could be brought to bear to make the new president conform to the Chicago platform. Any disagreements could be ironed out after the election was won.

THE MOST GIGANTIC UNDERTAKING

While the Democrats were busy nominating George B. McClellan as their presidential candidate, events were taking place south of Atlanta that would have as much of an impact on the November election as anything the Democrats were doing in Chicago.

John Bell Hood did not anticipate any threat from the Union forces in the Jonesborough area. He instructed one of his subordinates to ease Lieutenant General William Hardee's mind by advising that "General Hood does not think there can be a large force advancing upon Jonesboro [sic]."[27] This assessment might have been the result of faulty intelligence or just plain wishful thinking. But whatever the reason, Hood could not have been more wrong.

On August 30, the same day that Hood advised Hardee not to worry about the threat of any large enemy force, the armies of George Thomas, John Schofield, and Oliver Howard were heading straight for the Macon and Western Railroad. They would hit the rail line at three different places. Howard's Army of the Tennessee was bearing down on the railroad at Jonesborough, east of the Flint River and less than two miles away from the town. "Old Woodenhead" Hood had got it wrong again.

Only a few hours after sending his message to General Hardee, Hood received a sobering telegram that finally made him face the truth—Federal troops had crossed the Flint River and Jonesborough was in danger. The report was totally unexpected. Hood realized that he would have to rethink both his evaluation of the enemy and his plans to defend Jonesborough.

General Hood ordered General Hardee and Stephen D. Lee, one of Hardee's corps commanders (and no relation to Robert E. Lee), to join him in Atlanta for a strategy meeting. Hood needed to come up with some sort of scheme to confront the enemy forces and what he had to say was too long and drawn out be communicated via telegraph.

The meeting was straightforward enough—John Bell Hood was nothing if not straightforward. Hardee and Lee were instructed to go after the Federals at Jonesborough in the morning and push them back across the Flint at bayonet point. If everything worked out as planned, it would be the kind of slugging match that Hood relished. Hood was no strategist—there were many who would have said that Hood was no thinker—but he had no equal when it came to an old-fashioned bare-knuckles brawl.

The only trouble was that Lee's men were absolutely exhausted. They had been walking all night long over rough and uneven roads. Some of the men had not had any sleep at all during the previous two nights. All of them were famished—they had not had very much to eat during the past two days, either. Hundreds had not been able to keep up with the march and had dropped by the side of the road from fatigue or hunger or both. Now they were expected to go on the attack against an entrenched enemy in the morning.

The Federals had the advantage of rifle pits. They had dug trenches that morning, which were at least chest deep, and had piled logs and fence rails in front of their trenches for added protection. Hardee's men were in no condition to go into combat that morning, especially against men in rifle pits. The result of their attack on the Federal lines was predictable.

Lee's men got to within 80 yards of the entrenchments when the Federals opened fire—"the most terrible and destructive fire I have ever witnessed," according to one of the Federal corps commanders.[28] Some of the attackers saw what was happening and refused to advance any farther toward the enemy trenches. "The men seemed possessed of some great horror of breastworks," a Confederate officer commented, "which no power, persuasion, or example could dispel." One of the division commanders was wounded twice while trying to rally his men, which added to the panic. When Lee's troops finally withdrew from in front of the Federal position, they left hundreds of dead and wounded behind.[29]

But that had been only one attack. While Lee's troops were being driven back from in front of the Federal rifle pits, Hardee's corps was not having any better luck over on Lee's left. Hardee's advance was broken by "murderous fire of grape shrapnel and musketry"—Federal artillery and infantry drove the rebels to cover in a ten-foot wide gully.[30] The gully seemed like a ready-made shelter to the retreating Confederates, but it quickly turned into a trap. Men of the 66th Indiana regiment bounded into the trench and killed or captured all the rebels, except for a few who were lucky enough, or nimble enough, to escape.

To the left of the fight in the gully, a Confederate division commanded by Brigadier General Mark Lowery tried to break through the Federal defenses in a separate attack. For a while, it looked as though Lowery would succeed. But a Federal cavalry division armed with Spencer repeating carbines turned back Lowery's men. With the failure of this attack, the day became a complete disaster for the Confederates. The slugging match that John Bell Hood had planned had left his army battered, bruised, and bloodied almost beyond recognition.

Hood's naturally sad expression must have seemed even more downcast than usual at the end of the fighting on August 31. He was not happy with what he saw as the lack of aggressiveness in the attacks against the Federal positions. The casualties that had been suffered by Hardee and Lee made him even more dejected. Confederate killed, wounded, and missing that day came to between 1,300 and 2,200, depending upon which source is consulted. Most of them came from Lee's corps. Had he known that General Howard claimed that he lost only 172 of his men, poor Hood's distress would have increased even further. (But Howard also reported that the Confederates lost 6,000 men, so his estimates might be considered overly enthusiastic.)[31]

Although the two sides spent most of the afternoon doing their best to kill each other, there were occasional incidents of humanity in the middle of all the fighting. A private with the 54th Virginia regiment named Sam Chinault left the safety of his trench to rescue wounded men lying between the lines. Private Chinault ran out three times; every time, he brought back a wounded companion. One of the soldiers was shot a second time while Private Chinault was trying to carry him out of danger.

On a different part of the field, Federal troops actually stopped shooting while another rescue operation was in progress. Three members of a Kentucky regiment ran out to no-man's-land to carry wounded men back to their lines. Each time, Federal troops held their fire and actually cheered the rescuers. The Federals and rebels soon went back to their killing. But for a little while, at least, compassion prevailed on the field of battle.

General Hood received Hardee's account of the fighting at Jonesborough just after midnight on September 1. After reading what Hardee had to say, Hood realized that Atlanta was now in jeopardy and might have to be abandoned unless he could come up with another plan to defend it. He tried his best to convince General Hardee that the fate of Atlanta rested upon Hardee's ability to push the Yankees across the Flint River. But Hardee was unwilling to do what Hood wanted and expected him to do, at least it seemed that way to Hood, and now Old Woodenhead would have to think of some sort of idea to keep the Federals at bay.

The way that Hood saw it, his best bet would be to keep Hardee at Jonesborough to protect the Macon and Western Railroad and to send Lee's corps north to defend Atlanta. In other words, he intended to weaken an already-outnumbered army by dividing it in two. Hardee did not think very much of Hood's order, but he was too much of a soldier to disobey it. He sent a telegram to President Jefferson Davis informing him of Hood's plan, and ordered Stephen Lee to prepare to move out. Lee and his men began walking toward Atlanta during the early hours of September 1, skirting east of the Federal troops that blocked the rail line. Hardee's three divisions would have to face all of Sherman's forces by themselves.

With Lee and his men gone, Hardee had only about 12,000 troops. He did his best to form a line of battle, but it was only the skeleton of a line. In some places, his men were spaced six feet apart. The only thing between them and Sherman's troops was a rail fence—not much in the way of fortifications. Sherman slowed his advance to tear up more rail line, which helped Hardee by giving him time to dig a line of trenches. But when

Sherman began his attack at around 4:00 p.m. on September 1, Hardee was well aware that the odds were not with him. All he could do was put up a good fight and hope and pray for the best.

Brigadier General Jefferson C. Davis's 14th Corps led the Federal attack. Davis had been a brigadier for the past two years and had been trying to prove to Grant or Sherman or anyone who would pay attention that he deserved a second star. Now he would have another chance. His corps rushed the Confederate line where it made a 90-degree turn to the east, about a mile or so north of Jonesborough, and crossed the Macon and Western Railroad. This bend in the line was defended by an Arkansas brigade commanded by Brigadier General Daniel Govan.

"General Davis formed his divisions in line about 4:00 p.m., swept forward over some old cotton-fields in full view, and went over the rebel parapet handsomely, capturing the whole of Govan's brigade, with two field batteries of ten guns," Sherman observed. Sherman was "on the spot," and was able to observe Davis's movements for himself.[32]

Govan's men fought the oncoming Federals with bayonets and clubbed rifles and actually managed to turn back the first attack. But Davis regrouped and came at the rebels again. This time, the Federals simply overwhelmed the enemy. "They ran over us like a drove of Texas beeves, by sheer force of numbers," a private in Govan's brigade remembered.[33]

Govan had no choice but to surrender—about 600 of his men were taken prisoner, including Govan himself. This left a sizeable gap in the Confederate line, and at a critical place. But the coming of darkness put a stop to the fighting that day, September 1. General Hardee began to withdraw his men from the lines around Jonesborough around midnight, moving them south and out of Sherman's reach.

But by that time, it did not really matter—there would be no fighting on the following day. At about 5:00 p.m. on September 1, while Davis and Govan were going at each other, John Bell Hood made up his mind to evacuate Atlanta. He finally came to the conclusion that Sherman's army actually did pose a major threat and that if he did not withdraw from Atlanta he would lose both the city *and* his army. He ordered all his forces to move south to Lovejoy's Station, where Hardee and his men would regroup, and where

Hood would be able to figure out what to do next. Rear guard units would stay behind, setting fire to weapons, ammunition, and anything else that might be useful to the enemy. After carrying out their disagreeable job, the rear guard would also pull out and leave Atlanta to Sherman and his men.

Sherman had absolutely no idea that Hood was pulling out. Unable to sleep, he had spent the night making plans for the next day's fighting. At around midnight, he heard what sounded like rifle fire and exploding shells coming from the direction of Atlanta. Earlier in the day, Sherman had ordered General Henry Slocum to take his 20th Corps and make a probing march toward Atlanta to see exactly how many rebel troops stood between his army and the city. It sounded as though Slocum had stumbled into Hood's army in the dark, starting a full-scale battle.

Sherman walked to the nearby house of a farmer, roused him out of his sleep, and asked the startled man if he had ever heard such explosions coming from the north before. He certainly had, the farmer said. They were the sounds of a battle. It sounded like heavy fighting up Atlanta way.

But Sherman was still not sure if they were the sounds of battle or of the Confederates blowing up their own munitions. The noise died down and then stopped altogether, but it started all over again at about four o'clock in the morning. Before dawn, the explosions stopped again, leaving Sherman as puzzled as he had been before.

In the morning, General Thomas and General Schofield began their advance against General Hardee's corps and discovered that Hardee had disappeared during the night. The two armies pursued Hardee and ran up against his lines just north of Lovejoy's Station. Hardee's men were well dug in, and a Federal attack at about four o'clock in the afternoon was turned back. Sherman sent word that he did not want to force a second attack. Until he received information regarding the state of affairs in Atlanta, he had no intention of risking any more lives on attacks that might turn out to be pointless.

The information that Sherman wanted would soon arrive. While Thomas and Schofield were confronting General Hardee, Henry Slocum's 20th Corps had slowly made its way into Atlanta. At an abandoned Confederate works that had been ironically named Fort Hood, Slocum's lead column was met by a delegation of civilians carrying a white flag. The group's spokesman was the mayor of Atlanta, the honorable James M. Calhoun, who formally surrendered the city to Colonel John Coburn of the 33rd Indiana regiment. Mayor Calhoun told Colonel Coburn that the fortunes of war had placed Atlanta at his mercy and asked protection for noncombatants and private property.

Colonel Coburn immediately reported Mayor Calhoun's surrender to General Slocum. As soon as Slocum entered the city, he could see that the preceding night's explosions had been caused by Hood's rear guard destroying the Confederate ammunition trains. With the Macon and Western Railroad in Federal hands, there was no way that the trains could have escaped falling into the hands of Sherman's advancing troops. The fires from the 81 ammunition-filled rail cars that had been detonated by the retreating Confederate troops continued to burn for hours, long after the men who set them had left Atlanta to join up with the rest of Hardee's forces.

The first communiqué sent by Slocum from inside Atlanta was to the War Department in Washington: "General Sherman has taken Atlanta."[34] He also sent a courier pounding south with a handwritten note for General Sherman, firmly stating that he had entered Atlanta unopposed. The note was dated inside the city; Sherman had no doubt that Atlanta was now in Federal hands.

Sherman sent a slightly rambling telegram of his own to General Henry "Old Brains" Halleck in Washington. "HOOD, at Atlanta, finding me on his road, the only one that could supply him, and between him and a considerable part of his army, blew up his magazines in Atlanta, and left in the night-time, when the Twentieth Corps, Gen. SLOCUM, took possession of the place." His message ended with, "So Atlanta is ours, and fairly won."[35]

Before issuing a general order to inform the rest of the army that Atlanta had been captured, Sherman sent one of his staff officers to General George H. Thomas's tent with Slocum's note. He wanted to share the exciting news with somebody, preferably somebody he had known for many years, and General Thomas had been Sherman's friend since their West Point days. The officer returned a few minutes later, followed by a visibly agitated Thomas. The news seemed too good to be true; Thomas wanted to be absolutely certain that the note was genuine and not some sort of trick.

Sherman convinced his old friend that the note certainly was genuine, and he assured him that General Slocum was inside Atlanta at that very moment. With Sherman's assurances, Thomas's doubts turned to pure joy. George Thomas was a tall, serious West Point graduate from Southampton County, Virginia, who had remained loyal to the Union after Fort Sumter and had been disowned by his family for it. He was anything but an extrovert—the word most often used to describe him was "staid," and his nickname was "Old Slow Trot." But when he was finally convinced that John Bell Hood actually had evacuated Atlanta, staid old George Thomas did everything but jump in the air and turn handstands. "He snapped his fingers, whistled, and almost danced," Sherman would later recall with pleasure. It was the best and most exciting news he had heard in months, and Old Slow Trot did not even try to restrain himself.[36]

When the rest of the army heard the news, they reacted just like George Thomas, except with a lot more noise. Sherman wrote, "The shouts that arose from our men, the wild hallooing and the glorious laughter, were to us a full recompense for the labor and toils and hardships through which we had passed in the previous three months."[37]

The men had good reason to shout and raise their share of hell—they had survived. They had fought at Dalton, Resaca, Alatoona, Kennesaw Mountain, Peachtree Creek, Jonesborough, and what seemed like a thousand other places, and they were still alive. They had outmaneuvered Joe Johnston, had outslugged John Bell Hood, and had taken Atlanta. There would be more fighting ahead, the men could be certain of that. But for the moment, at least, they knew they would have a few weeks to rest and unwind before it started all over again.

To celebrate Sherman's capture of Atlanta, President Lincoln ordered every military installation in the United States, including Washington Navy Yard, to fire a 100-gun salute. This was Lincoln's tribute to one of the turning points of the war. Ulysses S. Grant celebrated the news of Atlanta in his own unique way. He ordered his artillery batteries to fire 100 rounds of live ammunition into the rebel works at Petersburg—this was Grant's idea of a 100-gun salute. "In honor of your great victory," he telegraphed Sherman, "I have ordered a salute to be fired with *shotted* guns from every battery bearing upon the enemy."[38]

Grant was almost giddy with excitement over Sherman's achievement. In a second telegraph, he told Sherman, "I feel you have accomplished the most gigantic undertaking given to any general in this war, and with a skill and ability that will be acknowledged in history as not surpassed, if not unequalled." This was an unheard-of compliment from the usually reserved and unemotional Grant.[39]

If Grant was giddy, the North was almost beside itself with excitement. A historian later wrote, "The news that Atlanta had fallen was a mighty intoxicant for the people back home."[40] It was the most significant news of the war so far, and everybody knew it. Church bells rang across the country, from Michigan to Maine. Edward Everett gave one of his famous orations to commemorate the occasion—the same Edward Everett who had spoken for two hours at Gettysburg less than a year before, just prior to Abraham Lincoln's famous two-minute address.

This was bigger news than either Gettysburg or Vicksburg. "Five telegraphic words—'Gen. SHERMAN has taken Atlanta,' on Saturday, thrilled the nation," the *New York Times* pronounced. "Four months of constant and vigorous campaigning, a contested march of full two hundred miles, ten pitched battles, and two score of lesser engagements by night and day, make up the price we paid for Atlanta." But Atlanta was well worth the cost, the article continued. "At once the workshop, the granary, the storehouse and the arsenal of the Confederacy" were now "ours."[41] Most of the men in Sherman's army would have agreed.

First there had been Admiral Farragut's "Damn the Torpedoes!" message from Mobile Bay a month earlier, and now "General Sherman has taken Atlanta." Throughout the North, morale reached its highest point since the beginning of the war. Everybody realized that General Sherman had done more than just win an important battle. By taking Atlanta, he had permanently damaged the Confederacy's very ability to wage war, and he had probably dealt a fatal injury to the Confederacy itself. After Atlanta, there was no longer any doubt in anyone's mind that the North was going to win the war. Though it might take a while yet, the outcome of the war was now inevitable—the Union would win! "The public's temper is buoyant and hopeful," one editorial observed. "The friends of the Government, the defenders of the Constitution, the supporters of the Union ticket, are full of courage and confidence."[42]

When word of the fall of Atlanta reached the British Isles, most people also saw its significance. Not everybody was prepared to admit that the loss of Atlanta would be a fatal blow to the South, however. Members of the British upper classes had almost unanimously backed the Confederacy, fervently hoping for Confederate independence. But with the surrender of Atlanta, enthusiasm for a Southern victory began to evaporate.

The editor of the weekly *Army and Navy Gazette*, W. H. Russell, had gleefully been predicting disaster for both Grant and Sherman since the spring. In common with most other British observers, Russell had been writing that the Confederate armies, led by the brilliant Robert E. Lee, were superior and more determined than the Union forces, and that the North had no chance of winning. Russell's opinions were respected and were widely repeated throughout the British press. He quickly changed his tune about Southern invincibility when he heard that Sherman had taken Atlanta, however.

"General Sherman has fully justified his reputation as an able and daring soldier," Russell wrote, "and the final operations by which he won Atlanta are not the least remarkable of the series which carried him from Chattanooga . . . into the heart of Georgia."[43]

Southern newspapers tended to agree. "We have suffered a great disaster," lamented the *Atlanta Chronicle & Sentinel*. "We cannot conceal from ourselves the magnitude of the loss we have sustained in the fall of Atlanta."[44] The article went on to say that the damage done by Sherman was not irreparable and that it was still possible to push the Federals out of Georgia, but most people recognized this as nothing more than an advanced case of wishful thinking. "Neither the fall of Vicksburg nor the repulse at Gettysburg produced so painful an impression here as the loss of Atlanta," a resident of western Georgia remarked.[45]

Some were farsighted enough to recognize that the effects of Sherman's success would be felt far beyond Georgia. "I am afraid that the fall of Atlanta will secure Lincoln's re-election," a North Carolina soldier wrote home to his father. The head of the Confederate Ordinance Bureau in

Richmond pondered this, writing that "there will be little left for the peace party [in the North] to stand on."[46] Throughout the South, more and more people were beginning to suspect that the Confederacy's days were numbered, in spite of any belligerent talk that might come out of Richmond.

If civilians and ordinary soldiers could guess what the loss of Atlanta meant to the fortunes of the Confederacy, President Jefferson Davis was all too conscious of its significance. He was also becoming increasingly aware of the consequences resulting from his decision to replace Joseph E. Johnston with John Bell Hood as commander of the Army of Tennessee. At that point in time, Davis probably wished that he had never feuded with Joe Johnston at West Point, and especially that he had never replaced Johnston with Hood. His most fervent wish probably was that he had never even heard of John Bell Hood. After relieving Johnston of command, Davis reflected that he was "fully aware of the danger of changing commanders of an army while actively engaged with the enemy."[47] But he made the change just the same, partly for personal reasons and partly because he thought he was making a sound military judgment. Now he had to live with the fact that his decision had lost Atlanta, and might have cost the Confederacy the war.

The news of Atlanta could not have come at a better time for Abraham Lincoln. The election was only two months away. Sherman's "Atlanta is ours and fairly won" message was the best and most effective political endorsement Lincoln ever could have hoped for. Just a few weeks before, Lincoln's political prospects appeared to be a dead issue. But now all that had changed, suddenly and dramatically. With the fall of Atlanta, his fortunes had taken a 180-degree turn for the better. After the first week of September, it began to look as though nothing could derail Lincoln's drive to the White House.

Sherman had certainly taken the steam out of the Democrats' peace platform. Nobody could claim that the war was an undiluted failure anymore, not with the Confederacy's second most important city in Union hands. Only the capture of Richmond could have made more of an impact. No record exists of what Clement Vallandigham said and did when he heard "Atlanta is ours," but it can be safely assumed that he did not join in the mood of national rejoicing. And on September 8, George B. McClellan submitted his letter stating that the Union "must be preserved at all hazards." It was not a good time to be a Peace Democrat.

It certainly was a good time for Abraham Lincoln. He declared the first Sunday after the fall of Atlanta a day of thanksgiving and requested that all churches throughout the North offer prayers of thanks for the victory in Georgia. He also wrote a letter praising Sherman for capturing Atlanta. Although Lincoln did not say as much, he was also thanking Sherman for saving his re-election campaign.

"The national thanks are rendered by the President to Major-General W. T. Sherman and the gallant officers and soldiers of his command before Atlanta," Lincoln wrote, "for the distinguished ability and perseverance displayed . . . which, under Divine favor, has resulted in the capture of Atlanta."[48]

Four months earlier, when the spring campaigns were just beginning in Virginia and Georgia, Lincoln thought that he would be writing such a letter to Ulysses S. Grant, not to Sherman. In May, Lincoln told a member of the White House staff that Grant was the first real general he had ever had, a general who would fight. He had expected great things from Grant against Lee in Virginia, possibly that Grant might even win a victory as spectacular as Gettysburg. Instead, it was the tall, nervous Sherman who had won the spectacular victory that gave his re-election campaign renewed hope and vitality. In May, William Tecumseh Sherman was just another general. Now, he was a national hero and the cause of Lincoln's celebration of thanksgiving.

Now that he had his long-awaited stunning military victory, Lincoln could concentrate on politics. He freely admitted that he knew a lot more about politics than strategy and that it was a lot easier to manipulate politicians than to control generals. The first item on Lincoln's political agenda was to placate the Radicals within the Republican Party.

The Radical Democracy party, led by their presidential candidate John C. Fremont, probably constituted the greatest threat to Lincoln after Atlanta fell. Fremont was an almost-legendary figure, an explorer and army officer known as "the Pathfinder." He was in a position to do real damage to Lincoln's re-election. Senior Republicans feared that if Fremont ran for president as a third-party candidate, he would split the Republican/ National Union Party vote in November, draining enough votes away from Lincoln and Andrew Johnson to give George B. McClellan and the Democrats the election.

But on September 21, Fremont announced that he was withdrawing from the presidential race. A senator from Michigan named Zachariah Chandler convinced Fremont to bow out of the race. He had no chance at all of being elected, Chandler informed Fremont—third-party candidates rarely attract enough votes to win a general election—and he would make powerful enemies among the Republican hierarchy if he decided to stay in the race. After Atlanta, Fremont saw that it would be expedient to throw his political support to Lincoln. He had no hope of winning, he could see that, and he did not want to cost Lincoln the election—Fremont knew what that would mean.

As a sort of peace offering in exchange for Fremont's withdrawal, Lincoln asked Postmaster General Montgomery Blair to resign from office. Both Fremont and the Radicals had no use for Blair, and the feeling was more than mutual. Blair was not enough of an abolitionist to suit them— he had opposed the Emancipation Proclamation. The Radicals had long wanted him out of the Republican political picture. Lincoln asked for Blair's resignation on September 23, three days after Fremont's withdrawal. Blair tendered his resignation in accordance with the president's request. Lincoln had nothing against Blair, and the two remained on good terms after the resignation. But politics were politics, and Lincoln considered Blair's resignation a fair exchange for Fremont's departure from the race.

For the first time, Lincoln's political fortunes seemed to be secure. He did not have any more adversaries in the Republican Party, at least none that had enough power and influence to sabotage his re-election campaign, and Sherman's capture of Atlanta had completely turned public opinion around concerning the war. There was still no guarantee that he would win the election, but at least Lincoln could relax a little. In spite of his naturally melancholy disposition, he knew that he could now afford to indulge in some hard-earned optimism.

The National Union Party staged hundreds of rallies and parades throughout the North to promote the Lincoln/Johnson ticket, but Lincoln did not take part in any of them. Lincoln did not campaign at all; Sherman had done all his campaigning for him. In a letter to a man from Kentucky, Lincoln explained, "I claim not to have controlled events, but confess plainly that events have controlled me."[49] He was a war president, and the ups and downs of the war had made his campaign. All the rallies and speeches in the world would not have done him any good if Sherman had still been bogged down outside Atlanta. Lincoln was enough of a professional politician to realize this.

But even though his chances of being re-elected had improved dramatically, thanks to Sherman, Lincoln knew that he was not out of the woods yet. One question mark would not go away, and that was the soldier vote—would the army vote for Lincoln or for McClellan? This was very much a point of concern because it looked as though the army was still leaning toward McClellan and the Democrats.

It was not that the army did not like Lincoln; they liked him well enough. But he was a politician, somebody from Washington. McClellan, on the other hand, was one of them. The army loved Little Mac. The soldiers of the Army of the Potomac still thought of themselves as McClellan's boys. If enough soldiers voted for the former general, like the ex-GIs of 1952 voted for Dwight D. Eisenhower, they might just have enough of an impact to knock the election out of Lincoln's grasp.

WHIRLING THROUGH WINCHESTER

Lincoln could be well satisfied that Atlanta was now in Union hands and that public opinion had swung so heavily—and seemingly so convincingly—to his advantage. But he realized that the war was still far from being won. Robert E. Lee and his army were still very much alive in the trenches south of Petersburg and Jubal Early continued to be a threat in the Shenandoah Valley. And public opinion was a strange and volatile thing. The same crowds that had run church bells and set off fireworks when they heard that "Atlanta is ours" might very well turn against Lincoln if either Lee or Early managed to mount a dramatic offensive. Both generals still had a lot of fight left in them and were more than capable of delivering a bloody nose to Northern morale—and to Lincoln's re-election hopes.

Lincoln was not all that worried about Lee at Petersburg. Grant was grinding down Lee and his army, just as he had said he would—although he was taking a lot longer than Lincoln would have liked. But Jubal Early in the Shenandoah was another matter. Even though Phil Sheridan had reduced the valley to a desert of fire-blackened earth, Early still controlled it. Newspapers that backed George B. McClellan and the Democrats were now picking on Sheridan, saying that the war was still a failure in spite of Atlanta because Sheridan could not dislodge Early from the Shenandoah.

Lincoln's nerves started to get the better of him again. On September 12, he telegraphed General Grant about Phil Sheridan. He wanted to know if something could be done to energize Sheridan, to encourage him to launch some sort of an attack in the Shenandoah. Sheridan had been instructed to follow Early "to the death," but he seemed to have forgotten his objective.

General Grant had been thinking along these same lines. He intended to contact Sherman on this very subject, but did not want to send orders to Sheridan via Washington. Secretary of War Edwin M. Stanton or Henry Halleck might intercept his communiqué and tamper with its contents. Halleck still did not fully trust Grant, even if he was a three-star general and the hero of Vicksburg and Fort Donelson, and Stanton tended not to trust any general. Both Stanton and "Old Brains" Halleck were much more cautious than Grant when it came to planning an offensive—cynics would say that they were feeble and dithering—and Grant did not trust either one of them. To get around Washington and its bureaucrats, he planned to visit Sheridan and talk to him in person.

Grant arrived at Sheridan's headquarters on September 15, with what he called "a plan of campaign."[50] But Sheridan already had a plan of his own. He took a map out of his pocket and opened it, a map that showed all the roads and streams of the area as well as the camps of the two armies. The two men looked at the map and talked about the plan that Sheridan had in mind. Sheridan did most of the talking, gesturing nervously at the map, while Grant listened and chewed his cigar. Grant always had the talent for being silent in several languages, and his talent was never more evident than on this occasion.

Grant liked what Sheridan had to say, and kept his own ideas for a campaign buttoned up inside his coat. He always did have a high opinion of Sheridan—the little Irishman liked to fight as much as he did. Could he be ready to move out on Tuesday, Grant asked? Sheridan assured Grant that he could start before daylight on Monday. That was exactly what Grant wanted to hear. He nodded his approval and, never one to waste words, told Sheridan "Go in." And Phil Sheridan went in, as only Phil Sheridan could.[51]

At about two o'clock in the morning on September 19, the cavalry of Brigadier General James H. Wilson splashed across Opequon Creek, about six miles east of the town of Winchester, and ran into the defensive line of Jubal Early's Army of the Valley. A few hours later, just as the sun was coming up, Wilson's cavalry was followed by the 24,000 men of the 6th Corps. The battle that both Grant and Lincoln had been waiting for had finally begun.

Sheridan's Army of the Shenandoah outnumbered Early's forces by 39,000 to 14,000. Besides the 6th Corps, Sheridan also had two other full corps—the 8th Corps and the 19th Corps—under his command. The 6th Corps was the most experienced and battle-tested corps—they would have said that they were the best—of Sheridan's army. They had been detached from the Army of the Potomac in July and had walked from Petersburg to the northernmost corner of Virginia, only a few miles from West Virginia. No sooner had they arrived in the Shenandoah Valley than Grant recalled them to Petersburg. Just as the troops reached Washington, marching 20 miles and more per day in the intense summer heat, their orders were changed yet again—they were to go back to the Shenandoah. By mid-August, the 6th Corps was back in the vicinity of Winchester.

Most of the men liked Winchester. The residents of the town were friendly and treated the soldiers with courtesy and respect. On their way to Winchester, the men passed through Harpers Ferry and saw the spot where the radical abolitionist John Brown was hanged in 1859. A band played "John Brown's Body." Everybody knew the tune, and the soldiers sang,

"John Brown's body lies a-mouldering in the grave, but his soul goes marching on," as they passed through the town.

On the evening of September 18, the men of the 2nd Rhode Island Volunteers received orders to get ready to leave camp at a moment's notice—they were veterans enough to know this meant to prepare for an impending battle. They checked their weapons and made sure that cartridge boxes had been filled before leaving camp at about 2:00 a.m. on September 19. At about 8:00 a.m., after marching all night, the Rhode Islanders could see the white puffs of smoke from the enemy's guns on the opposite side of Opequon Creek.

Sheridan's attack had started promisingly enough, with the 6th Corps cavalry and infantry surprising and scattering Early's forces. But the infantry and the train of supply wagons had become tangled up together on the same road, which slowed the advance to a crawl. And three divisions of the 6th Corps managed to get themselves separated from the 8th Corps, which left a gap between the two units. As soon as the rebels saw the gap, they threw a hard counterattack that brought the advance to a dead stop.

Phil Sheridan himself came up to separate the infantry from the supply wagons, cursing and shouting and ordering and threatening until the mess was straightened out. Then he sat up straight in the saddle, all five feet five of him, and urged the men "to kill every son of a bitch" that got in front of them.[52] Encouraged by Sheridan, the men did their best to carry out his order to the letter.

"About noon, our division was ordered in," recalled Captain Elisha Hunt Rhodes of the 2nd Rhode Island Volunteers, "and we drove the Rebels back towards the city" of Winchester.[53] Rhodes was ordered to join forces with the 37th Massachusetts Volunteers, which was about a mile off to the right. The "37th Mass." was armed with the Spencer repeating rifle. The lever-action Spencer was loaded via a cylindrical magazine that held seven metallic cartridges, which made it far superior to any muzzle-loading rifle. The muzzle-loading rifled musket used by both sides could be fired and reloaded about twice per minute. The Spencer could be fired seven times in about 15 seconds. When that seven-round magazine ran out, the rifle could be quickly reloaded by inserting another magazine through a chamber at the end of its stock, giving the rifleman another seven rounds. While the muzzle-loader was being fired once, the Spencer could be fired 14 times.

About 40 of Elisha Hunt Rhodes's men also carried the Spencer and had used it in combat. They had a great deal of respect for this weapon, which represented the latest and most advanced technology in 1864. Confederates who had encountered the Spencer in the hands of Union troops probably had even more respect for it. They knew even better than the Federals what it was capable of accomplishing in battle.

Two months earlier, near Leesburg, Virginia, Rhodes's men had used their Spencers for the first time. The rifles had apparently been a new experience for the rebels as well. When the Rhode Islanders opened fire, and kept on firing at the rate of one shot every couple seconds, the rebels knew that they had come up against something new and unexpected.

"I say, Yankees, what kind of guns have you got?" one of the rebels had shouted across the lines. The Yankees replied with another volley.[54] After watching the repeating rifle in action, Rhodes had concluded that the Spencer gave his men the firing capacity of five times that many Confederates.

Just outside Winchester on September 19, the Confederates became reacquainted with the Spencer and its firepower. Elisha Hunt Rhodes's unit, along with the Massachusetts volunteers, had been ordered to capture a battery of rebel horse artillery. A brigade commander gave the men the order to move forward. "Away we went," Rhodes said, "the 37th Mass. and the 2nd R.I. heading for the battery."[55] The attack was pressed with such force and determination that the rebels unhitched their horses and headed for the rear, leaving the cannons behind. Persuaded by the rapid-firing Spencers, the Confederate line broke and ran.

The rebels were breaking all along the entire line. Two divisions of Sheridan's cavalry charged the Confederates with drawn sabers, giving the infantrymen a sight they would always remember—"two divisions of Yankee cavalry massed in solid columns, drawn sabres flashing in the sun like sheets of flame, thundering down at a full gallop to strike the flank and rear of the Confederate line."[56] Supporting artillery tried to break the charge, but the momentum of the advancing horsemen carried them right through the line. The cavalrymen, those who did not stay behind to take prisoners and capture enemy battle flags, chased the running Confederates off the field toward the town of Winchester.

"With loud shouts, they dashed into the mass of fleeing Rebels," Rhodes observed. "Friend and foe mingled together, cutting and slashing right and left. The infantry stood still and looked on." Artillery fire gave the Confederates an additional reason to run for safety. "Down through the streets of Winchester fled the Rebels, and our Cavalry pursued, and firing up and down the streets took place."[57]

Phil Sheridan watched the battle as well, except he did not stand still. He seemed to be everywhere at once, riding his big black charger Rienzi, attended only by one orderly who carried his personal red-and-white battle standard. Wherever he went, the men cheered him. "There goes Sheridan," and "Hurrah for Sheridan!" they would shout while they waved their caps. Sheridan waved right back and told them to keep moving forward.[58]

The men kept moving forward, driving Jubal Early's men in front of them. Sheridan's cavalry chased Early's rear guard right through Winchester. They kept going south along the Valley Turnpike until they reached Fisher's Hill, about 20 miles away. Early managed to get what was left of his army away from Sheridan and total destruction, along with most of his artillery, but he had lost about one-quarter of his army—just under 4,000 men. Sheridan lost 1,000 more men than Early, a total of 5,018 casualties, but this only amounted to one-eighth of his command.[59]

One of the men that Sheridan lost at Winchester was Major Peter Vredenburgh of the 14th New Jersey Volunteers, who had written to his mother outside Richmond in June. Following the battle, a friend wrote to Vredenburgh's mother to express his sympathy. "All his comrades attested to his bravery even to rashness, and his was the pure patriotism which nobly sacrificed his life in the defense of his country," the letter said. "We cannot restrain our tears when we think of our friend as no more on earth."[60] This is just one of hundreds of similar letters written after the battle.

When the fighting was finally over on September 19, Phil Sheridan sent a message of a completely different sort to General Grant. In a telegram from "Winchester, 7.30 p.m.," Sheridan fairly bristled with enthusiasm: "I have the honor to report that I attacked the forces of General Early . . . and after a sanguinary engagement which lasted from early in the morning until 5 o'clock, completely defeated him and, driving him through Winchester, captured about 2,500 prisoners, 5 pieces of artillery, 9 army flags and most of their wounded."[61]

Sheridan's chief of staff sent a similar telegram, worded to catch the attention of newspaper editors throughout the North. "We have just sent them whirling through Winchester, and we are after them tomorrow. This army behaved splendidly." The phrase "whirling through Winchester" was copied by just about every newspaper north of the Mason-Dixon Line, and served as yet another boost for already-surging morale.[62]

Grant was also glad to hear Sheridan's news, but he was not all that surprised by it. September 19 had been a quiet day around Petersburg, with Lee showing no signs of taking any sort of offensive action. He was encouraged by Sheridan's success against Jubal Early, but remarked to a group of officers that Sheridan had only been following orders—he had ordered Sheridan to move out and whip Early. One of the officers was slightly taken aback by what Grant had just said and spoke up to correct the general. "I presume the actual form of the order was to move out and attack him," he said.

Grant corrected the young officer's misunderstanding at once. "No, I meant just what I say," he responded. "I gave the order to whip him." As far as Grant was concerned, when Sheridan chased Jubal Early south for 20 miles, he was only following orders.[63]

As Sheridan's communiqué from Winchester had stated, he certainly had attacked Early and his army. His cavalry went first, straight down the Valley Turnpike, with the rest of the army right behind. At around 4:00 p.m. on September 22, Sheridan's troops lined up and charged the dug-in Confederates at Fisher's Hill, about 21 miles south of Winchester. As usual, Sheridan himself was out in front, with his orderly and his battle standard riding a short distance behind him. Everybody could see their commanding general as he rode up and down the lines, shouting at his men to keep moving forward and not to stop for anything.

Early's troops did their best to hold off the charging Federals. But there were just too many of them, and they came howling in with such determination that the entire Confederate line gave way. Elisha Hunt Rhodes did not take part in the battle, but word of its outcome reached him in Winchester on the following day. "We have glorious news today," he wrote in his diary. "General Sheridan has again defeated the Rebels at Fisher's Hill, twenty-one miles from here and has taken 16 cannon and a large number of prisoners."[64]

But Jubal Early managed to get away with his surviving troops once again. He disengaged from Sheridan's army and took refuge in the Shenandoah Valley, along with what was left of his infantry and cavalry. Even though he had been beaten twice in three days, Early was not about to give up.

When General Grant heard what Sheridan had accomplished at Fisher's Hill, he ordered another 100-gun live-ammunition salute fired into the rebel positions. "I congratulated Sheridan upon his recent great victory and had a salute of a hundred guns fired in honor of it, the guns being aimed at the enemy around Petersburg." Just as he had done after Sherman had taken Atlanta, Grant also ordered "other commanders throughout the country" to fire a volley of artillery at the enemy to celebrate Sheridan's victory.[65] The Confederates probably did not appreciate Grant's sense of humor this time any more than they did when he commemorated the fall of Atlanta.

General Grant was not the only one who celebrated. When President Lincoln was told about Winchester, he lost no time in sending a congratulatory telegram to Phil Sheridan. "Have just heard of your great victory. God bless you all, officers and men."[66] He was well aware that Sheridan had not only won a victory over Jubal Early but had also scored a major victory for him in his re-election campaign.

A writer for *Harper's Weekly* saw a man reading one of the dispatches from Sheridan to Grant on a news bulletin board. The writer overheard the man say, "A few more such victories, and Abe Lincoln will be re-elected in November."[67] It was certainly an apt observation. Lincoln was still not doing any campaigning of his own or taking part in any political rallies, even though the election was only six weeks away. He did not have to. Sheridan and Sherman were doing all the campaigning he ever could have hoped for.

Just a few weeks earlier, Lincoln had all but given up any hope of ever being re-elected. Now his prospects were looking sunnier with each passing day. But Lincoln was a canny politician who knew that no election is over until all the votes have been counted.

Chapter Seven

THE GAME OF ALL OR NOTHING

ELECTION NERVES

After submitting his letter accepting the Democratic Party's nomination for president in September 1864, George B. McClellan remained almost eerily silent regarding his election prospects. He made only one campaign appearance, in Newark, New Jersey, shortly after he had accepted the nomination. Following this one campaign stop, McClellan promptly dropped out of sight. Leaders of the Democratic Party did their best to persuade McClellan to appear at party gatherings, but their presidential candidate refused to take part in any activities that had been arranged on his behalf.

McClellan seemed determined to keep aloof from his campaign and separate himself from the Democratic Party and all its members. He corresponded with senior party officials when he had no choice in the matter, but he did not want to associate with any of them. It was as though he wanted to be president but did not want to get his hands dirty with the business of politics. This attitude did not make any friends for McClellan among the party officials. Everybody from party chairman August Belmont down to the lowest local campaign worker were all doing their part to sell their candidate to the public, everything from raising campaign funds to making speeches to handing out pamphlets. But McClellan himself remained in seclusion in New Jersey, having made the decision to stay out of his own campaign.

Because of Sherman's capture of Atlanta and Sheridan's convincing victories over Jubal Early at Winchester and Fisher's Hill, the Democrats could no longer insist that the war effort had been an abject failure. The war, and the presidential race, had taken a dramatic turn since the Chicago convention. The Democrats had to alter their strategy accordingly. Beginning in mid-September, they began to shift the focus of their campaign— instead of being anti-war, the Democrats decided that it would be smarter to be anti-Lincoln.

According to Democratic campaign literature, Lincoln was nothing short of a tyrant and radical abolitionist. Pamphlets pointed out that Lincoln had misused his executive power to suspend habeas corpus, to order thousands of people into prison without trial for the vague charge of suspected disloyalty, and had generally bent the Constitution to suit his personal whims—all of which happened to be true. The Democrats were now saying that another four years of Lincoln in the White House would result in anarchy, tyranny, and Negro equality.

It did not take very long for the Democrats to find out whether people were paying attention to the new campaign verbiage and whether they were taking it seriously. Local elections were being held in Ohio, Pennsylvania, and Indiana on October 11. Both political parties realized that the results of these contests should give some indication of which way public opinion was leaning—for the Republicans and the continuation of the war or for the Democrats and Confederate independence.

The outcome of all three elections demonstrated exactly how much public opinion had shifted since the summer. In Ohio—Clement Vallandigham's home state—the Republicans won by 50,000 votes. Before October 11, the state had 14 Democratic congressmen and five Republicans. But after all the votes had been tallied, only two Democrats still held their seats. When Congress reconvened after the New Year, Ohio would be sending 17 Republicans to Washington—three times as many as had been elected two years earlier.

Indiana also went to the Republicans, although not nearly as dramatically. Lincoln's party gained four seats in the House of Representatives and managed to oust the outspoken Copperhead Daniel W. Voorhees from his seat. Republican governor Oliver P. Morton was re-elected by 20,000 votes.

Unfortunately, the election was not exactly a model of decorum or integrity. The Democrats charged that the voting had been fraudulent and that the Republicans had stuffed the ballot boxes—charges that seem to have been substantiated by some of the voters.

A soldier with the 60th Massachusetts regiment, which was stationed outside Indianapolis to guard a contingent of Confederate prisoners, reported that his unit had been ordered to the polls with instructions to vote for Oliver P. Norton. The men seemed to have carried out their assignment with relish. "Most of our regiment went down to the city and voted," a Massachusetts man said in a letter home. "Some of the boys voted twenty-five times each."[1]

The Pennsylvania elections caused the greatest amount of anxiety for the Republicans. President Lincoln kept a vigil at the telegraph office all day long, monitoring returns and trying to determine which party had the lead. His patience was rewarded with good news—the Republicans had gained four seats in Congress and had picked up several seats in the state legislature as well. Lincoln could breathe a sigh of relief—on October 11, his party had won all three elections. The hopelessness and despair of August, when winning any election seemed a distant dream, now looked to be a thing of the past.

But just because the Republicans had won three local elections in October did not necessarily mean that they would carry these states in November. Their main concern was over Pennsylvania. Even though Republican candidates had won Pennsylvania by a combined total of 13,000 votes, party leaders were not all that confident about carrying the state in the upcoming presidential election. The outcome of the November election looked to be uncomfortably close, with neither party able to claim a clear advantage. And if George B. McClellan decided to come out of seclusion and make some campaign appearances, his presence could very well swing Pennsylvania to the Democrats.

Lincoln's anxiety over the impending election showed itself a couple days after October 11. He went back to the War Department's telegraph office and tried to work out his chances of being re-elected four weeks hence. On a blank sheet of telegraph paper, Lincoln drew two columns. In the left-hand column, he jotted down the number of electoral votes he thought McClellan would be likely to win and in the right-hand column he wrote the number of electoral votes that he would probably win. The telegraph operator watched as Lincoln struggled with his figures. The president wrote slowly and thoughtfully, stopping from time to time to think about what he was doing. He knew that his numbers not only would provide a very clear signal of who might be president during the next four years, but would also give an indication concerning his own political future.

The figures that Lincoln produced were not very encouraging. He determined that he would probably win the election, but only by six electoral votes—120 to 114. He also predicted that he would lose both Pennsylvania and New York, which carried 59 electoral votes between them. This margin would hardly provide the mandate he would need if he hoped to carry the war through to the end. Lincoln was clearly disappointed. He reflected that "the moral effect" of such a narrow victory would severely compromise his power as a war president and that his "power to prosecute the war and to make peace would be greatly impaired."[2] Winning the election by such a slim majority would be almost as bad as losing it.

Lincoln sent an edgy telegram to General Grant in Virginia to report on the results of the state elections, as well as to express his worries over the coming presidential election. "Pennsylvania very close, and still in doubt on home vote—Ohio largely for us . . . Indiana largely for us. . . . Send what you may know of your army vote."[3]

This was not just an idle request. Lincoln was very much concerned with the "army vote," not only in Pennsylvania but in every other state as well. In Pennsylvania, the "home vote," that is, the civilian vote, had been fairly evenly divided between the Republicans and the Democrats on October 11. It was the army vote that had tilted the election toward the Republicans. The prognosticators were predicting that the soldiers voting in the field would play a large role in deciding the presidential election.

The political experts also predicted that the army would cast its votes overwhelmingly for George B. McClellan. The soldiers had voted for the Republican candidates in Pennsylvania, but McClellan had not been on the ballot in Pennsylvania. This is what was in the back of Abraham Lincoln's mind when he telegraphed Grant—he was really asking whether the soldiers were leaning toward him or toward McClellan.

If the army were to vote overwhelmingly for McClellan, as Lincoln feared, it would almost certainly make all the difference between re-electing Lincoln and sending George B. McClellan to the White House. McClellan himself was of the opinion that the army would vote for him. He informed August Belmont that he had been in touch with friends in the army and, from what he had been told, the soldiers were all definitely behind him. Which seemed logical. The troops had always cheered Little Mac in the field and on the parade ground, and they had always loved and respected him. "McClellan was our first commander, and, as such, he was worshipped by his soldiers," wrote a private from Maine.[4] Because they had worshipped him, the soldiers were also expected to vote for him.

And the soldiers would be voting by the thousands on November 8. Seventeen of the 22 Northern states would be allowing their residents in uniform to cast absentee ballots on Election Day. Only five states— Delaware, Illinois, Indiana, Oregon, and New Jersey, McClellan's home state—still required all registered voters, including those in the army, to return home and cast their ballots in person. This would be the first time that the army would be allowed to vote in the field. Prior to this, any soldier who was stationed away from home lost the right to vote.

As far as the Democrats were concerned, the absentee soldier vote was a boon, a godsend. They saw their party as the beneficiary of this new law and they predicted that most of the soldier votes would go to George B. McClellan, the Hero of Antietam and the former commander of the Army of the Potomac. "We are as certain of two-thirds of that vote for General McClellan as that the sun shines," wrote the editor of the *New York World*.[5]

Lincoln heard all the predictions about which way the army would vote and seemed to take them in stride. He had already resigned himself to a close election, regardless of what the army did. "I would rather be defeated with the soldier vote behind me than be elected without it," was his reaction to the laws that would allow soldiers to cast their ballots in camp.[6]

But Lincoln also did not seem to believe all the things that were being said about the supposedly mystic bond between the army and McClellan—

that the soldiers would support Little Mac just because he once commanded the Army of the Potomac. Lincoln credited the army with better judgment than that. Above all, Lincoln was not about to concede anything. The experts could say anything they wanted, and could make all the predictions they liked. Election Day was November 8, only a few weeks off. The results of the balloting on that Tuesday would be the only opinion poll that counted. Everything that was said before then would be nothing but an exercise in guesswork and conjecture.

POLITICS AND STRATEGY

In Virginia, the Army of the Potomac was also well aware of the impending election, as well as of its implications. A good many soldiers would be voting for the first time in their lives, and they realized that their vote would be a referendum on the war. But mid-October also brought thoughts concerning the approach of winter and the end of the season's campaigning. Before long, the rain and snow of December and beyond would turn the roads into quagmires, making any kind of movement just about impossible. The dull routine of winter quarters was also just ahead. Making camp for the winter meant a few months without having to face Robert E. Lee— Bobby Lee, as the Army of the Potomac called him—which was a lot more important to most of the men than voting in the presidential election.

The coming winter would be anything but luxurious. The army would be living in tents and in canvas-roofed huts on the cheerless landscape outside Petersburg. But the men remembered the Wilderness and Spotsylvania and Cold Harbor and the Crater, and even wintering at Petersburg represented an improvement over what they had been through since May. Everyone, officers and men alike, hoped this would be the last winter of the war.

General Grant knew that winter was coming, as well, but he had no intention of going into winter quarters so soon. Although he had battered Lee and worn him down since May, the Army of Northern Virginia was still intact and Richmond remained maddeningly out of reach. Seven months earlier, in Cincinnati, he and his friend Sherman had mapped out their strategy: Sherman would go for Joe Johnston while Grant would go for Lee. Now it was autumn, and Sherman had certainly had his way with Johnston's Army of Tennessee, and had taken Atlanta, and had outfought John Bell Hood. But Grant was still bogged down in the Petersburg trenches. Grant was not the sort of general, or the sort of man, who would take such a situation lightly. "Time is passing and Richmond is still not ours," Grant wrote to his wife Julia. "I think it cannot be long now before the tug will come which will put us where the end will be in sight."7

General Meade came up with the idea that his Army of the Potomac should make another attempt to isolate Petersburg by cutting the Southside Railroad and the Boydton Plank Road, both of which were vital to keeping the city open and connected with Richmond and the rest of the Confederacy. This seemed like a good idea to Grant, who was always looking for another opportunity to strike at Lee. He had been trying to squeeze the life out of Petersburg since summer, and this looked like a good time to try again. On October 24, he sent a telegram to Meade: "MAKE PREPARATIONS TO MARCH OUT AT AN EARLY HOUR ON THE 27TH TO GAIN POSSESSION OF THE SOUTH SIDE RAILROAD AND HOLD IT."8

As he had been ordered, Meade had three full army corps, cavalry and infantry, on the road shortly before 3:00 a.m. Grant and Meade, along with their staffs, rode out to watch the battle as it unfolded. The entire assemblage, including generals, staff officers, and escorts, totaled more than 100 horses and riders. As this impressive-looking detachment rode past, all glittering gold braid and polished brass buttons in the early-morning drizzle, General Grant was the only officer who was not imposing in his appearance. An onlooking soldier pointed out that Grant was the plainest-looking general in the group.

This conspicuous plainness was not anything deliberate on Grant's part. Grant was wearing his usual mud-spattered plain blue uniform, the same uniform he wore every day. He had no time for things like gold braid or polished brass, which he considered a waste of time. Grant was only interested in one thing: results. He did not give a damn about appearances.

The general was certainly not impressed by what he saw on October 27.

Confederate resistance turned out to be a lot heavier and more spirited than anyone had expected, and it managed to stop the Union advance all along its line of attack. To get a clear picture of the situation, Grant determined to ride to the front of the attacking columns and make a personal reconnaissance of the rebel position. After coming under fire himself—for which he was roundly scolded by one of his aides—Grant reached the conclusion that the enemy was too well entrenched for the attack to succeed. No Federal unit managed to get any closer than six miles from the Southside Railroad, in spite of the fact that over 1,700 men had been lost.

Just before 4:00 p.m., Grant made up his mind to withdraw all troops. All three army corps were ordered to return to the positions they had occupied early that morning. The offensive had failed. Grant decided that there was no point in wasting any more time, or lives, in pursuing a failed objective.

But there was another reason behind Grant's decision to withdraw. The election was now only 11 days off. He understood that "the enemies of the nation of the North were certain to exaggerate every mishap."[9] The Copperheads and the anti-Lincoln newspapers, including the *New York World*, would do their best to turn any Union setback into a major Confederate victory.

Grant had become enough of a politician to realize that he had the power to upset Lincoln's re-election. If he should launch another ill-fated offensive that resulted in the loss of thousands of lives, the Democrats would almost certainly use this against Lincoln. The Ulysses S. Grant of October 1864 was not the Ulysses S. Grant of Spotsylvania and Cold Harbor. "Success at the polls was just now even more important than a victory in the field," Grant's secretary remarked, "and it would have been most unwise to risk greatly on this occasion."[10]

Grant noted that the fighting of October 27 "closed active operations around Richmond for the winter."[11] If he was disappointed by his failure to cut the Southside Railroad, he did not let it show. This setback was only temporary. Even though this latest attempt to isolate Petersburg had not worked out, there would be others.

Lee and his army would still be in the Petersburg trenches come spring. Grant had painted Lee into a corner from which there was no hope of escaping. The Army of Northern Virginia was tethered to Petersburg and Richmond, which meant that it was a stationary target for the Northern forces. By the spring of 1865, "we would . . . have Lee so surrounded that his supplies would be cut off entirely," Grant would later write, "making it impossible for him to support his army."[12]

Grant was fully aware that Lee's army was declining, along with the fortunes of the Confederacy. He also knew that the end of the war would probably come in the spring—Lee's surrender might possibly be a matter of just one more campaign. He had not only the army with which to finish off the Confederates, but also the backing of the enormous wealth and power of the North. An Episcopal bishop visiting Grant at City Point, Virginia, was nearly overwhelmed by the abundance of supplies he saw there: "not merely profusion, but extravagance; wagons, tents, artillery, ad libitum. Soldiers provided with everything."[13] Following his visit to the great supply depot, the bishop was convinced that the South no longer had any chance of winning the war.

But the South was still alive, and Robert E. Lee gave no indication that he was even thinking about surrendering. Grant knew that if the Democrats were to win the November election, there would not be a spring campaign against Lee and his army. Putting Lincoln back in the White House for another four years was as important as defeating Lee in the field. Lincoln was the key—the key to putting down the rebellion, to restoring the union, and to reuniting the country.

SHERIDAN'S RIDE

Ulysses S. Grant was not the only general who did not want to retire to winter quarters in mid-October. Jubal Early was not about to give up the Shenandoah Valley to General Philip Sheridan without at least one more fight before winter set in. Even though he had been soundly beaten twice within a month, Old Jube still had plenty of fight left. And before the first winter rains began, he would let Phil Sheridan know that he was still a force to be reckoned with.

Sheridan's first hint that there would be trouble ahead came on the morning of October 14, when he was handed a message that had been intercepted by the Signal Corps on the previous day: "Lieutenant-General Early: Be Ready to move as soon as my forces join you and we will crush Sheridan. (Signed) Longstreet."[14] Nobody, including Sheridan, knew if the communiqué was genuine or some sort of trick. Just to be on the safe side, Sheridan warned the commander of the 6th Corps to be prepared for an attack.

If nothing else, the intercepted message alerted Sheridan that General Longstreet was in the Shenandoah. General James Longstreet was Lee's most famous, and probably best, corps commander. At Gettysburg, he had been George E. Pickett's commander and had reluctantly given the order for Pickett to begin his storied and ill-fated charge against the Union position on Cemetery Ridge. Ten months later, Longstreet was badly wounded during the fighting in the Wilderness, where he was accidentally shot by one of his own men. As a result, he missed all the fighting of the spring and summer of 1864, and had only just returned to command his famous 1st Corps. Longstreet's right arm remained paralyzed and in a sling, but he would eventually train himself to regain the use of his crippled arm. If both Early and Longstreet were active, Sheridan knew it would be critical to keep his army on alert.

In mid-October, Sherman's army was encamped around Cedar Creek, in an area about 15 miles south of Winchester. On October 14, the same day he was shown Longstreet's "crush Sheridan" message, Sheridan left for Washington to confer with Secretary of War Edwin M. Stanton. Stanton was on his way to City Point and wanted to speak with Sheridan before proceeding to a meeting with General Grant. Sheridan was not happy about leaving his army at that time, with Jubal Early making threatening noises, but he had to obey Stanton's directive—an order from the Secretary of War was an order, even for a major general.

The conference in Washington did not take as long as Sheridan feared it might. He discussed the Shenandoah Valley with both Stanton and General Henry W. Halleck, politely answered all their questions, and, traveling by train and by horseback, returned to his army as quickly as he could get there. Sheridan was back in Winchester on October 18, where he spent the night as the guest of a local tobacco merchant. Before retiring for the night, he sent an officer to Cedar Creek to find out if the enemy was on the move. The commanding general of the 6th Corps, Horatio Wright, sent word that all was quiet. This was exactly what Sheridan wanted to hear. He went to bed with his mind at ease.

His peace of mind did not last very long. At 6:00 a.m. the next morning, an officer on picket duty woke Sheridan to report that artillery fire was coming from the direction of Cedar Creek. The officer said that "it was not a sustained fire, but rather irregular and fitful."[15]

The news worried Sheridan and convinced him that he had better change his plans. He had not intended to rejoin the army until later in the day, after a leisurely breakfast and a quiet morning, but word of the artillery fire changed everything. Before Sheridan went downstairs, the same officer came back to report that the firing was still going on. Sheridan thought it best to ride out to Cedar Creek to find out for himself what the firing was all about.

After a quick breakfast, Sheridan and his staff left Winchester and began heading toward the sound of the guns. Shortly after leaving Winchester, the column picked up a cavalry escort, 300 troopers from the 17th Pennsylvania Cavalry. A few miles after starting out, Sheridan and his escort were unexpectedly met by what Sheridan described as "the appalling spectacle of a panic-stricken army."[16] Blue-uniformed troops were running away from Cedar Creek as fast as they could go: men, horses, wagons, artillerymen without their guns, all heading north toward Winchester in various states of panic and confusion. Sheridan managed to stop and talk to some of them, and everyone he spoke with told him the same thing—Jubal Early had surprised them and had given them one hell of a beating. The army was in full retreat. Sheridan called the situation a disaster.

Now that he understood what had happened, Sheridan had to make up his mind what he should do about it. His first thought was to form a defensive line to stop Early in the vicinity of Winchester, but he quickly thought better of it. Sheridan knew that the men had confidence in him. He would use their confidence to take the battle to the enemy. Instead of going on the defensive, Sheridan decided to rally his men and launch a counterattack against Early. "I took two of my aides-de-camp, Major George A. Forsyth and Captain Joseph O'Keefe, and with twenty men from the escort started for the front."[17]

With everyone else streaming north toward Winchester, Sheridan and his posse were the only riders traveling south and were not hard to spot. As always, the orderly who carried his personal red-and-white swallow-tailed battle standard also accompanied Sheridan. The general wanted to make absolutely certain that everybody knew he was on the field and that he did not intend to retreat. "Turn back, men! Turn back! Face the other way!" Sheridan bellowed at any stragglers he met on the road.[18] "If I had been with you this morning this disaster would not have happened. We must face the other way; we will go back and recover our camp."[19]

He rode through his retreating troops, a small black-haired man riding his large black charger Rienzi, waving the jaunty flat-topped hat he always wore and shouting at everyone within earshot to stand and face the enemy. Sheridan was angry that his army had been routed, but he was also embarrassed that Jubal Early had caught him off guard. He was not about to accept any defeat, whether at the hands of Jubal Early or anyone else.

The men reacted to Sheridan "with enthusiasm and cheers," in Sheridan's own understated words. They certainly did cheer, waving their hats in response to the general and shouting, "Sheridan! Sheridan! Sheridan!"[20] Even more to Sheridan's liking, they picked up their rifled muskets, turned themselves around, and began following the general south toward the enemy. Major William McKinley, future president of the United States, saw Sheridan and his orderly ride past with the general's personal red-and-white battle standard. Major McKinley began passing the word: Sheridan was back. ?, PVT Mckinley

"Oh I tell you things looked bad but Sheridan made his appearance on the ground about noon," a private with a New Jersey regiment wrote to his father. "His presence seemed to put a different heart in the boys and to use his own words, 'Boys by God you must go back to where you came from by four o'clock.'"[21]

The men followed Sheridan's urgings, running forward toward Cedar Creek with enthusiasm that exceeded the terror with which they had run from it that morning. The Confederates had stopped to pillage the Union camp they had overrun. While the rebel lines were thinned out by pilfering troops, Sheridan's men struck.

"We charged the [rebels] and were successful and away we went," wrote the same New Jersey private, "driving them to where they came from and the cavalry came in their rear and captured 9 pieces of artillery, 2,800 prisoners and lots of wagons. After all proved to be a defeat to them and a gain to us."[22]

Cedar Creek certainly did prove to be a defeat, a decisive defeat, for Jubal Early and the Confederates. Sheridan had done what he had set out to do. Early's troops had been pushed south beyond the Union campgrounds they had captured that morning. The Federal troops spent the night back in their own camp. It had been Early's third defeat within the month. His army was finished as a fighting force and a threat to the Union.

After the battle, the New Jersey private mused, "Now then I suppose they will want to send us to Petersburg but as soon as they do, away go the Rebels to Pennsylvania."[23] Actually, Early's army was in no condition to go to Pennsylvania or anyplace else. Lee's army, trapped in its lines at Petersburg, would not be going anywhere, either. There would be no more attacks on Pennsylvania, or Maryland, or Washington, DC, by the Confederates.

If anyone in the North still had any doubts that their side was winning the war, Cedar Creek firmly put an end to them. Newspaper headlines shouted out the word of another Confederate defeat at the hands of a surging Union army. "VICTORY! Another Great Battle in the Valley," announced the *New York Times* on October 21. "Longstreet Whipped by Sheridan. VICTORY WRESTED FROM DEFEAT." Longstreet was mentioned more prominently than Jubal early, probably because he was better known.

In case anyone did not get the message, a War Department dispatch was also printed. "Another great battle was fought yesterday at Cedar Creek, threatening at first a great disaster, but finally resulting in a victory for the Union forces under Gen. SHERIDAN, more splendid than any heretofore achieved."[24]

Sheridan was the man of the hour. "The nation rings with praises of Phil Sheridan," the *Chicago Tribune* stated.[25] Four days after the battle,

Assistant Secretary of War Charles A. Dana woke Sheridan out of a sound sleep to inform him that he had been "appointed a major-general in the United States Army."[26] He had been a major general of volunteers, which is basically the equivalent to being an officer in the National Guard. Now Sheridan was a two-star general in the regular army, a highly prized and much-sought-after promotion. As a general in the regular army, Sheridan would be able to keep his stars and the salary that went with them after the war's end.

When General Grant heard about Cedar Creek, he did not seem all that surprised by the news. Grant had sided with Sheridan against General Meade in May when Sheridan said that he could beat Jeb Stuart if only Meade would leave him alone. Sheridan had killed Jeb Stuart, just as he had promised, and now he had driven Jubal Early out of the Shenandoah Valley. Sheridan had more than justified Grant's faith in him, as Grant knew he would. As a token of his confidence, Grant sent Secretary of War Edwin M. Stanton a telegram stating that Philip Sheridan was one of his ablest generals. He also fired another 100-gun live-ammunition salute into the Confederate lines at Petersburg to celebrate Cedar Creek. Even crusty old General Meade, who was hardly a friend of Sheridan's, sent congratulations to his cavalry commander.

Abraham Lincoln sent a letter of his own to Sheridan, a handwritten note of thanks.

Executive Mansion
Washington, Oct. 22, 1864

Major General Sheridan,

    With great pleasure I tender to you and your brave army the thanks of the Nation, and my own personal admiration and gratitude, for the month's operation in the Shenandoah Valley; and especially for the splendid work of October 19, 1864.

    Your Obt. Servt.

    Abraham Lincoln[27]

Lincoln could afford to be generous with his gratitude. He was well aware that Sheridan's accomplishment was one more nail in the coffin of the Democratic Party. Another Confederate army had been overwhelmed, which meant that the Peace Party's campaign looked even more out of touch with the reality of the war than ever. The Democrats had been keeping very quiet of late, mainly because they had very little to say.

Sheridan's action in the Shenandoah also produced a poetic contribution to Civil War literature, which turned out to be another boost to Lincoln's re-election campaign. This literary tribute came from a completely unexpected source. An actor named James E. Murdock had read an account of Sheridan's ride from Winchester in *Harper's Weekly* and had also seen an illustration of Sheridan on Rienzi in the same magazine. Murdock had become friends with Sheridan before the war. "He was an actor at one of the Cincinnati theatres at the time," Sheridan recalled, "when I had known him."[28] At the battle of Missionary Ridge, at Chattanooga, Tennessee, on November 25, 1863, Murdock lost a son in the fighting and had visited Sheridan when claiming the boy's body.

When he read the story in *Harper's Weekly*, Murdock asked the poet Thomas Buchanan Read to write something "new and appropriate" for him to recite in public. In addition to being an actor, Murdock was also well known for giving poetry recitals. The story of Sheridan's journey from Winchester to Cedar Creek was just the sort of subject he was looking for—dramatic, moving, and patriotic. As soon as Read heard the story of Sheridan and Rienzi, he "jumped up, locked himself in his room, wrote the poem off-handed in an hour, got his wife to make a copy, and had it over to Murdock's before dark."[29]

Murdock recited the poem in Cincinnati that night, November 1. Called simply "Sheridan's Ride," it created an instant sensation. Thomas Buchanan Read had indulged in a certain amount of poetic license in his narrative—he increased the distance of the ride from 12 miles to 20 miles and neglected to mention the fact that Sheridan made several stops along the way from Winchester. Read instead made the trip one long, nerve-tingling gallop. But the public did not care about these details. They loved the poem, loved the way Read's lines bounced along, and loved the story itself.

Even though "Sheridan's Ride" is not exactly great poetry, it is hard to resist. Metrically, it resembles Alfred, Lord Tennyson's "Charge of the Light Brigade," and it was just what the public in the North was looking for. Read starts out by describing how the news of Early's attack came

> Up from the South at break of day,
> Bringing to Winchester fresh dismay . . .
> Telling the battle was on once more,
> And Sheridan twenty miles away.

But Sheridan's horse, Rienzi, "A steed as black as the steeds of night," carries Sheridan south toward the battle at breakneck speed,

> As if he knew the terrible need,
> He stretched away with his utmost speed.
> Hills rose and fell, but his heart was gay,
> With Sheridan fifteen miles away.

Sheridan and Rienzi keep up their relentless pace toward Cedar Creek, with the last lines of each stanza giving an update on their progress:

> Every nerve of the charger was strained to full play,
> With Sheridan only ten miles away.

> He is snuffing the smoke of the roaring fray,
> With Sheridan only five miles away.

Finally, Sheridan reaches Cedar Creek.

> The first that the general saw were the groups
> Of stragglers, and then the retreating troops.

He rallies the men "'mid a storm of huzzahs," and turns the retreat into a decisive Union victory. Sheridan turns the tide of the battle, but Rienzi is just as much of a hero.

He seemed to the whole great army to say:
"I have brought you Sheridan all the way
From Winchester down to save the day."

Read's last stanza celebrates both the general and his charger.

Hurrah! Hurrah for Sheridan!
Hurrah! Hurrah for horse and man!
And when their statues are placed on high
Under the dome of a Union sky,
The American soldier's Temple of Fame,
There, with the glorious general's name,
Be it said in letters both bold and bright:
"Here is the steed that saved the day
By carrying Sheridan into the fight,
From Winchester—twenty miles away!"[30]

"Sheridan's Ride" was much loved throughout the North, just as "Over There" and "Praise the Lord and Pass the Ammunition" would catch the public's imagination in two subsequent wars. The poem also turned out to be another ringing endorsement for Abraham Lincoln and his re-election, since it gave still another encouraging view of the war and of the men who were running it. The summer before, when the war seemed all but lost, the public had been ready to disown Lincoln. But now that the Union seemed to be well on its way to winning the war and destroying the rebellion, all that had changed. The same voters who were ready to run Abe Lincoln out of Washington on a rail now heartily approved of Lincoln and the way the war was being fought.

Thomas Buchanan Read's narrative poem is probably one of the best and most effective examples of campaign literature, or at least campaign verse, in the history of American politics. With the election only one week away, the poem gave Lincoln's already-surging approval rating an additional boost. It helped to make up the minds of thousands of voters who had been undecided to that point as to whether to vote for Lincoln or for McClellan.

A success by one of Lincoln's commanders, especially a well-publicized success, served as a testimonial for the commander in chief. "Hurrah! Hurrah for Sher-i-dan, Hurrah! Hurrah for horse and man!" was also catchy enough to capture the imagination of Northern voters. It became the "I Like Ike!" of the 1864 presidential election campaign.[31]

Hardheaded Phil Sheridan would not let his head be turned by anything as trivial as a poem, even if he was the hero of it. He thought the main reason behind its popularity was his horse. Sheridan had been given the gelding in August 1862 and had named the horse "Rienzi" after the town in Mississippi where he had just won a small skirmish. After their famous ride, Sheridan renamed the horse "Winchester." Sheridan wryly admitted that the horse had probably become as famous as Sheridan himself.

Lincoln was finally becoming optimistic about his chances on Tuesday, November 8. Events of the past two months, in Georgia and in the Shenandoah Valley, had turned his innate pessimism completely on its head. It began to look as though the fickle voters in the North were going to ask him to stay on for another four years after all.

FOR THIS APPROVAL OF THE PEOPLE

Election Day, November 8, 1864, turned out to be grey and rainy, making Washington, DC, seem even gloomier than usual. Elisha Hunt Rhodes, of the 2nd Rhode Island Volunteers, complained that it had been raining for the past three days. Captain Rhodes was stationed near Middleton, Virginia, sixty-odd miles to the west of Washington as the crow flies, but he had the same thing on his mind as everyone in the capital—casting his ballot in the election that day. "Today we have held an election for President," he noted in his diary, "under the law that allows soldiers to vote."[32]

According to conventional wisdom, rain on Election Day is supposed to bode well for Republicans, since bad weather keeps the Democrats at home. (Although there are Democrats who claim that the opposite is true.) But apparently Abe Lincoln never heard this old saw. His outburst of optimism of only a few days earlier had completely disappeared. It was replaced by an outlook as dismal as the weather itself. Even though he was still fairly certain that he would win the election, he was not 100 percent certain. Several key states, including New York and Pennsylvania, still remained too close to call. A visitor to the White House reported that Lincoln was anxious and ill at ease.

To add to the city's gloom, it seemed that everybody in Washington had gone back to their home states to vote. The White House itself was also very nearly deserted and strangely quiet, which did not help to calm Lincoln's nerves. A reporter found the president all alone, as though everybody was avoiding him. First election returns would not be coming in until much later in the day. Until that time, there was nothing for Lincoln to do except sit and listen to his anxieties.

His son Tad broke the monotony when he stormed into Lincoln's office and pointed out the window to a unit from a Pennsylvania regiment, which was visible on the south lawn. The men were voting, under the supervision of a team of commissioners from their home state. Tad's pet turkey, Jack, decided to go out on the lawn and join the soldiers, much to their hilarity. Lincoln wanted to know if Jack intended to vote. Tad said no, the turkey was not old enough. Lincoln thought the remark was funny. It was probably the only laugh he had all day long.

Voter turnout was heavy, in spite of the rain—Republican rain—but there was no news as to which way the voters were inclining. The only excitement during the early part of the day came from New York, and involved the Democratic Party's national chairman August Belmont. Belmont's vote had been challenged on the grounds that he had bet on the outcome of the election. The challenge was upheld and Belmont lost his vote. He was outraged by this unexpected turn of events—August Belmont was not accustomed to being turned away, not by anyone—and left the polling place shouting and protesting, but there was nothing he could do about it.

At about seven o'clock that evening, Lincoln and his secretary, John Hay, finally left the White House for the War Department telegraph office. The weather was just as bad as it had been all day long—it was still pouring rain—but anything was better than staying cooped up in the White House waiting for something to happen. The two men made their way through the downpour to the side door of the War Office, which was guarded by a rain-soaked sentinel in a rubber raincoat.

The telegraph office was upstairs. As soon as Lincoln climbed the stairs and stepped into the room, he was handed a telegram from John W. Forney, a pro-Republican newspaper editor from Pennsylvania. Forney's dispatch claimed that Lincoln and Andrew Johnson had a 10,000-vote majority in Philadelphia. This was very good news, except that the practical and sober-sided Lincoln did not believe it. "Forney is a little excitable," was Lincoln's reaction to the telegram.[33] But at least it was encouraging.

The results kept coming in—from Philadelphia, from Boston, from Baltimore—and all of them gave Lincoln the lead. The rain and wind were causing problems with the telegraph wires, slowing the receipt of election returns, especially from the more distant western states. This played hell with Lincoln's already-frayed nerves. He did his best to relieve the stress, his own and everyone else's, by telling stories and anecdotes to the assemblage in the War Office.

Among those present were Secretary of War Edwin M. Stanton and Assistant Secretary of War Charles Dana. At one point, Lincoln called Dana over to join him and asked if he had ever read any of the writings of Petroleum V. Nasby. Dana replied that he had read some of Nasby's work and thought it was quite funny. That was all the encouragement Lincoln needed. He had a copy of one of Nasby's pamphlets in his coat pocket, which he pulled out and began reading to Dana.

Petroleum Vesuvius Nasby—a pseudonym created by humorist David R. Locke—was one of Lincoln's favorite writers. His writings always seemed to be able to make the president laugh—no easy chore, especially on this particular day. The booklet Lincoln had in his pocket was probably *The Nasby Letters*, in which Petroleum V. Nasby, a semiliterate preacher and Copperhead, gives his pro-Confederate views in a crude and usually misspelled style. Dana did not seem to mind hearing Nasby's rough and sometimes vulgar wit, but Edwin Stanton was visibly irritated by what he considered Lincoln's inappropriate conduct. Stanton did not have a very high opinion of Lincoln and also did not have much of a sense of humor. As far as he was concerned, Lincoln should have known better than to read stupid and tasteless jokes at such a time.

Lincoln was not all that concerned with Stanton's opinion of him and went on reading Petroleum V. Nasby's letters throughout the night, stopping from time to time to look at election telegrams. He would read Nasby for a while then allow himself to be interrupted by the latest news from the election front, and then he would go back to his joke book. The jokes helped to steady Lincoln's nerves.

As the results continued to come in, Lincoln could see that the election was going his way. Returns showed the Lincoln/Johnson ticket leading in Massachusetts and all of New England, and in Indiana, Ohio, Michigan, Maryland, and Wisconsin. First reports from New York indicated a 10,000-vote lead, but Horace Greeley sent a telegram giving the lead as 4,000 votes—a number that sounded much more believable to Lincoln. Problems with the telegraph wires were still delaying reports from most of the western states, but word from Chicago reported a 20,000-vote lead throughout Illinois.

By midnight, there was no doubt that Lincoln had been re-elected. Both Pennsylvania and New York were leaning toward Lincoln; he would carry both states, although not by overwhelming margins. New England had voted solidly for Lincoln, along with the West and the Midwest. New Jersey, George B. McClellan's home state, had gone to the Democrats, along with Delaware and Kentucky. Results would continue to trickle in during the next two days, but by the early hours of Wednesday, November 9, 1864, the outcome of the election was certain.

Everybody in the telegraph office congratulated Lincoln on his re-election. Noah Brooks thought that the president reacted very calmly, both to the election news and to the good wishes, "showing not the least elation or excitement." But Lincoln did admit that "he was glad to be relieved of all suspense" and "grateful that the verdict of the people was likely to be so full, clear, and unmistakable that there could be no dispute."[34] After a late supper of fried oysters, which the president self-consciously served his guests, Lincoln finally departed the War Office.

The weather had cleared by that time—about two o'clock in the morning—and the rain had stopped. Outside the War Office, Lincoln found a small crowd and a brass band waiting for him and calling for him to make a speech. Lincoln did his best to oblige, even at that time of day.

"I earnestly believe that the consequences of this day's work . . . will be to the lasting advantage, if not the very salvation, of this country," Lincoln told the gathering. "I am thankful to God for this approval of the people," he continued, "but, while deeply grateful for this mark of their confidence in me . . . my gratitude is free from any taint of personal triumph." In summing up, he gave thanks to the Almighty "for the evidence of the people's resolution to stand by free government and the rights of humanity."[35]

And that was that. The campaign, which had begun six months before, when General Ulysses S. Grant and General William Tecumseh Sherman had begun their long and eventful journeys on the same hopeful May morning, had finally ended. Sometimes it had looked as though it would never end, especially during that relentless summer, when Lincoln had himself lost all faith in his re-election. But the summer was over, and Atlanta had been captured, and Phil Sheridan had chased Jubal Early right out of the Shenandoah Valley, and Grant had trapped Robert E. Lee and his Army of Northern Virginia in the trenches at Petersburg. Every time one of his generals had won a battle, voters throughout the North had gained confidence in Lincoln and in his war effort. Now they had decided that Lincoln should stay on as president and commander in chief and that the war should continue. Lincoln said good night to the gathering outside the War Office and walked home through the rain-soaked streets. He was relieved that it was all over at long last.

Abraham Lincoln had every reason to be both relieved and thankful. The war had not destroyed his political career, after all. He had stood by his convictions and carried on fighting the Confederacy, even when it looked as though both the war and the White House were as good as lost, and he had still been re-elected. Maybe if Lyndon B. Johnson had had a Sherman or a Sheridan or a Grant in Vietnam, he would not have committed political suicide in Southeast Asia.

Even though Lincoln had won the popular vote, he did not win by anything resembling a crushing majority. The Lincoln/Johnson ticket received a total of 2,203,831 votes. George B. McClellan's vote count totaled 1,797,019. This gave Lincoln and his Union Party a majority of just over 406,000 votes, which was enough to give Lincoln the White House for another four years but was not exactly a landslide. As far as percentages are concerned, Lincoln received 55.09 percent of the vote, while McClellan's share of the ballots came to 44.91 percent.[36]

Lincoln did not receive very much support from America's growing immigrant population, especially from recent immigrants who lived in cities along the eastern seaboard. The Irish voted heavily against Lincoln. Irish immigrants were competing against blacks for the most menial jobs in New York, Boston, and other cities, and had no intention of voting for any candidate who advocated freeing the slaves. Adding freed blacks to the work force would mean more job competition and even fewer opportunities for any sort of employment. The fact that McClellan came from Irish ancestry had undoubtedly helped turn the Irish away from the Republicans as well.

The majority of voters who supported Lincoln were, in the words of a biographer, "native-born farmers in the countryside, better off skilled workers and professional men in the city, and voters of New England descent everywhere."[37] New England voters tended to be solidly anti-slavery. The Democrats' position of supporting Confederate independence and allowing the seceded states to keep their slaves completely alienated the no-nonsense folk from that part of the country, who thought of slavery as nothing less than an unmixed evil.

One of Lincoln's main worries had been how the soldiers would vote. The way things turned out, he need not have worried at all. Veterans throughout the Union army cast their ballots against McClellan in over-whelming majorities, voting for the war to go on. The army might have worshipped George B. McClellan, but not many soldiers voted for him.

Even more than their civilian counterparts, these men in uniform knew exactly what they had been voting for. The soldiers were fully aware that sending Abraham Lincoln back to the White House for another term meant that the war would go on to the bitter end. They had known that voting for Lincoln would mean more mud marches, more sleeping outdoors in the rain, more worm-infested rations, and more dying. A vote for George B. McClellan, for Little Mac, would have meant an end to all of that.

But voting for McClellan would also have meant giving up and declaring that the war had been a failure. And it would have meant telling the world that all the sacrifices and hardships they had endured for the past three and a half years had been for nothing. The men were not about to do this. They did not look forward to more fighting—they had already seen more than enough—but they could not bring themselves to quit, either, or to agree with the Democrats that the war was a failure. So the army cast its votes for Lincoln, for more fighting and dying, and for restoring the Union. Soldiers refused to lay down their arms to Robert E. Lee or any other Confederate general, and would not vote for any political party that believed in surrender and defeat.

Even the soldiers of the Army of the Potomac, who still considered themselves to be McClellan's boys, gave their former commander a drubbing. Seventy percent of McClellan's former command voted for Lincoln. Pennsylvania had 51 regiments in the field, but only six of them voted for McClellan. Forty-five of Pennsylvania's regiments backed Abraham Lincoln. Down in Georgia, Sherman's army had even less enthusiasm for McClellan and the Democrats—only 20 percent of Sherman's men voted Democratic. A total of 150,635 votes were cast by troops in the field. Of these, 116,887 voted for Lincoln while 33,748 cast their ballots for McClellan.[38]

Albert Harrison, of the 14th New Jersey Infantry, spoke for the majority of his fellow soldiers when he wrote, "I cannot chew that Chicago Platform," meaning Clement Vallandigham's peace platform, "fine enough to swallow it." Although young Private Harrison declared himself to be a Democrat, he saw no reason why he should vote for a Democratic candidate whom he did not trust and who insisted that Lee and his Army of Northern Virginia could not be defeated. Even though George B. McClellan never insisted any such thing, the fact that he belonged to the same party as Clement Vallandigham and his fellow Copperheads made him a Copperhead in the eyes of army veterans. If Vallandigham thought the South would win the war, then McClellan must think so too. "Take the majority of soldiers in the field, they would sooner vote for Jeff Davis himself," Harrison said. "Uncle Abe, the soldier's friend, retains the chair for the next four years, if the Good Lord spares his life." Reporter Henry Wing told Lincoln that the soldiers would vote as they shoot; they were not about to abandon the Union cause after three and a half years of fighting for it.[39]

When the election results were announced, the army was delighted. Elisha Hunt Rhodes wrote in his diary, "The band at Brigade Headquarters is playing 'The Star-spangled Banner' in honor of the re-election of President Lincoln."[40] General Grant telegraphed Lincoln to say that his defeat of George McClellan counted more than a great battle won. But any celebrating was kept short and restrained. The election was over and Uncle Abe had been re-elected. Now it was time to get on with the war.

Lincoln may not have won a resounding victory in the popular vote, except with the soldiers, but he made up for it by swamping McClellan in the electoral college. The Lincoln/Johnson ticket received 212 electoral votes while the three states that McClellan carried netted him only 21 votes. The results had not been unanimous for Lincoln, but they were a one-sided humiliation for the Democrats.

But the outcome might have been a humiliation for the Republicans. It was certainly too close for comfort, in spite of the electoral college results. The states that had the greatest number of electoral votes, New York, Pennsylvania, and Ohio, had gone to Lincoln by a combined total of only 86,407 votes. These three states had 80 electoral votes between them. Had they been carried by McClellan, along with two or possibly three other states, the Democrats would have had enough electoral votes to win the election. If George B. McClellan had decided to leave his ivory tower in New Jersey to do some energetic stump speaking throughout the North, the outcome of the balloting on November 8—and the outcome of the war—might have been very different.

On the morning of November 9, the public throughout the North—and the South—received official word of the election results in the morning newspapers. The headlines told the story. "GLORIOUS RESULTS YESTERDAY," shouted the *New York Times*. "Election of Lincoln and Johnson. Terrible defeat of McClellan. The Union Triumphant."[41] The *New York Herald* was just as emphatic, although a good deal less enthusiastic. "The Result of the Great National Contest," the headline stated matter-of-factly, "Abraham Lincoln Reelected President of the United States and Andrew Johnson of Tennessee Elected Vice President of the United States."[42]

Of course, not everybody was glad that Abraham Lincoln would be president for another four years. As might be expected, the *New York World* did not even try to hide its unhappiness. "We will not attempt to conceal the profound chagrin and sorrow with which we contemplate the result," it pouted. The Democratic *Springfield State Register* came out against Lincoln, even though Springfield, Illinois, was Lincoln's hometown. The *Register* called the re-election "the heaviest calamity that ever befell this nation . . . the farewell to civil liberty, to a republican form of government, and to the unity of these states."[43]

This was not a very encouraging editorial, especially coming from the town that Abraham Lincoln had left less than four years before. It was a prediction for continued suppression of habeas corpus and other civil liberties, which Lincoln had invoked, and showed a total lack of confidence in Lincoln's ability to reunite the country. Maybe no one can ever be a hero in his own hometown, not even Abe Lincoln.

In Britain, word of the election results was met with resignation by the anti-Lincoln faction, including the editorial staff at the *Army and Navy Gazette*. "Abraham Lincoln I reigns in succession to Abraham Lincoln II, the first Republican monarch of the Federal states, and as far as we are concerned we are very glad of it because the manner of the man is taken and known."[44] The staff at the *Gazette*, along with their readers, had hoped that Lincoln would lose. Now they were prepared to make the best of a bad situation.

Lincoln's re-election came as a deep disappointment throughout the South. The great and abiding hope of Southerners was that the "McClellanites," as the Democrats were sometimes called, would displace Lincoln and his war party and negotiate an armistice with Richmond. That hope was now gone beyond recall. After November 8, it was painfully obvious to everybody, even the most optimistic, that there would be no armistice and no peace, at least not on the terms proposed by the Confederacy.

Confederate president Jefferson Davis considered the re-election of Abraham Lincoln nothing less than an absolute disaster—like General Grant, he thought that it counted for more than a major Union victory in the field. Along with everyone else in the South, Davis had hoped that the Democrats would win, which would likely have led to a negotiated peace and, soon afterward, independence for the Confederacy. But Lincoln had made it clear that he would only negotiate if peace terms included cessation of all fighting, the restoration of the union, and the abolition of slavery— "the restoration of peace, the integrity of the whole union, and the abandonment of slavery," is how Lincoln phrased it.[45]

Davis considered this proposal not only unacceptable but also an insult. "If we would break up our government, dissolve the Confederacy, disband our armies, emancipate our slaves," Davis wrote sarcastically, "take an oath of allegiance to it and disloyalty to our own states, the government of the United States proposed to pardon us and not to deprive us of anything more than the property already robbed from us, and such slaves as still remained."[46] As far as Jefferson Davis was concerned, Lincoln had gone out of his way to be as offensive as possible so that his proposal would certainly be rejected. And reject Lincoln's proposal is exactly what President Davis did; he refused even to negotiate with Lincoln. In Richmond, Davis gave a speech that urged all Southerners to unite and not to give up hope, predicting that it would be the North that would be asking for a negotiated peace by midsummer. His message was plain and sobering: the war would end only when one side or the other had been hammered into surrendering.

"The Yankee nation has committed itself to the game of all or nothing," said the *Richmond Examiner*, "and so must we."[47] Southern newspapers did their best to make light of Lincoln's re-election. Editors called Lincoln a gorilla and joked that his election would be a great day for all the abolitionist clubs in Washington. But in spite of themselves, every newspaper from Virginia to Mississippi ran the same message, only in different words and headlines: the war would go on. At this stage, more and more people wondered how much longer it *could* go on.

A historian from Michigan said basically the same thing about Lincoln's re-election as the *Richmond Examiner* had, only, being a Northerner, he had done so from a completely different point of view. "On November 8," he said with relish, "the people of the North re-elected Abraham Lincoln and endorsed a war to the finish."[48]

Chapter Eight

THE NEXT FOUR YEARS

LET 'EM UP EASY

Now that the election was over, Abraham Lincoln could relax, at least for a little while. Two days after he was re-elected, he was serenaded at the White House by a small crowd of supporters. Lincoln enjoyed the little entertainment; he was calm enough that he was able to take pleasure in such things again. Afterward, he told the gathering his thoughts about the election and about the fact that it had taken place at all.

The election "demonstrated that a people's government can sustain an election in the midst of a great civil war," Lincoln told the gathering. "We cannot have free government without elections," he went on, "and if the rebellion could force us to forego or postpone a national election, it might fairly claim to have already conquered and ruined us."[1] Now he was safely back in the White House for another four years and could stop worrying.

Lincoln could also stop worrying about George B. McClellan. After the election, McClellan and his family left the United States for an extended trip to Europe. He returned in 1868, but did not become involved in politics again until 1877, when he was elected governor of New Jersey. After serving one term, from 1878 to 1882, McClellan never held another political office. With the election and McClellan out of the way, and with the Democrats in full disarray after their defeat, Lincoln was now able to concentrate on winning the war.

Lincoln was well aware that there were other vital concerns that had to be dealt with besides the fighting in Virginia and Georgia. The issue of slavery had to be settled, once and for all. Also, there would be the problem of making peace with the South, a peace of reconciliation without bitterness and without reprisals. But before either of these things could even be considered, the Confederate armies in the field would either have to be destroyed or reduced to the point where they had no option but surrender. After November 8, 1864, Lincoln and his generals had only one goal: continue fighting without letup until the war was over.

The Army of the Potomac was spending a severe winter in Petersburg. The winter of 1864–1865 was the coldest in years, which made life in the trenches even more uncomfortable than usual. To keep everyone's mind off their miseries, and to keep the army sharp, daily drills were held throughout the dreary months—drilling and dress parades and cavalry maneuvers and artillery practice and more dress parades and more drills. Emphasis was on preparing for the spring campaign, which everyone knew would be upon them before they knew it.

To relieve the monotony, there was also a genuine winter offensive. In January 1865, after a naval bombardment that lasted three days, two infantry divisions, 6,500 men, captured Fort Fisher, North Carolina. Fort Fisher stood guard over the port city of Wilmington, which was the last seaport still open to the Confederacy. When the fort's garrison surrendered to Federal troops, the South had become all but completely isolated from the outside world. The Confederacy could no longer export cotton or receive desperately needed food, clothing, weapons, or medical supplies from Europe. One more nail had been driven into the coffin of Jefferson Davis's government and the Confederate war machine.

The capture of Fort Fisher had an additional and totally unexpected bonus for General Grant: it finally gave him the excuse to rid himself of Major General Benjamin F. Butler. Ben Butler, having been given the job of capturing the fort in December, immediately rose to his full level of incompetence. As a sort of prelude, he had planned to soften up the fort's defenses by detonating a ship filled with explosives close to its outer walls. This was actually not a bad idea—Grant himself had given his approval, and the navy had also been intrigued by the thought—except that it did not work. The ship blew up dramatically enough, but it did no damage—the rebels manning the garrison thought that some Yankee ship had burst a boiler out in the bay. Next, Butler landed troops to begin their assault on the fort. But apparently things did not go quickly enough or efficiently enough to suit General Butler, so he ordered all troops back on the transports and sailed away. Butler reported that it would be impossible to take the fort because it was just too difficult an objective.

Ben Butler probably would have gotten away with this little stunt had it taken place a few months earlier. Butler was more politician than general—much more—and had a great deal of influence within the Republican Party. He certainly had enough influence to give aid and assistance to Lincoln's enemies, including Thaddeus Stevens or anyone else who might have benefited by standing in the way of Lincoln's re-election. Grant had placated Ben Butler, along with everybody else in the army, to keep him from working against the president's re-election campaign.

But with the election over, there was no longer any need to handle Ben Butler with tender loving care. As soon as Grant found out what happened at Fort Fisher, he lost no time in removing Butler. He wrote to Secretary of War Edwin M. Stanton on January 4, 1865, requesting the removal of Major General Benjamin F. Butler from his command for the good of the service. When he learned that Stanton was not in Washington, Grant immediately telegraphed President Lincoln.

Both Lincoln and the War Department acted as quickly as humanly possible—the president always did his very best to comply with any request made by General Grant. On January 8, General Butler was officially notified of his removal, and before long he was on his way home to Massachusetts and out of the army. Grant was absolutely delighted. As he wrote to an old friend, "The failure at Fort Fisher was not without important and valuable results."[2]

The Fort Fisher expedition was the last fighting done by the Army of the Potomac during the winter of 1864–1865. The weather continued to be freezing cold. But General Grant already had his plans for a spring offensive in mind, and what he was planning was nothing less than the destruction of the Army of Northern Virginia. "Lee's present 55,000 is not at all the old material. It is all he can rake and scrounge—clerks, Government employees, departmental men and all," were his observations regarding his opponents in the Petersburg trenches. "Of his old fighting stock"—that is, the army that Grant and Meade had faced at Spotsylvania and Cold Harbor—"he has about 22,000 men left."

Grant had definite ideas of what he intended to do about this core of 22,000 veterans. "These men *we must kill* before the country can have peace. They are old soldiers and fierce slave-holders. These men have got to be used up."[3] Lincoln probably would have shuddered at this cold-eyed logic, even coming from Grant, although he also would have agreed with it.

"Lee can keep his army just where it is, but he can't attack, nor can he fight a battle," Grant went on. "Victory or defeat would be alike ruinous."[4] Lee's once-proud Army of Northern Virginia had been reduced to a band of half-starved scarecrows waiting outside Petersburg for a miracle to save them from Grant's juggernaut. As soon as the winter rain and snow ended and the knee-deep mud dried up beneath the spring sun, the Federals would be at them again. By this time, everybody knew what that would mean.

The war had been a bitter fact of life for nearly four years. But by the early months of 1865 anyone who had an eye for realism could see that it was finally beginning to wind down. Both north and south, but especially north of the Mason-Dixon Line, people began to think and talk of other things. In Washington, Congress began looking beyond the war; members debated such items as the completion of the Pacific railway, the availability of land for settlers and railroads, and the resettlement of Indian tribes. The end of the war finally seemed to be within reach. The phrase "after the war" began to enter conversations.

But the war was not over yet. Phil Sheridan and his army, about 9,400 officers and men, were spending their winter in the Shenandoah Valley. What was left of Jubal Early's army, about 2,000 men, was also haunting the valley, hanging on grimly and hoping for the best. At the end of February, Sheridan received word that Early was at Waynesboro, about 75 miles south of the Cedar Creek battlefield.

Sheridan could have left Early right where he was and ignored his small force, but Grant had ordered Sheridan to follow the enemy "to the death," and that included following him to Waynesboro. His men slogged their way through two days of rain and arrived at Waynesboro on March 2, 1865, soaking wet and covered with mud. Sheridan sent a cavalry division under the command of a young general named George Armstrong Custer to put an end to Early's presence in the valley.

Custer dismounted three of his cavalry regiments and sent them against Early's flanks, just as though they were infantry units. The rest of his cavalry mounted up and galloped straight for the center of the Confederate line, four columns advancing in-line abreast as buglers sounded the charge. All four columns broke through the line and rode straight into the town of Waynesboro to the shock and dismay of the local citizens. The dismounted troopers did not accomplish anything as dramatic as this, but they did manage to break both the right and left flanks of Early's line. The outnumbered Confederates broke and ran, at least those who were able. Old Jube managed to hide out in the house of a nearby resident along with a few of his men. Most of Early's soldiers, about 1,600 of them, were taken prisoner and sent south to Petersburg along with 11 pieces of artillery, about 200 wagons, and 17 battle flags.

Phil Sheridan could be well satisfied with what he had accomplished that cold March day. When he rode into the Petersburg lines with his trophies, he could report that he had finally been able to close the Shenandoah Valley to the enemy, something that Union generals had been trying to do since 1862. Grant sent his congratulations and asked Sheridan to join him at his headquarters at City Point. Sheridan would stay in Virginia and would be with Grant when he met with Robert E. Lee at Appomattox Court House a few weeks later.

In Georgia, William Tecumseh Sherman had no intention of going into winter quarters. He had another idea—he would make Georgia howl.

His idea was to march through Georgia, from Atlanta to the Atlantic coast. But before he could begin his march, he first had to persuade both General Grant and Abraham Lincoln that his idea was feasible. Lincoln was skeptical about Sherman's plan at first. But after thinking about it, he decided not to interfere—"nothing risked, nothing gained," he reflected.[5]

General Grant took a while longer to reach his decision. He was mainly concerned with John Bell Hood and his army of about 41,000 men, which was still in northwestern Georgia and was still dangerous. "If you can see a chance of destroying Hood's army," he telegraphed Sherman early in November, "attend to that first, and make your other move secondary."[6]

Though Sherman had made an effort to catch Hood and his army, Hood had always managed to elude him. In October, he decided to send generals George H. Thomas and John M. Schofield to chase down Hood while he took 62,000 men across Georgia in a "march to the sea." After he understood what Sherman intended to accomplish, Grant finally approved Sherman's planned march. "Great and good fortune attend you," he telegraphed Sherman. "I believe you will be entirely successful, and, at worst, can only make a march less fruitful of results than hoped for."[7]

As for John Bell Hood, he did exactly what Sherman wanted him to do—as Sherman himself said, Hood "played into our . . . hands perfectly."[8] He moved his army to the north, toward Tennessee, in an attempt to divert Sherman's army away from Atlanta. But Sherman had no intention of being sidetracked from his intended march to the Atlantic coast, by Hood or by anybody else, and was delighted to see Hood leave. "Damn him, if he will go to the Ohio River I will give him rations." Old Woodenhead had got it wrong again.[9]

The march from Atlanta began on November 15. Before he left the city, Sherman ordered the destruction of all factories, railroad installations, and anything else that might be of use to the Confederacy and its war effort. His soldiers went about their business with more enthusiasm than Sherman expected. Their goal seemed to be the destruction of everything in Atlanta. Crews pulled down factory walls and then proceeded to set fire to what they found inside. They also destroyed theaters, hotels, a laboratory, and private residences. Sherman had assured Grant, "I can make this march, and make Georgia howl."[10] Even before leaving Atlanta, Sherman was already making good on his promise.

Sherman himself rode out of Atlanta at about 7:00 a.m. on November 16, moving along Decatur Road. When he reached the former rebel lines just outside the city, Sherman and his party paused at the battlefields of the past summer. They visited the site of the battle of July 22, where Sherman's friend James McPherson had been killed. He wished that young McPherson could have lived to see the capture of Atlanta, and he wished that McPherson could have joined him now as he began his march to the sea.

The day was clear and sunny. Off in the distance, the gun barrels of a column of infantry gleamed in the sun and the white-topped supply wagons stretched away into the distance. Just in front of Sherman, the 14th Corps marched along at a good pace, heads held high, happy to be on their way. As Sheridan rode past, a group of soldiers called out, "Uncle Billy, I guess Grant is waiting for us at Richmond!" That was how the army felt—Atlanta today, Richmond tomorrow.[11]

A band began to play the tune "John Brown's Body," and the men began singing to it. But the words they sang were "Glory, glory, hallelujah!" Sherman remarked that he had never heard it sung with more spirit, or in better harmony.

> Mine eyes have seen the glory of the coming of the Lord;
> He is trampling out the vintage where the grapes of wrath are stored;
> He hath loosed the fateful lightning of His terrible swift sword;
> His truth is marching on.[12]

"Then we turned our horses' heads to the east," Sherman remembered. "Atlanta was soon left behind the screen of trees, and became a thing of the past."[13]

Sherman and his men marched between 10 and 15 miles every day, 62,000 men moving in two columns toward the port city of Savannah, 225 miles away from Atlanta. Along the way, they continued their war against the rail lines of Georgia, burning the wooden ties and making "Sherman's neckties" out of the iron rails, destroying about 300 miles of track. The troops also looted every house and farm and mansion they came across. One writer estimated that Sherman's foragers—called "bummers," probably from the German word *Bummler*, meaning waster or vagrant—"confiscated almost seven thousand horses and mules, more than thirteen thousand head of cattle, a half million pounds of grain, and nearly eleven million pounds of fodder."[14]

To residents of the South, William Tecumseh Sherman was a latter-day

Attila the Hun, burning, pillaging, and looting everything in his path. But his soldiers were enjoying themselves hugely. One of them remarked that the army "had come to look on the trip as a grand picnic, and were not getting tired but more anxious to prolong it if anything." And army rations could not even come close to comparing with the food being foraged along the march. One soldier noted, "We live on sweet potatoes, turnips, flour, meal, beef, pork, mutton, chickens, and anything else found on the plantations."[15]

Sherman intended his march to be a psychological blow to the South as much as a campaign against its military resources. He wanted to convince all Southerners that continuing with the rebellion would not only result in the destruction of the Confederacy but would also bring about their own personal ruin. But even Sherman could relent once in a while.

At one point during the march, Sherman passed the front gate of a plantation called Shelman Heights, near Cartersville. An elderly black retainer met Sherman at the gate and expressed his relief that "Miss Cecelia" was not at home to witness the arrival of the dreaded Yankees at her very doorstep.[16]

Sherman was taken by surprise when he heard the name. "Not Miss Cecelia Stovall?" The old slave assured Sherman that it was the same person, only now she was Mrs. Shelman, the wife of Captain Charles T. Shelman of the Confederate army.

Miss Cecelia Stovall had been the love of Sherman's young life when he had been a West Point cadet back in 1836. The sister of Sherman's room-mate, Marcellus Stovall, she had attended many academy dances with Cadet Sherman. Sherman knew that she was from Georgia, and he also knew that she had married someone else, but he never expected to come across the plantation where she lived.

When he had courted Cecelia in his West Point days, 28 years before, Cecelia had remarked that his eyes were so cold and cruel that she pitied anyone who ever became his foe. Sherman had gallantly replied to Cecelia, "Even though you were my enemy, my dear, I would ever love and protect you." Now, in the middle of a march that would vilify his very name to gen-erations of Southerners, Sherman intended to make good his promise.

He ordered his men to return any items that had been taken from

Shelman Heights and he placed a guard around the plantation house to prevent any further looting. Before moving on, Sherman left a note for his former love, which remains in the family's possession.

"You once said that I would crush an enemy and you pitied my foe. Do you recall my reply?" Sherman asked. He wanted her to know that *he* recalled his reply, all those years later. "Although many years have passed, my answer is the same. I would ever shield and protect you. That I have done. Forgive all else. I am only a soldier." Even the implacable General Sherman, the scourge of Georgia, had a sentimental side.[17]

The retainer at Shelman Heights knew more about Sherman and his army than anybody in the North, including Abraham Lincoln—at least he knew where Sherman was. After leaving Atlanta, Sherman cut off all communication with the outside world. Nobody knew where he was or which way he was going. Some of the South's newspapers gave sketchy reports of Sherman's movements, but these tended to be highly biased and inaccurate. Some papers actually said that the army was fleeing for its life, heading for the Atlantic coast so that the US Navy would rescue it from pursuing Confederate forces.

Some Southerners believed this line of propaganda. Senator Benjamin H. Hill of Georgia encouraged the people of Georgia to rise up against the Yankee invader. "Every citizen with his gun, and every Negro with his spade and axe, can do the work of a soldier," the senator wrote, apparently believing that Sherman's army was on the verge of collapse. "You can destroy the enemy by retarding its march."[18] But General Sherman did not pay much attention to these "arise and take up arms" appeals. He knew full well that no Confederate force had either the numbers or the ability to interfere with him.

Even though Sherman had confidence in his men, people in the North were becoming increasingly concerned about what was being called the "lost army." One person who was not worried about Sherman, or at least he pretended not to be, was Abraham Lincoln. When Senator John Sherman, General Sherman's brother, asked the president if he had heard anything from Georgia, Lincoln gave a glib reply. "I know what hole he went in at," Lincoln said, "but I can't tell what hole he will come out of."[19] But if Sherman and his army had disappeared into the wilds of Georgia in late

October, before Election Day, instead of mid-November, Lincoln's reaction would not have been nearly as calm or composed.

Even though Lincoln did not know where Sherman was, at least he could rest assured that the army he commanded would not be bothered by John Bell Hood's Army of Tennessee. Hood's plan to draw Sherman's army away from Georgia had failed conspicuously and had finally ended in disaster. On November 30, 1864, at Franklin, Tennessee, he attacked two Federal corps commanded by General John M. Schofield. Overaggressiveness, Hood's downfall when he fought Sherman outside Atlanta, would prove to be his ruin at Franklin as well.

Hood ordered a series of suicidal charges against the Federal line, even though his generals warned that the enemy was too well entrenched for such an attack to have any hope of success. Unfortunately, Old Woodenhead refused to listen to his generals. Eighteen thousand Confederates came at the enemy in perfect marching order, more men than General George E. Pickett had at Gettysburg. The results were the same as Pickett's charge. A quarter of Hood's army was wiped out, including six generals. A captain in a Texas regiment confided to his diary exactly what he thought of General Hood. "And the wails and cries of widows and orphans made at Franklin Tenn Nov 30th 1864 will heat up the fires of the bottomless pit to burn the soul of Gen JB Hood for murdering their husbands and fathers at that place that day," he wrote. "It can't be called anything else but bloody murder."[20]

Hood continued to move north into Tennessee even though his movements were having no effect on General Sherman's march through Georgia. His depleted army arrived at Nashville, Tennessee, early in December. Federal forces under General George Thomas attacked Hood for two days on December 15 and 16, hammering the Confederates until they broke and ran. Hood watched the Federal onslaught and its results from the rear and could hardly believe what he was seeing. Later on he would recall in shock that he had never seen a Confederate army abandon the field in such confusion.

Following the disasters of Franklin and Nashville, the Army of Tennessee could no longer be considered an effective fighting force. Instead, it had become a shattered, demoralized mob, no longer a threat to Sherman, Grant, or anybody else. When Hood had succeeded Joseph E. Johnston as commander in July 1864, the army's effective strength had stood at over 40,000 men. After Franklin and Nashville, only about 21,000 were left, and these were in no condition to fight.

John Bell Hood had been given command of the Army of Tennessee because of his reputation for aggressiveness. Instead of trying to outmaneuver Sherman's army, as his predecessor Joseph E. Johnston had, Hood attempted to attack and destroy it. But his tactics against Sherman had resulted in the loss of Atlanta and, more than any other single factor, had put Abraham Lincoln back in the White House for a second term. And his idea of diverting Sherman away from Georgia by moving north toward Tennessee had failed completely, resulting in the destruction of his army at Franklin and Nashville. Hood's tenure as commander had been a complete disaster. It became clear that Hood had to go.

Even Old Woodenhead himself understood his predicament this time; he could see that he had reached the end of the line. "He looked at the tattered, shattered ranks, the shot-torn flags, and the gunless batteries," one writer commented, "and could scarcely recognize what he himself had once commanded."[21] On January 13, 1865, Hood respectfully requested to be relieved of command of the Army of Tennessee. Richmond complied immediately. Hood's career in the Confederate army was finally over.

Now that Hood was gone, there was no question at all over who would be his successor. The War Department's choice of a replacement for John Bell Hood was a masterpiece of irony—they selected General Joseph E. Johnston to replace Hood as the general commanding the Army of Tennessee. A member of the War Department noted, "A great pressure has been brought to bear after Hood's overthrow for the reassignment of Johnston."[22] Johnston had been fired in July for not being aggressive enough against Sherman. Now he was about to replace Hood because Hood had been too aggressive.

Three days after Hood submitted his resignation, the Confederate Senate approved two items on its agenda. The first was a motion calling for the appointment of Robert E. Lee as general in chief of all Confederate armies. This gave Lee the same authority as Ulysses S. Grant, although Lee would not have anything close to the men or resources that Grant had at his disposal. The second item was a resolution reinstating Joseph E. Johnston as the Army of Tennessee's commander. The Senate approved both resolutions, followed by the House four days later, and sent them off to President Jefferson Davis for his signature.

If Jefferson Davis had been a more reflective man, he might have wondered what would have happened at Atlanta if Joe Johnston had been left in command. But Davis still held his old West Point grudge, and he was not about to indulge in what-might-have-beens. He also was not about to reappoint Joe Johnston to his old command. Instead, he wrote a long note explaining exactly why he would not agree to the resolution passed by both houses of Congress.

Davis's main excuse was that he did not trust Johnston with such an important position. "My opinion of Genl. Johnston's unfitness for command has ripened slowly and against my inclination so settled that it would be impossible for me again to feel confidence in him as the commander of an army in the field," was how Davis put it.[23]

But Robert E. Lee disagreed with President Davis. He strongly recommended that Johnston be reinstated on the grounds that Johnston was the only officer who had the confidence of the army and the Southern people. (Lee was being modest. He knew very well that both the army and the South also had absolute faith in him.) Because of Lee's recommendation, Davis reluctantly signed Johnston's reappointment. On February 23, 1865, General Joseph E. Johnston received orders assigning him command of the Army of Tennessee.

Joe Johnston was glad to have his old command back, although he was not exactly elated—he knew exactly what had happened to the army in the seven months since he had been replaced by General Hood. He was also realistic enough to see what lay in store for his army, and for the Confederacy, once the spring campaigns began.

William Tecumseh Sherman would face Joe Johnston again, but not until after he had captured Savannah. Sherman would end his march to the sea on December 21, 1864, when he entered an evacuated Savannah and took the salute as his army marched past in review.

Savannah must have seemed a very strange place to these men, who came from cities in the North and had never seen anyplace like it before. Even though it was mid-December, flowers continued in full bloom throughout the city. Streets were lined with palm trees, and orange trees grew in residential gardens. Seeing such an exotic city put the war in a completely different perspective to men from Illinois and Indiana and Ohio. If Georgia had towns where flowers still grew in December, maybe the South was not such a bad place after all.

General Sherman informed Abraham Lincoln what "hole" he came out of on December 22. In a jubilant note addressed to "His Excellency, Pres.t Lincoln," Sherman wrote, "I beg to present you as a Christmas gift the city of Savannah with 150 heavy guns & plenty of ammunition & also about 25,000 bales of cotton."[24] Actually, Sherman had already given Lincoln his Christmas present over three months earlier—the city of Atlanta, along with the White House. Savannah was just a nice stocking stuffer.

After the North celebrated the capture of Savannah—and after General Grant ordered another 100-gun salute to be fired into the Confederate works at Petersburg—Sherman began another march. This time his movement was northward from Savannah through South Carolina and North Carolina and finally into Virginia to join Grant and Meade. At least, that was the plan.

Sherman rested his army for just over a month before moving his army across the Savannah River into South Carolina in early February 1865. The men were fully aware that South Carolina was where secession had begun and where the first shots of the war had been fired in 1861. In December 1860, South Carolina was the first state to secede from the Union, and the bombardment of Fort Sumter in Charleston Harbor the following April had actually begun the war. The entire state had become the target for the army's collective rage. Sherman's men determined to do a lot more damage in their march through this state than they had done in Georgia. Houses were burned, crops were destroyed, and barns were torched. Everything in the army's path was demolished. The men did not want only to conquer South Carolina; they wanted to destroy it.

Confederate general Joseph E. Johnston remarked of Sherman's men, "There had been no such army in existence since the days of Julius Caesar."[25]

Johnston did his best to impede Sherman, and even gave the Federals a real battle at Bentonville, North Carolina, beginning on March 19. But the Confederate army could not stop the Union force, and suffered nearly twice as many casualties in the three-day battle. Both Johnston and Sherman knew that there was not very much that the Confederates could do about the blue army that continued to push its way relentlessly toward Virginia.

Sherman knew better than to think that his army was invincible— Robert E. Lee had a notion that his men were unbeatable at Gettysburg and found out the hard way that they were anything but. Sherman was well aware, however, that he had a larger and better-supplied force than his opponent, which was another point that Johnston was reluctantly forced to concede. Johnston grudgingly informed Lee that Sherman's army could go pretty much wherever it wanted in North Carolina without much interference. "I can do no more than annoy him," he said.[26]

As it would turn out, Sherman would never make it as far north as Virginia. The Confederacy was shrinking with every mile that his army advanced into North Carolina. Except for two widely dispersed Confederate armies—one west of the Mississippi River and another in lower Mississippi and Alabama—which were too isolated to have any impact on the outcome of the war, there was nothing left of the once-proud Confederate States Army. Apart from northern North Carolina and southern Virginia, there was not very much left of the Confederacy. In a small farmhouse near Greensboro, North Carolina, on April 17, 1865, William T. Sherman and Joseph E. Johnston would sign a surrender agreement that would end the war. By that time, Robert E. Lee and Ulysses S. Grant had already had their meeting at Wilmer McLean's house in Appomattox Court House.

Sherman wanted to be with his friend Grant at the end, but it was not to be. He was still preoccupied with Joe Johnston. But they did meet again at City Point at the end of March, a year after they had last seen each other in Cincinnati. In March 1864, it had been decided that Grant would go for Lee and Sherman would go for Joe Johnston. Now they would talk about all that had happened during the past eventful year. Or, rather, Sherman talked and Grant listened, the same as in their suite in the Burnet House 12 long and decisive months earlier.

"Their encounter was more like that of two school boys coming together after a vacation than the meeting of two actors in a great war tragedy," was how one witness described the meeting.[27] The two addressed each other as "Grant" and "Sherman." As they walked toward Grant's headquarters, the short stumpy man and his tall red-haired friend, no casual onlooker would have guessed that they were both generals, at least not by their appearance. Grant, as usual, wore his plain blue uniform and seemed to go out of his way to look as disheveled and undistinguished as possible. "He looked rather like a Scottish terrier," one writer described Grant, "a short, broad, blunt man with a bristly stubbly beard and sharp eyes."[28] Sherman's appearance did not offer any improvement—he wore a shabby coat, a slouch hat, and wore his trousers tucked inside his boots. They were probably the two most famous men in America after Abe Lincoln, but they dressed like a couple of rag pickers.

At headquarters, Sherman entertained his old friend and members of Grant's staff with stories of his march through Georgia and the Carolinas. He made a special point of mentioning that South Carolina's state capital, Columbia, had been completely burned out. Grant listened quietly, smoking a cigar, letting his friend go on with his story.

The main part of Grant and Sherman's reunion at City Point came when they sat down with Abraham Lincoln aboard the president's steamer *River Queen*, along with Admiral David Porter, to discuss war strategy. Admiral Porter's Mississippi Squadron had been part of Admiral Farragut's fleet at Vicksburg in 1863, and he had been friends with General Grant ever since. Porter was on hand to offer any advice on naval matters, even though the discussion would mainly involve the armies of Grant and Sherman. Plans on what terms to offer the South after the surrender were also on the agenda, and these were just as vital.

The strategy and postwar discussion took place on the following day, March 28. General Philip Sheridan, who had also come to City Point, was struck by the anxiety he saw on the president's face. Lincoln was concerned that General Johnston might slip away from Sherman's army and join forces with Lee and his army while Sherman was away, which would not only upset plans for the spring campaign but would also prolong the war. The fighting had already gone on for too long, and Lincoln wanted to end it with as little additional killing as possible.

Sherman and Grant assured the president that there was no chance of Johnston getting away to join Lee, which put Lincoln's mind at ease. Lincoln also hoped fervently that the war could be brought to a close without another major battle and its resulting major casualties, but neither Grant nor Sherman could guarantee this. The two generals would continue to battle the enemy in the field—Grant and Meade against Lee, and Sherman against Johnston— until both Confederate armies surrendered and the war was over.

This was the agreed-upon strategy, which was basically the same as it had been the year before—Grant would go for Lee and Sherman would go for Joe Johnston. The big difference in 1865 was that Lee's army was badly weakened after a year of hammering by Grant and Meade, and what was left of Joe Johnston's forces were in North Carolina after having lost Atlanta. Also, there was no presidential election to worry about.

But besides winning the war, restoration of the Union and securing a lasting peace also preoccupied the president. Sheridan asked Lincoln what would happen to the Confederate armies after they surrendered and what would happen to Jefferson Davis and the other Southern political leaders. Lincoln knew exactly what he intended to do. All he wanted was to defeat the opposing armies, to bring Joseph Johnston and Robert E. Lee to bay, and then to allow every Confederate soldier to go home. As far as Jefferson Davis was concerned, Lincoln hinted that he would be inclined to look the other way if Davis decided to sneak out of the country. He only insisted upon two conditions for peace: the seceded states would be required to rejoin the Union and slavery would have to be abolished. He made it clear that he wanted to destroy the Confederacy, but he did not want to destroy the South. And he did not want to inflict any additional punishment on the Southern people—they had already been punished enough. "Let 'em up easy," was the way Lincoln put it.[29]

But before the Confederates could be let up easy, they had to be knocked out. Sherman hurried back to his army in North Carolina. Grant told Sheridan, "I feel now like ending the matter," and instructed his tough little cavalry commander to get on Lee's right flank.[30] Grant intended to knock his opponent out of the war once and for all and as quickly as it could be done.

That was probably the main difference between the spring of 1865 and the spring of 1864. Everyone—on both sides—knew that the war was winding down at long last. After four years of slaughter, after Fredericksburg and Chancellorsville and the Wilderness and Cold Harbor and thousands of dead and wounded and crippled and maimed, the killing and the maiming were about to end. "There was hope in the air," a soldier with the 6th Corps wrote, "All were beginning to feel that the next campaign would be the last."[31]

Just one more push and it would all be over. Lee still held his lines at Petersburg, but his army was not even half the size of the Army of the Potomac and more and more "Johnnies" deserted every day. The Federals looked at the state of the deserters and could see that the Confederates did not have a chance. Lee might be a great general, but even Bobby Lee could not win a war with an army of half-starved skeletons. Soon Grant would have his victory, Lincoln would have his peace, and everybody would be able to go home.

When Lincoln left City Point on the morning of March 29, Grant watched the president's departure. Grant took his cigar out of his mouth and said to an aide, "I think we can send him some good news in a day or two."[32]

Grant was being just a little overoptimistic. Sending the news that Lee and his army had surrendered would take 11 days, not one or two. But it had been nearly 11 months since Grant and the Army of the Potomac had stepped off into the Wilderness, a journey that had now put him on the road to Richmond and Appomattox, and he had already put Lincoln back in the White House. A few extra days would not make much difference.

TO BIND UP THE NATION'S WOUNDS

Even before he had met with Grant and Sherman and Admiral Porter aboard the *River Queen*, President Lincoln had already set down his intentions for the postwar South. By the time of his *River Queen* conference, when he said, "Let 'em up easy," Lincoln had already begun his second term, having been inaugurated as president three weeks earlier. In his Second Inaugural Address, he informed the country what he had in mind for the defeated and devastated former Confederate States of America. Charles Francis Adams Jr., the son of the American ambassador to Great Britain, called Lincoln's Second Inaugural speech "the keynote of the war."[33]

Inauguration Day was March 4, 1865, a cold and rainy Saturday. Exactly four years earlier, on March 4, 1861, Lincoln had delivered his First Inaugural Address on another gloomy, rainy day. In that speech, Lincoln had urged the Southern people not to secede—"we are not enemies but friends"—but to be touched by "the mystic chords of memory" and by "the better angels of our nature" and remain in the Union.[34] Now, the war that Lincoln had hoped to avoid was nearly over, and he was making plans for a lasting peace.

The president had spent most of the morning of March 4 signing bills in a room of the Senate wing. Outside, the rain was making a mess of everything. An Inauguration Day parade had bogged down in the mud of Washington's unpaved streets. Horses, soldiers, several patriotic floats, and still more soldiers waded their way through several inches of mud. Sometimes the mud got the better of the whole affair—horses, soldiers, and all—as everything sank into the goo and came to a complete stop. Women who came to the inauguration in all their finery quickly found themselves splashed with dirty water, "crinolines smashed, skirts bedaubed, velvet and lace streaked with mud."[35] But everyone seemed to be having a good time and enjoying themselves in spite of the mud and the weather.

The first order of business on the inauguration agenda was the swearing in of the new vice president. By about noon, Lincoln had finished his bill-signing chores and was seated in the front row of the Senate chamber. Members of the House and the cabinet were also present, along with members of the diplomatic corps in their gold lace and the Supreme Court in their black robes. The army was represented by General "Fighting Joe" Hooker; the navy had sent Admiral David G. Farragut, the hero of Mobile Bay. All in all, it was quite an impressive gathering.

As the Senate clock struck twelve, Vice President Hannibal Hamlin entered the chamber, accompanied by Vice President-Elect Andrew Johnson. Hamlin began the proceedings by thanking everyone present for their kindness and consideration during the past four years. After finishing his remarks, Hamlin asked Andrew Johnson if he was ready to take the oath of office. Johnson replied that he was, and walked slowly toward the rostrum. Actually, Johnson was anything but ready.

Earlier that day, Johnson had told Hannibal Hamlin that he really was not well enough to be in Washington. Having only just recovered from an attack of typhoid fever, he had asked Lincoln for permission to take the oath of office in Nashville instead of traveling to the inauguration ceremony. But Lincoln, wanting Johnson to be in Washington for the event, had urged his future vice president to make the trip in spite of his being unwell.

Because of his illness, Johnson was shaky to begin with. When he arrived at Hamlin's office that morning, some well-meaning individual had brought Johnson what is usually described as a tumbler full of whiskey. The large glass of whiskey was supposed to quiet his nerves and help him get over any lingering effects of the typhoid fever. Before entering the Senate, he had had a second large glass of whiskey. According to some accounts, he had also had a third. By the time he stood before President Lincoln and the assembled dignitaries to take the oath of office, Vice President-Elect Andrew Johnson was well and truly plastered.

He stood unsteadily at the rostrum, without any notes, and began his rambling address by reminding Mr. Secretary Seward (Secretary of State William H. Seward), Mr. Secretary Stanton (Secretary of War Edwin M. Stanton), and the secretary of the navy (he could not remember Gideon Welles's name) that they did not derive their greatness or their power from President Lincoln. "Humble as I am, plebeian as I may be deemed," he went erratically on, "permit me in the presence of this brilliant assemblage to enunciate the truth that courts and cabinets, the president and his advisors, derive their power and their greatness from the people."[36]

Gideon Welles leaned over and told Edwin Stanton that Johnson was either drunk or crazy. Most of the other onlookers had already reached the conclusion that Johnson was clearly under the influence. Vice President Hamlin kept pulling on his successor's coattails, and the Senate clerk also tried unsuccessfully to catch Johnson's attention. All attempts to stop the drunken speech failed. Poor President Lincoln sat with his head down throughout the speech, staring at the tops of his shoes and wishing that Johnson would stop.

But Johnson kept on talking, his voice becoming increasingly raspy as he went on. At one point, he thanked God that his native Tennessee had not seceded from the Union, declaring, "No state can go out of this Union and, moreover, Congress cannot eject a state from the Union."[37] Finally, after what seemed like hours, Johnson either ran out of words or was stopped from any further rambling by Hamlin's coattail tugging. The clerk came forward with a Bible, and the oath of the vice president was administered. After taking the oath, Johnson seized the Bible in both hands and bellowed, "I kiss this Book in the face of my nation of the United States."[38] He then proceeded to give the Bible a large, wet kiss.

A few days later, Lincoln was asked what would happen to the country if anything were to happen to him and, under the Constitution, Johnson were to replace him as president. Lincoln sensed the alarm in the question. "I have known Andy for many years," Lincoln replied with an unusual amount of gravity. "He made a bad slip the other day, but you need not be scared. Andy ain't a drunkard." But as he rose and walked outside on Inauguration Day with the rest of the procession, he was overheard telling a marshal, "Do not let Johnson speak outside."[39]

When he stepped out onto the inaugural platform, Lincoln was struck by the size of the crowd, which seemed to stretch as far as the eye could see. As soon as they caught sight of Lincoln, the mass of people let out with a roar of applause. A band played "Hail to the Chief" and the sergeant at arms signaled for the crowd to quiet down. The sun broke through the overcast as Lincoln advanced onto the platform, which most of those present took to be a good omen, and he walked slowly and deliberately toward the rostrum.

At six feet four inches tall, he was considerably taller than those around him. Many in the crowd thought that Lincoln also looked considerably older than his 56 years. Lincoln's aide John Hay observed that Lincoln had become a very different man from the youthful president-elect of 1861.

"He continued the same kindly, genial and cordial spirit he had been at first," Hay later declared, "but the boisterous laughter became less frequent year by year; the eye grew veiled by constant mediation on momentous subjects; the air of reserve and detachment from his surroundings increased."[40] Four years of war had turned Abraham Lincoln into a tired, worn old man.

The president adjusted his steel-rimmed glasses, looked down at the single sheet of paper he held in his hands, and began reading.

"Fellow countrymen," he started out, "at this second appearing to take the oath of the presidential office, there is less occasion for an extended address than there was at the first."[41] The First Inaugural Address certainly had been a far different speech, all about reconciliation and trying to avoid war. Now, Lincoln said that "the progress of our arms, upon which all else chiefly depends, is as well known to the public as to myself; and it is, I trust, reasonably satisfactory and encouraging to all."

The progress of Northern arms certainly was satisfactory and encouraging now that the North was clearly winning the war. The public above the Mason-Dixon Line remembered the fighting of the past summer and autumn as a series of slogans: "I propose to fight it out on this line if it takes all summer"; "Damn the torpedoes!"; "Whirling through Winchester"; and, especially, "Atlanta is ours, and fairly won." Lincoln was all too aware that if General Sherman had not taken Atlanta, he would not be standing where he was. He did not need anyone to tell him that his re-election had been decided on the battlefield.

Lincoln continued by reminding his audience that when he was delivering his First Inaugural Address four years before, "all thoughts were anxiously directed to an impending civil war. All dreaded it—all sought to avoid it." But there could be no mistake about who was to blame for it. "Both parties deprecated war; but one of them would *make* war rather than let the nation survive; and the other would *accept* war rather than let it perish." The South wanted war, and the North accepted war to preserve the Union. "And the war came."

Next, Lincoln addressed the issue of slavery. "One-eighth of the whole population were colored slaves, not distributed generally over the Union, but localized in the southern part of it. These slaves constituted a peculiar and

powerful interest." He elected to leave out the economic reasons for the break
between North and South, which were every bit as responsible for the war as
slavery, and greatly oversimplified the story of the road to Fort Sumter.

"All knew that this interest was, somehow, the cause of the war. To
strengthen, perpetuate, and extend this interest was the object for which
the insurgents would rend the Union, even by war; while the government
claimed no right to do more than to restrict the territorial enlargement of
it." This refers to Lincoln's own expressed intent, which he had stated in his
First Inaugural Address, to prohibit the expansion of slavery but not to
abolish it.

"Neither party expected for the war, the magnitude, or the duration,
which it has already attained." This was certainly true. In April 1861
everyone on both sides expected the war to be over by Christmas. "Neither
anticipated that the *cause* of the conflict might cease with, or even before,
the conflict itself should cease." This was political talk. Lincoln knew that
his Emancipation Proclamation had not freed any slave—the "colored
slaves" in the South were still in bondage and could still be bought and sold,
even while Lincoln stood before the crowd and spoke.

Still on the subject of slavery, Lincoln told his attentive audience that
both sides read the same Bible and prayed to the same God but that each
side, Union and Confederate, invoked God's name against the other. Para-
phrasing Saint Matthew's gospel, he said, "It may seem strange that any men
should dare to ask a just God's assistance in wringing their bread from the
sweat of other men's faces; but judge not, that we be not judged." "The
prayers of both could not be answered," he continued, "that of neither has
been answered fully. The Almighty has his own purposes."

Lincoln continued in the same vein, quoting from Matthew again.
"Woe unto the world because of offenses! For it must needs be that offenses
come; but woe to that man by whom the offense cometh." Blacks in the
audience reacted vocally to what Lincoln was saying. "Negroes ejaculated
'bress de Lord' in a low murmur at the end of every sentence," according to
the *New York Herald*.[42] If American slavery could be counted as one of the
offenses caused by the country, and now God had given the country this
civil war as the woe for causing the offense, "shall we discern therein any

departure from those divine attributes which the believers in a living God always ascribe to Him?" As far as Lincoln was concerned, the living God was punishing both North and South for the offense of slavery.

"Fondly do we hope—fervently do we pray—that this mighty scourge of war may speedily pass away." Again, Lincoln was referring to the war as an instrument of God's punishment—a mighty scourge. "Yet if God wills that it continue, until all the wealth piled by the bondman's two hundred and fifty years of unrequited toil shall be sunk, and until every drop of blood drawn with the lash shall be paid by another drawn with the sword, as was said three thousand years ago, so still it must be said, 'The judgments of the Lord are true and righteous altogether.'" This last quote, from Psalm 19, produced another chorus of "Bless the Lord!" from the audience, along with a long and enthusiastic round of applause.

Lincoln saved the main point of his speech for last. It is also the best remembered and most often quoted part of the address, as well as the most eloquent. "With malice toward none; with charity for all; with firmness in the right, as God gives us to see the right, let us strive to finish the work we are in; to bind up the nation's wounds; to care for him who shall have borne the battle, and for his widow, and his orphan—to do all which may achieve and cherish a just and lasting peace, among ourselves, and among all nations."

This is what Lincoln would tell Grant and Sherman three weeks later, aboard the *River Queen*. He wanted clemency for the defeated South, not retribution. He intended to bind up the nations wounds, to heal the bloody four-year breach between North and South, to "let 'em up easy."

In his short speech, Abraham Lincoln summed up what had taken place during the past four years. Both sides were equally to blame for the war, and neither side had expected that it would go on for as long as it did or cost as much as it had in blood and treasure. God had given "to both north and south this terrible war," Lincoln said, and he hoped and prayed that it would soon end. Although he did not say so, Lincoln knew that the country had changed forever, especially the South. The former Confederate states not only had lost their slaves, but had also seen their entire way of life disappear.

But if both sides were equally guilty of causing the war, both sides should also be equal partners after the war. North and South had often behaved like two separate countries long before Fort Sumter. The industrial North and the agricultural South had almost always disagreed with each other since the beginning of the republic over taxes and tariffs and imports, not just over slavery. Lincoln hoped that when the fighting ended the country would be really united for the first time in its history, which is one reason why Lincoln did not want to punish the South. "If there was a triumph to celebrate," one historian noted, "it was not the triumph of one set of men over another set, but of all men overcoming a common affliction."[43]

Lincoln did not know it, but his Second Inaugural would be his last major speech. It was a hopeful look into the future, which he would not live to see, as well as a farewell glimpse at the past. The war had not turned out as planned. "Neither party expected for the war, the magnitude, or the duration, which it has already attained," but if everything turned out the way he imagined, maybe the four awful years that had just passed would not only bring "a just and lasting peace," but would also produce a unified country as well as an end to slavery.

When Lincoln ended his speech, the crowd was taken by surprise. It had been only 703 words long and had only lasted six or seven minutes. Some people, still arriving when the president finished, were startled by the artillery salute that punctuated the end of the address and the burst of applause and cheering that accompanied it. Expecting that his inaugural address would go on for some time, like most political speeches, everyone was disappointed by Lincoln's brevity.

After the ovation faded away, Chief Justice Salmon P. Chase stepped forward to administer the oath of office. The clerk of the Supreme Court brought a Bible. Lincoln had appointed Chase as Supreme Court chief justice just three months earlier, in December 1864. Lincoln placed his right hand on the Bible and repeated the presidential oath, ending with a ringing "So help me God!"[44] He kissed the Bible, which was then presented to Mrs. Lincoln, and the two of them left the Capitol building for the White House. Lincoln had begun his second term of office as president of the United States, an event that had seemed as remote as the mountains of the moon seven months earlier. The impossible had come to pass.

Reactions to the inaugural address varied wildly. The *Philadelphia*

Inquirer thought the speech was characteristic of the president. "It exhibits afresh the kindness of his heart, and the large charity which has ever marked his actions toward those who are his personal enemies as well as enemies of his country."[45] The *New York Herald* did not like it as much, calling the address "a little speech of 'glittering generalities' used only to fill the program."[46] As might be expected, the *New York World* had absolutely nothing good to say. Although the paper's editors printed the speech, apparently out of a sense of civic duty, the paper's management made no secret of the fact that they hated it. "It is with a blush of shame and wounded pride, as an American citizen, that we lay before our readers to-day the inaugural addresses of President Lincoln and Vice President Johnson."[47]

British newspapers tended to treat the inaugural speech with approval, along with the fact that Lincoln would be in office for four more years. The *London Spectator*, which had shown anything but approval toward Lincoln when it looked as though the North was going to lose the war, said that the speech was "by far the noblest which any American president has yet uttered to the American Congress."[48] The *Times*, which had been pro-Confederate and anti-Lincoln for most of the war, remarked, "This short inaugural speech reveals Abraham Lincoln's dispositions and opinion more completely than many verbose compositions of his predecessors."[49] Which goes to prove that there is nothing like winning a national election and being on the verge of winning a war for reversing public opinion.

Throughout the North, many were disappointed by the inaugural address and did not see anything noble about it. Most Northerners had expected a rousing narrative of Union victories in the field, not dishwater about charity and reconciliation. Thousands who read the speech on the front pages of their local newspapers, and not just Radical Republicans, did not want charity for the South—they wanted revenge. "With malice toward none" had a hollow ring for those who had lost loved ones in the war. Countless widows and relatives of dead soldiers felt a great deal of malice toward the Confederacy and did not give a damn for the president's message of reconciliation. They wanted to reconcile the South with a bayonet.

Lincoln did not think of the Confederates as traitors. As far as he was concerned, they were fellow countrymen who should be welcomed back into the Union as soon as the war ended. There were many Northerners, including many in high places, who did not agree. Henry Adams, son of the ambassador to Great Britain, thought that Robert E. Lee should be hanged. But Lincoln saw the main task of his second term as reuniting the country, not dividing it further. He really did intend to bind up the nation's wounds. This was not just political posturing.

Abraham Lincoln was not always so generous or open-minded toward the South or its sympathizers. On April 27, 1861, in an effort to suppress "disloyalty," Lincoln issued a proclamation that did away with habeas corpus. He had also used his authority as president to arrest and imprison indefinitely, without trial or formal charges, anyone suspected of "disloyal practices." An angry neighbor could have a person thrown in jail for whistling "Dixie" in the bath on the vague charge of "disloyalty," and that unfortunate citizen might stay in jail for months.

In his proclamation, Lincoln had declared that "all rebels and insurgents, their aiders and abettors," or anyone "guilty of any disloyal practice ... shall be subject to martial law." The heart of the proclamation stated that "the writ of Habeas Corpus is suspended in respect to all persons arrested, or who are now, or hereafter during the rebellion shall be, imprisoned in any fort, camp, arsenal, military prison, or any other place of confinement by any military authority."[50]

Lincoln had more than 13,000 people jailed as the result of this proclamation. Most of them were Peace Democrats. He was afraid that the courts would not convict anyone on such a vague charge as "disloyalty," so he ordered the accused to be thrown into jail without the inconvenience of having to take them to court. This might not have been Lincoln's most ethical decision, but it did keep his critics from vocally opposing the war. And keeping many of his political enemies in prison probably helped him to be re-elected.

The most famous case involving Lincoln's suspension of habeas corpus involved a state legislator from Maryland named John Merryman. John Merryman, brazenly secessionist and pro-Confederate, had actively campaigned for Maryland to secede from the Union and join the Confederacy. When Lincoln heard about Merryman and his activities, he decided to take steps to shut him up. Federal soldiers arrested Merryman in May 1861 and confined him in Fort McHenry in Baltimore Harbor, which Francis Scott Key had made famous. He was charged with nothing more specific than sympathizing with the Confederacy, and he was not given any definite date for a trial.

When John Merryman's predicament came to the attention of Supreme Court Chief Justice Roger B. Taney, the eighty-four year-old judge questioned the legality of Merryman's arrest and demanded that the accused be brought before him. President Lincoln cordially ignored the demand.

An angry and frustrated Chief Justice Taney, sitting as a circuit court judge, responded to Lincoln's defiance by writing *ex parte Merryman*, which challenged the president's authority to suspend habeas corpus on both legal and constitutional grounds. Lincoln had clearly overstepped his authority, Taney ruled, since no president had the power to suspend habeas corpus. This time, it was later rumored, Lincoln not only ignored the ruling, but also issued a warrant for Taney's arrest. Lincoln's biographers generally dismiss that any such warrant was ever issued, but the story suggests what many at the time felt—that Honest Abe could be ruthless and arbitrary when it suited his purposes. In any case, although Lincoln may have abused his executive power, he also effectively defused all secessionist activities in Maryland. The state remained in the Union.

By the spring of 1865, Lincoln's attitude had been completely reversed. After four years as a war president, he was no longer the feisty newly elected president doing his best to keep the Union together. Now that the war was almost won, Lincoln wanted nothing more than to end the bloodshed and bring the seceded states back into the Union.

Reconstruction had not yet become a dirty word in American history. Within a few years, it would mean carpetbaggers, corruption, settling of scores with a conquered South by Northern politicians, and keeping all former slaves from enjoying any of the benefits of their new freedom. But Abraham Lincoln intended Reconstruction to mean amnesty for all Southerners, including army officers and political leaders, and the restoration of all seceded states to the Union.

He certainly made a bright start. On March 11, Lincoln issued an order pardoning all deserters from the Confederate army, wherever they happened to be and regardless of their reason for leaving the Confederate forces. A short while afterward, pedestrians along Pennsylvania Avenue were treated to the spectacle of a Confederate regimental band marching past the White House while playing a medley of Union songs. The band had deserted en masse, instruments and all, and was entertaining the citizens of Washington as musicians, not as prisoners. Seven months earlier, these same musicians might have entertained Jubal Early's men as they planned their attack on the capital. But now they moved down one of the city's main streets, free and easy and without any armed Union soldiers in sight to stand guard over them.

Although the pardoning of Southern deserters was a good beginning, Lincoln knew that it was only a beginning. Implementing his version of reconstruction was going to require a lot of persuasion and political manipulation and deal making with the opposition. And there would be a good deal of opposition to Lincoln's policy of leniency toward the South, including from members of his own party. Crusty and cynical old Thaddeus Stevens, leader of the Radical Republicans, went on record saying that, as far as he was concerned, Abraham Lincoln should not be president. The Radicals accused Lincoln of squandering all the victories won by Union armies in the field, and of selling out to the Peace Democrats, in his wrongheaded desire to allow the Confederate traitors to escape all punishment.

But Lincoln was not all that worried about Thad Stevens or any of his friends. He would deal with the Radicals in his own way when the time came. He knew that he was more than a match for Stevens or any of the Radicals when it came to political infighting, and that he was unscrupulous enough to do anything that needed to be done. He also knew that he had plenty of time, and he was certain that he would be able to carry out his agenda for reunification and reconciliation during the next four years,

NEVER DEAD

"If it were not for Lincoln's victory," a British writer considered, "there might not have been a U.S.A. capable of pulling so many European irons out of the fire."[1] This has to be considered a minor masterpiece of British understatement. If Abraham Lincoln had lost the 1864 election and the Peace Democrats had granted the seceded Confederate states their independence, the world would have been deprived of an undivided United States, which would have affected a lot more than just pulling European irons out of the fires of the First World War and the Second World War.

Had Lincoln not been re-elected, the continental United States, the 48 states not including Alaska and Hawaii, would have evolved into several separate countries, not just the United States of America and the Confederate States of America. The United States never would have developed into the superpower of the mid-twentieth century and beyond. In addition to the Confederacy, the "lower 48" would have been divided into the Republic of California, a Mormon church-state of Utah, and another confederation of western states, made up of modern-day North and South Dakota, Nebraska, Oklahoma, Montana, Wyoming, Colorado, Idaho, Washington, Oregon, and Nevada. New Mexico and Arizona would have been reoccupied by Mexico in 1916 in a war to reclaim the territory led by Pancho Villa. And the Republic of Texas would have seceded from the Confederacy and become a sovereign nation for the second time in its history. Alaska would have remained a possession of Russia, and Hawaii would have become a territory of California.

If the Confederacy had become independent at the end of 1864, the South would not have been as badly ravaged by war as it was by the spring of 1865. There would have been no march to the sea by General Sherman, no march through South Carolina, no burning of Columbia, South Carolina, no destruction of Richmond, Virginia. All Union forces would have been withdrawn north of the Mason-Dixon Line shortly after the election and all the burning and destruction that took place in Georgia and Virginia and throughout the South between November 1864 and April 1865 never would have taken place.

If Abraham Lincoln had not been re-elected to the White House and George B. McClellan had become president of the United States, history might have happened something like this.

When Confederate forces under John Bell Hood defeated General Sherman's armies south of Atlanta in a surprising counterattack, Sherman decided to lay siege to the city and wait for its residents to surrender. The siege lasted throughout the summer and autumn of 1864, with Union forces unable to break through the Atlanta defenses. As a consequence of the resulting stalemate, voters in the North turned against Lincoln and the war. The Democrats were overwhelmingly elected to power in the November election. The Copperheads—the Peace Democrats—took over the leadership of the party and implemented their platform of "peace without victory." George Brinton McClellan was sworn in as seventeenth president of the United States on Inauguration Day, March 4, 1865. McClellan gave in to the Peace Democrats and agreed not to dispute Confederate independence.

In his inaugural address, President McClellan explained that even though he supported the idea of restoring the Union, he could not stand by while thousands of Federal troops, including soldiers in his beloved Army of the Potomac, were being slaughtered in Georgia and Virginia every day. As such, he would agree to give the Confederate States of America its independence. "The seceded Southern states shall be granted their full and sovereign independence," is how McClellan phrased it. He proposed to ask Congress to approve this measure at a date to be named in the very near future. The North had become tired of the stalemates in Georgia and Virginia, and the Democrats, especially the Peace Democrats, did not hesitate to end the war by giving the Confederates everything they wanted. They proudly called the legislation giving the Confederates their sovereignty the "Copperhead Legislation."

After becoming independent, the Confederate States of America developed into an association of states resembling the European Union, with each state having the right to negotiate its own trade agreements and regulate its own economy. Virginia and Georgia emerged as the most influential states, just as they had been during the war, and just as France and Germany became the leading members of the European Union over 100 years later.

Following the war, the Confederacy and its economy needed time to recover from the war's destruction. The Shenandoah Valley was a fire-wracked shambles. The farms that had been destroyed by General Philip Sheridan required many years before returning to prewar production. Cotton and tobacco continued as the Confederacy's main exports, as well as the country's primary source of income. Slaves cultivated both these cash crops, since the institution of slavery remained intact. Lincoln's Emancipation Proclamation was rendered null and void when the Confederate states were granted self-rule.

Abraham Lincoln left Washington after the inauguration and returned to Springfield, Illinois. He was elected to the US Senate, where he served for more than 20 years. Among his many accomplishments in the Senate was the drafting of a trade bill with the Confederacy, which became the Lincoln Trade Law. This agreement, which gave generous trade concessions to the newly independent South, was pushed through Congress in spite of determined opposition by Democrats, and it was instrumental in helping the devastated Confederacy recover from the war.

During his years as a senator, Lincoln also wrote his *White House Reminiscences, 1861–1865*. In his memoir, Lincoln did his best to give his views on the war and on slavery, and he also tried to explain why he lost the White House in 1864. The book became a sensation, selling nearly a half million copies in its first year of publication. More copies were sold in the Confederacy than in the United States. Confederates were more interested in reading about why they won the war than Northerners were in reading about why they lost it.

George B. McClellan served one term as president. To his profound embarrassment, he became known as "the man who lost the Civil War." One of the most unpopular presidents in American history, McClellan was succeeded by William T. Sherman, who entered politics on the advice of his friend Ulysses S. Grant. In 1869, McClellan returned to his home state of New Jersey and served as governor for a single term. He also wrote a memoir that offered his views on why he granted the Confederacy its independence. Unlike Lincoln's *Reminiscences*, McClellan's memoir did not even sell out its first printing and was quickly forgotten.

Ulysses S. Grant stayed in the army after the war. In 1865, he became an instructor of strategy at West Point. He was appointed superintendent of the United States Military Academy in 1867, 12 years after the end of Robert E. Lee's tenure in the same position.

Philip Sheridan also stayed in the army. In 1870 he was transferred as a "military adviser" to the armies of the Western Confederacy. In the West, Sheridan acquired a fearsome reputation as a fighter against the plains Indians, especially against the Apaches.

Robert E. Lee was appointed President Jefferson Davis's special envoy to the United States—Lee thought "ambassador" was too formal a title for the position. Because he was admired in the United States almost as much as in the Confederacy, Lee was considered to be the ideal diplomatic representative between the two former enemies.

Lee had a much easier time as special envoy during his first four years, when he worked with President McClellan and a Democratic congress, than when William T. Sherman was president. Sherman was as short-tempered as he had always been, and he often let Lee know that he did not particularly enjoy having to deal with a former enemy. As far as Sherman was concerned, the United States should have won the war, an attitude that often led to heated arguments between the two. Lee and Sherman also had many angry encounters over points of protocol, such as whether the Stars and Bars, the official Confederate flag, which resembles the US Stars and Stripes, or the rebel battle duster, the battle flag of the Army of Northern

Virginia, should be flown next to the Stars and Stripes on state occasions. These frequent and emotional disagreements are reportedly what led to Lee's death in 1870 from a heart attack, less than a year after Sherman was sworn in as president.

For the next four decades, the two countries kept a wary eye on each other. As the generation that fought in the war—known in the Confederacy as the War of Confederate Independence, and sometimes the War of the Northern Invasion—died off, bitter memories of the battles lost and won faded away. The Confederacy continued to be the principal trading partner of the United States, sending tobacco and cotton and whiskey north in exchange for farm equipment, building materials, and manufactured items.

Slaves continued to grow the staple crops throughout the Confederacy, and they also ran the machinery in the country's increasing number of factories. Slavery also continued to be a major bone of contention between the United States and the Confederacy. Clergymen and political leaders from the United States, especially the New England states, repeatedly called upon the Confederate States to ratify an emancipation proclamation of its own. Such criticism, especially on this particular subject, brought about predictably heated responses from Confederates, who sharply reminded the Yankees of which side had won the war. From time to time, a senator from one of the Confederate states would introduce legislation to end slavery, but the attempts always came to nothing. The Confederacy's explanation was always that it had too much money invested in slaves and the country simply could not afford the financial loss that abolishing slavery would cause. The country was as bound to slavery, it was widely repeated, as the slaves themselves were bound to their masters.

When the First World War began in 1914, both the Confederacy and the United States resolved to stay out of the fighting between Britain, France, and Russia, and Germany and her allies. But in April 1917, after nearly three years of steadily worsening relations, Germany declared war on the United States after a US Navy destroyer sank two German submarines off the coast of Maine. The United States Congress declared war on Germany the following day.

President William Howard Taft used all his powers of persuasion in an attempt to persuade his Confederate counterpart, President Woodrow Wilson, to join the United States in an alliance against Germany. But the Confederacy remained staunchly isolationist and refused to be drawn into what Confederate newspapers described as "the European war," or "the English war." Britain had refused to intervene on their behalf against the Yankees in 1862, when Robert E. Lee needed all the help he could get, so why should they help the British fight the Germans? Virginia-born Woodrow Wilson very firmly informed President Taft that he could expect no help from any of the Confederate states.

One "Southern" state that did send troops overseas was Tennessee. Tennessee held strong Union sympathies during the Civil War and had seceded from the Confederacy in 1866 to rejoin the United States. One of the most famous US heroes of the First World War was Alvin C. York of Tennessee, who was awarded the Medal of Honor for gallantry during the Meuse-Argonne offensive in 1918.

Alvin C. York's heroics were about the only bright note for the United States during that campaign. The Meuse-Argonne offensive began in September 1918 and ended when US troops were beaten back by a determined German counterattack. Had Confederate troops taken part, the outcome of the offensive probably would have been quite different. But the under-strength US Rainbow Division, no match for the veteran German units, was forced to retreat before the enemy advance. French and British generals had hoped that the US forces would help turn back the Germans, but they now openly expressed fears that the enemy would be in Paris by spring.

United States troops did make their presence felt during the spring offensive of 1919, when units of the Rainbow Division combined with British and French forces to annihilate the German army that had been just northeast of Paris since winter. By June 1919 all German forces had surrendered, although a formal armistice was not signed until October. The United States sent a delegation to the peace conference, which was held in Paris. The Confederacy was not invited to send any delegates and probably would not have sent any if it had been asked.

In the years following the First World War, relations between the United States and the Confederate States grew noticeably chillier and more distant. The Great Depression, which affected the Confederacy more severely than the United States, was the primary cause for this unfriendliness. The United States simply could no longer afford to buy Dixie cotton and other products in pre-Depression quantities, which led to a huge decline in the Confederacy's economic fortunes. Although there were any number of solid economic reasons for the lack of US buyers for Southern products, most Confederates attributed the drying up of trade between the two countries to Yankee revenge for having lost the war.

This general air of hostility took an unexpected turn for the better in 1935, when President Franklin D. Roosevelt invited Confederate president Huey Long to the White House for an economic summit. Both men were consummate politicians, and they genuinely seemed to like each other. At the end of the two-day meeting, President Long reported, "My friend Franklin and I have reached an agreement."

Roosevelt arranged a loan of millions of US dollars to help small farmers throughout the Confederacy, and he also agreed to increase imports of cotton, rice, and other "Confederate products," in Long's words. By the beginning of 1941, with the United States importing Dixie cotton in record amounts, diplomatic relations between Richmond and Washington were more cordial than they had been since 1864.

The Great Depression did more than just test the relationship between the United States and the Confederacy. It also led to an expansion of the United States, which grew to more than double its 1864 size. In 1937, the Western Confederation applied for admission to the Union, mainly for economic reasons. The Western "experiment," simply stated, had not worked. The states bickered and argued among themselves almost constantly and rarely agreed on anything. They could not even agree on a site for the capital of the Confederation—Denver, Colorado, Fargo, North Dakota, and Rapid City, South Dakota, had all been proposed and rejected.

The West also had no cash crop, such as cotton or tobacco, which could easily be exchanged for US dollars. The catastrophe of the Dust Bowl in the mid-1930s all but destroyed what was left of the Western Confederation's already-tottering economy. The Western Confederation needed a miracle to recover, but there were no miracles during the Depression. In July 1937, the states sent a delegation of bankers and politicians to Washington for the purpose of applying for admission to the United States. This "convention," as they called themselves, also lost no time in applying for economic aid under Franklin D. Roosevelt's National Recovery Administration.

With the states of the former Western Confederation a part of the Federal Union, the United States suddenly extended from the Atlantic coast to the Pacific Ocean. The US Navy now had a Pacific base at Bremerton, in Washington State. Colorado, Wyoming, the Dakotas, and the other Western "provinces"—as they were sometimes called—had joined the United States, for better or worse. California remained a sovereign republic, and it annexed the Territory of Hawaii in 1930. The Mormons who governed the State of Utah refused to acknowledge the US Constitution's separation of church and state provision, and would not even consider joining the Union.

None of the five American states, as they were sometimes called, showed any intention of involving themselves in the French and British war against Adolf Hitler and Nazi Germany, which had broken out in 1939. Only California showed any interest at all in the Japanese aggression in the Pacific. When the German army overran France in June 1940, leaving Britain to face Germany all alone, an editorial in the *Richmond Telegraph* declared that the descendents of Robert E. Lee and Jefferson Davis had no intention of pulling any British irons out of any German fire. None of the other American countries were inclined to disagree.

This opinion changed instantly in December 1941. During the first week of December, a Japanese carrier task force attacked the naval fleets of California and the United States, which shared facilities at Pearl Harbor, Hawaii. California declared war on Japan the following day, just a few hours before Franklin D. Roosevelt made his "Day of Infamy" speech before the US Congress. Within the week, the same Japanese task force also attacked both the US naval base at Bremerton, Washington, and the California fleet at San Diego. Both the United States and the Republic of California found themselves at war on the same day, totally unexpectedly.

On December 17, Japanese ally Adolf Hitler simultaneously declared war on the United States, the Confederate States, and the Republic of

Texas, for reasons that have always puzzled historians. Within less than two weeks, four of the five American countries had been blasted out of their peaceful isolation and were involved in a world war. California was not able to send troops to Europe to fight the Nazis. President Jack L. Warner explained that California did not have enough men or resources to fight a two-front war. And Utah president Brigham Young V declared neutrality on the grounds that the Church of Jesus Christ of Latter-day Saints had no quarrel with either Adolf Hitler or the Japanese Empire.

The war against Japan was fought largely by naval forces. A combined US/California task force fought a climactic battle against the Japanese navy several hundred miles off the coast of Washington in April 1942, sinking six enemy aircraft carriers for the loss of one US carrier. Japan never recovered from the loss, although Japanese forces continued to fight on for more than three years. In July 1945, Japan formally surrendered in an official ceremony aboard the giant aircraft carrier *Sacramento*, the largest ship in the Californian navy. The ceremony, which took place in San Diego Bay, was attended by President Warner and delegates from both the United States and California.

The war against Nazi Germany was carried out by troops from the United States, the Confederate States, and the Republic of Texas. All Confederate forces were commanded by General George S. Patton, United States troops were commanded by General Omar Bradley, and the Texans were led by General Dwight D. Eisenhower.

The climax of the war came in June 1944, when the ground troops of all three countries, along with British and French forces, landed on the northern coast of France. German army units fought back and inflicted heavy casualties among the Allied troops. But in the late summer of 1944, combined British, Confederate, and US forces broke through the German defenses and drove right across France, across the Rhine River, and into Germany. The spearhead of this drive was the 1st Virginia Division, better known as the Jeb Stuart Division, which was commanded by Jeb Stuart's grandson Jubal Early Stuart. The Jeb Stuart Division also had the distinction of being the first Allied unit to enter Berlin.

The war ended unexpectedly on Christmas Day 1944, when Adolf

Hitler was assassinated by a clique of German generals who no longer trusted him. Postwar Germany was divided into six zones of occupation: British, French, Russian, US, Confederate, and Texan.

The five American countries did their best to return to their prewar status when the war ended. The United States had the largest population of the five, along with the largest and most diverse economy, and emerged as the most dominant of the five. All the countries joined the United Nations when it was formed in 1945, although only the United States joined the Security Council, along with France, China, Russia, and Great Britain.

When Russian-backed North Korean troops invaded South Korea in 1950, only California did not send troops to South Korea to fight Communist aggression. The smallest but most enthusiastic member of the UN troops in Korea was the Joseph Smith Brigade from Utah, which was named after the founder of the Mormon Church. Utah regarded the war in Korea as a holy war against godless Communism. The war ended in 1953 with the signing of an armistice between the two Koreas. Although the Korean Conflict, as it came to be known, was officially declared a stalemate after three years of fighting, Texas president Dwight D. Eisenhower said that the armistice was a great day for democracy. Utah president Brigham Young VI declared it a victory for the armies of God.

Another war against Russian-supplied Communist troops broke out seven years later, when soldiers from Communist North Vietnam invaded the Republic of South Vietnam. The president of South Vietnam asked for assistance to repel the invaders. Once again, President Brigham Young sent a small contingent of troops to help fight the Communist forces. President Lyndon Johnson of Texas also sent several divisions of troops. But neither California, the Confederacy, nor the United States would commit soldiers to what US president Adlai Stevenson called a "pointless little war." North Vietnamese troops, armed with the most advanced Russian weapons, overwhelmed the combined forces in the south and occupied all of Vietnam by early 1961. President Johnson never forgave the United States for not backing his military efforts in Vietnam, which he considered a betrayal.

The United States and the Confederacy continued to be allies and close trading partners, but they were also two very different countries, with two economies, two currencies, two different cultures, and two different ways of life. The separateness of the two countries was never more evident than during the commemoration of the hundredth anniversary of the War of Confederate Independence, which began in 1961. The celebrations began on April 12, 1961, the anniversary of the bombardment of Fort Sumter, with a reenactment of the bombardment of the fort in Charleston, South Carolina. Festivities finally came to a patriotic conclusion on December 15, 1964, the centennial of Confederacy Day, the date when the United States Congress voted to withdraw all Federal troops from the seceded states.

For more than three and a half years, the Confederacy reveled in an endless procession of parades, fireworks displays, battle reenactments, and patriotic speeches. Descendents of Jefferson Davis, Robert E. Lee, and Jeb Stuart made appearances throughout the Confederacy. On Confederacy Day 1964, special ceremonies were held in Richmond and Atlanta, the two cities where the Yankee invasion was stopped. Texas president Lyndon Johnson visited Confederate president Robert D. Lee in Richmond to observe and remember Confederate independence. "Our cause was righteous and just," President Lee told a television audience, "and our victory over foreign domination was complete."

In the United States, the War of the Southern Rebellion, or just the Rebellion, was hardly mentioned. A few television documentaries recounted the main events of the war and covered the main points of why it was fought, but these tended to be very straightforward and low-key accounts. A good many newspapers ran stories on the war's major battles and its most prominent generals. A favorite editorial topic was what might have happened if Abraham Lincoln had won the 1864 election. A well-known historian even wrote a book called *Atlanta: The Victory That Might Have Been*. But overall, the United States did not give much coverage to the centennial. The country acknowledged the war but did not exactly celebrate its outcome.

United States history books generally treat the war as an unfortunate event, a gallant but failed attempt to restore the Union. Abraham Lincoln is usually portrayed as a minor president who tried his best to save the Union and free the slaves but did not have the ability to do either. The major battles are listed—Antietam, Vicksburg, Shiloh—and Gettysburg is always mentioned as the most costly battle in United States history.

Lincoln's short speech at the dedication of the Gettysburg National Cemetery understandably receives very little attention. It is considered a minor speech by a one-term president. People who know the speech at all will often remark sarcastically that Lincoln was right about the nation having "a new birth of freedom." But, unfortunately for him, the nation he was talking about was the Confederacy, not the United States. He came a lot closer to the truth, critics point out, when he said that the world would "little note, nor long remember" his address. Lincoln was absolutely right about that. Nobody wanted to remember the only war that the United States ever lost. Nobody north of the Mason-Dixon Line, at least.

A few years after the centennial of the war, the United States and the Confederate States had a major disagreement over the issue that had always divided the two countries: the issue of race. Slavery had finally been repealed in the 1920s, having been rendered obsolete and economically unfeasible—it had become cheaper to hire blacks as employees and pay them an hourly wage than to maintain a slave's upkeep. All slaves throughout the Confederacy were declared citizens and were given the right to own property. But blacks and whites remained segregated, with "blacks only" and "whites only" facilities employed in every state. Confederates considered this to be part of their normal way of life.

The US Congress had passed civil rights legislation in the early 1960s, which gave blacks and whites equal rights under the law. But very few blacks lived in the United States. The vast majority of former slaves chose to remain in the Confederacy. They were citizens of the Confederate States, not the United States, and had no desire to move to the United States, which they considered a foreign country.

The disagreement between the two countries over race was triggered by remarks made by US president Hubert Humphrey in a speech to the United Nations Commission on Human Rights. President Humphrey called on the Confederate States to pass legislation to give equal rights to their black citizens, just as the United States had done. The official Confederate policy of racial segregation, Humphrey insisted, did not constitute any improvement over the former policy of slavery. "Free your black citizens once and for all," Humphrey concluded, directing his comments to the Confederate Congress in Richmond.

Reaction to President Humphrey's speech was not long in coming. In an address to the Confederate Congress, President Robert D. Lee, serving an unprecedented second six-year term, scolded President Humphrey for criticizing the Confederacy's "racial policies," which had been a feature of everyday life for generations. President Lee also declared that President Humphrey's indignation over what he perceived as racial prejudice was nothing more than a Yankee excuse to undermine the Confederacy itself. The country needed all its citizens, black and white, Lee said. By sowing dissent among the country's black citizens, Humphrey was trying to weaken and divide the Confederacy. Even though the war had been over for more than 100 years, the Yankees were still trying to get even with the South. President Lee told Humphrey, and all Yankees, to stop refighting the War of Independence and leave the Confederacy alone.

The verbal skirmish between Lee and Humphrey accomplished absolutely nothing. The Confederacy continued with its policy of racial segregation and the United States continued to criticize the Confederacy for it. The difference of opinion served only to prove, if any further proof were needed, that the United States and the Confederacy were two completely different countries.

In spite of the occasional war of words, relations between the United States and the Confederate States continued to be cordial. Both countries also maintained friendly ties with Texas, California, and Utah, although the Mormon government of Utah tended to hold itself aloof from the four secular governments. California president Ronald Reagan caused a minor flap when he remarked that the Latter-day Saints from Salt Lake City frequently behaved as though they were saints from the New Testament, implying that they were humorless and took a holier-than-thou attitude. Reagan quickly apologized and sent President Brigham Young VIII a case of California oranges as a peace offering.

In the early 1980s, shortly after Ronald Reagan made his famous crack about the Latter-day Saints, the relationship between the United States and the Confederacy faced its first trial under fire. Both countries were threatened by aggression from the Soviet Union almost simultaneously, although in two separate incidents in two different parts of the world, and each country stood by the other throughout the military crises. All past feuds and bad feelings were put aside during the emergency.

The two incidents broke out in Alaska and in Cuba at almost exactly the same time. The first episode occurred in Alaska. Alaska had been a Russian territory for over 200 years and the Soviet foreign office had just formed an alliance with the pro-Soviet military dictatorship in Cuba. In 1982, Russian engineers secretly built missile bases in both Cuba and Alaska, and Soviet technicians armed the bases with the latest missile technology. When the Soviet government was confronted with US and Confederate opposition to the new bases, Moscow stated that the missiles were essential to national defense and refused to remove them.

The United States was thoroughly alarmed by the threat posed by these missile bases. The Soviets had built 35 bases in Alaska. Thirty-three of these were situated in the territory's southernmost part, the narrow panhandle of land that runs along the western border of Canada. Hundreds of nuclear warheads were now within striking distance of the western United States, including the US Navy's base at Bremerton, Washington.

The United States saw no alternative but to remove the Soviet bases in Alaska by force. The speed of the US response to the missile threat took the entire world by surprise. United States president Barry Goldwater sent a naval task force to Alaska with orders to do anything necessary to neutralize the missile sites. Confederate president Joseph Johnston, a direct descendent of the War of Independence general, broadcast that his country stood by "our allies and neighbors to the North in their gallant fight against foreign aggression." No one seemed to notice the irony of this declaration in light of his predecessor's 1964 speech celebrating Confederate victory over "foreign aggression" by the invader Yankees.

On the same day that the US task force arrived off the Alaskan coast, units of the 1st Marine Division landed on the northernmost part of the panhandle region, sealing it off from the rest of Alaska. A series of carrier-based air strikes, which were carried out during the next two days, effectively destroyed all 35 missile bases. This action was so swift and decisive that Soviet political and military leaders were caught completely off guard. President Goldwater gambled that the Soviets would be too intimidated to use nuclear weapons against US forces and would not want to run the risk of a nuclear counterstrike. A fiery speech by President Goldwater to the United Nations General Assembly nullified an earlier Soviet objection to Goldwater's military response to the missile bases, which the Soviet ambassador had called "United States imperialist aggression."

The US offensive not only removed the Soviet missile threat, it also successfully ended Alaska's role as a Soviet outpost in North America. Because the United States now controlled all but the very northern extremity of the territory, Alaska had now become a liability to the Soviet Union. The Soviet government offered to sell the entire territory to the United States for several billion dollars, along with trade concessions. Following a series of negotiations between a US congressional committee and a delegation from Moscow—talks that went on for several years and were usually described as "heated"—the United States and the Soviet Union reached an agreement, and the territory of Alaska officially changed hands. On January 1, 1988, Alaska formally joined the Union as the thirty-seventh state.

At the same time that the United States was dealing with the Alaskan crisis, the Confederacy was having its own trouble with the Soviets in Cuba. In fact, the Cuban/Confederate missile affair came close to being an exact copy of the US/Alaska emergency.

Between 20 and 24 missile bases, depending upon which source is consulted, were discovered in Cuba by aerial reconnaissance flights over the island. Each missile was capable of carrying several atomic warheads, which put hundreds of Russian nuclear devices within range of Richmond, Atlanta, New Orleans, and every major city within the Confederacy, as well as New York, Baltimore, and several other cities in the United States.

With the backing of President Goldwater, President Johnston ordered a flotilla of CS Navy warships to form a blockade around the island. But Goldwater did more than just lend moral support to the blockade. He also detached several warships from the United States Atlantic Fleet and ordered the ships to join the Confederate flotilla off Cuba. The combined

US/Confederate task force was instructed to isolate Cuba from the outside world—no ships would be allowed to enter or leave any Cuban port. Both countries wanted to make absolutely certain that Soviet and Cuban troops on the island did not receive any reinforcements. Both Richmond and Washington also wanted to guard against Soviet ships smuggling either missiles or troops out of Cuba undetected. The Soviet Union had denied that it had any bases in Cuba; both the United States and the Confederacy wanted the rest of the world to know the truth.

A force of Soviet warships challenged the blockade, which resulted in a naval battle off the Florida Keys on October 22, 1982. The guided missile cruisers USS *William T. Sherman* and CSS *Stonewall Jackson* were credited with sinking two Russian cruisers and damaging several others. On the same day, Confederate marines landed on two places along the southern coast of Cuba. Russian troops stationed on the island, mainly technicians and missile experts, offered no resistance. Meanwhile, Cuban troops were overwhelmed by the crack marine units.

Because the battles on both land and sea had been such one-sided victories for the Confederacy and for combined US/Confederate naval units, and because Cuba had effectively been isolated by the US/Confederate naval blockade, the Soviet government was forced to make a very difficult decision. Moscow came to the conclusion that it had no alternative but to abandon its missile bases in Cuba. Soviet officials demanded the return of their missiles and radar technology, but the Confederate government flatly refused to comply. The capture of so much Soviet military equipment turned out to be a windfall for Confederate intelligence. The information gained by seizing all this technology was later shared with US military intelligence.

The Confederates did agree to release all Soviet technicians and missile crews that had been taken prisoner—after they had been thoroughly questioned by their captors. The examination of the Soviet prisoners was carried out by a specially trained group of interrogation experts, consisting of military officers from both the United States and the Confederacy, which was officially known as the Joint Intelligence Committee. The members of the committee referred to themselves whimsically as the "Yankee/Dixie Cuban Rum Cartel," although they took their jobs a lot more seriously than they let on.

Within a month after the Russian withdrawal from Cuba, the Cuban military government was driven from power by a counterrevolutionary contingent. Confederate marines took no active part in the coup, but President Johnston let it be known that he stood by the insurgents, whom he called "freedom fighters," and that he would formally recognize any new government they formed. Johnston was as good as his word. In the spring of 1983, the new Cuban government received full diplomatic recognition from the Confederate States of America. Within the same week, the US government also officially recognized the new government in Havana. At the end of the year, with the full approval of the new government, Cuba became a territory of the Confederate States. Officially, the island became part of the Confederate States Commonwealth.

The Russian government, not at all happy about this turn of events, tried its best to dissuade the Confederacy from making Cuba a permanent territory, first by threats and then by diplomacy. But President Johnston made it clear that he had no intention of pulling out of Cuba. "Our forefathers, who gave us our freedom and our independence over one hundred years ago, would never have abandoned Cuba, and we stand obligated to follow in their valiant footsteps," Johnston declared in a television broadcast. "Our military accomplishment in Cuba follows in the proud tradition of Manassas, Fredericksburg, Chancellorsville, and Atlanta."

The Cuba/Alaska conflict was the last time any of the five American countries were involved in any sort of military alliance with each other. But relations continued to be congenial, with an occasional outburst of bad temper. Two decades after Ronald Reagan's Latter-day Saints remark, a congressman from Texas caused another small furor after visiting California. The Texan, unhappy with the results of his visit, called California "the oddball capital of the world." This statement led to a predictable show of indignation by the California Congress, which was followed by a predictable Texas apology. The Latter-day Saints from Utah still managed to ruffle a few feathers with their New Testament–saint attitude from time to time— less generous minds would call it pompousness.

Currently, all five sovereign nations carry on with normal diplomatic relations and also keep their economies in relatively good health by trading with each other. The United States continues to have the largest and most active economy among the five countries, as well as the largest army, navy, and air force, with the Confederacy doing its best to keep nipping at the heels of its northern neighbor in both categories.

Economics and trade relations occasionally caused problems, as well, such as the 1988 trade pact between the United States and the Confederate state of Georgia. The pact was ratified by both the US Congress and the Georgia state legislature, but it had not been approved by the Confederate Congress in Richmond. Richmond was more than just slightly annoyed by this omission.

Washington apologized for what had obviously been nothing but an embarrassing oversight, but the governor of Georgia, Joseph Brown, was not about to apologize to anybody. Governor Brown very sharply informed Richmond that the Confederate government had no right to interfere with the Georgia state legislature regarding this piece of legislation or any other, and he effectively told both houses of Congress to mind their own business. Eventually, Richmond did ratify the trade deal, but not before enduring several more tirades from Governor Brown, who repeatedly insisted that Georgia had the right to pass its own laws without any meddling from Richmond. After more than a hundred years, states' rights were still very much an issue in the Confederacy.

But, unlike the 1860s and before, economic disputes between the two countries had—usually—become nothing more than minor annoyances by the twenty-first century. The only real cause for bad feelings and hostility continued to be the issue of race, which still divides North and South.

The Confederate States resent US criticism of its racial segregation policy, which remains in effect throughout the Confederacy. Confederate political leaders contend that black and white citizens have the same rights under their constitution and that neither race complains about any kind of ill treatment at the hands of the other. When a US presidential candidate, well known for her outspoken views on race relations, implied that several Confederate states were guilty of human rights violations, Confederate president Jefferson Davis Clinton had a quick response. President Clinton accused the woman of reading *Uncle Tom's Cabin* too many times and invited her to come to Arkansas or any other state if she wanted to see how real people lived in the Confederacy.

The two countries regard the subject of race in two completely different ways, from two completely different backgrounds and points of view, and both sides remain convinced that their point of view is the only correct one. Some things have not changed since the 1860s.

Exactly what would have happened if Abraham Lincoln had not been re-elected in 1864 is open to the wildest sort of speculation. Would the First World War have been prolonged by almost a year? Who can say. But one thing is certain: if Lincoln had lost the election, the history of the United States, as well as the history of the world, would have been vastly different. In fact, the presidential election of 1864 is a pivotal event for both the United States and the world.

On the day after Lincoln's re-election, a man from New York called it "the most momentous popular election ever held since ballots were printed."[2] A constituent of Ohio senator John Sherman was just as emphatic about its importance. "Language cannot describe nor imagination conceive its importance to our country and the world," the senator was informed in a jubilant letter written just after the election. "It is the great political event in all history."[3] The letter was highly appropriate, since Senator Sherman's brother, General William Tecumseh Sherman, was directly responsible for Lincoln's re-election.

The influence of that election will always be with us. It has had an effect on the outcome of at least one war and the probable outcome of several others, as well as on race relations, states' rights, international relations, national and international economics, and national politics since 1864. And it will continue to be just as influential as long as the United States struggles with the issue of race and continues to be a world power. As the character Gavin Stevens says in William Faulkner's novel *Requiem for a Nun*, "The past is never dead. It's not even past."[4]

ACKNOWLEDGMENTS

This is my first book on the subject of the American Civil War. Most of my previous books have been about the Second World War, and were largely based upon eyewitness interviews—conversations with people who had lived through the London Blitz, or had lived on Long Island, New York, at the time of the landing of the German saboteurs. Obviously, it was not possible to interview anyone who remembered the 1864 election.

Instead, I had to rely upon a good many historians, librarians, and other helpful people to assist me in my gathering of information for *Decided on the Battlefield*. I would like to single out a few individuals who went out of their way to be helpful.

First of all, I would like to acknowledge both the assistance and the encouragement of Mr. James Cornelius, curator of the Abraham Lincoln Presidential Library and Museum in Springfield, Illinois. In addition to answering several of my questions, Mr. Cornelius also encouraged me to undertake this project in the first place. He told me that a book on the election of 1864 was a good idea, "needing exploration," and he was right.

I would also like to thank Mary Shepherd of the Abraham Lincoln Association, also of Springfield, for putting me in touch with Mr. Cornelius, which actually got the whole project rolling.

Kimber Fender, of the Public Library of Cincinnati and Hamilton County, gave me the story of the meeting of Ulysses S. Grant and William T. Sherman at Cincinnati's Burnet House in March 1864. The meeting took place in the hotel's Parlor A, which, according to Ms. Fender, turned the room into "a kind of shrine." Parlor A became the meeting place for the

Sons of Union Veterans for many years, until the hotel was pulled down in the 1920s. Details like this bring a book to life. Many thanks to Kim Fender for her help.

And, once again, I would like to express many thanks to the staff of the Union Township Public Library in New Jersey. They rode to my rescue many times, like General Phil Sheridan at Cedar Creek. Thank you to Eileen, Susan, Carole, Laura, and All Hands for all your help.

I am certain that I left out a number of people who have helped me, for which I offer many sincere apologies. It is not that I am ungrateful, just absentminded.

David Alan Johnson

NOTES

CHAPTER ONE: GENERALS AND POLITICIANS

1. Ulysses S. Grant, *Personal Memoirs of U. S. Grant* (Old Saybrook, CT: Konecky and Konecky, n.d.), p. 213.

2. Charles Bracelen Flood, *Grant and Sherman: The Friendship That Won the Civil War* (New York: Farrar, Straus, and Giroux, 2005), p. 3.

3. Union losses at Shiloh, as repoted in the *New York Times*, April 10, 1862.

4. Geoffrey Perret, *Ulysses S. Grant: Soldier and President* (New York: Random House, 1977), p. 250.

5. Quoted in Flood, *Grant and Sherman*, p. 74.

6. Carl Sandburg, *Abraham Lincoln: The Prairie Years and the War Years* (New York: Harcourt Brace Jovanovich, 1982), p. 531.

7. Shelby Foote, *The Civil War* (New York: Vintage Press, 1986), 3:13.

8. Grant, *Personal Memoirs*, p. 413.

9. Ibid., p. 416.

10. Ibid., p. 423.

11. Sandburg, *Abraham Lincoln*, p. 467.

12. Ibid., p. 274.

13. Clement Vallandigham, quoted in Michael Kent Curtis, "Lincoln, Vallandigham, and Anti-War Speech in the Civil War," *William & Mary Bill of Rights Journal* 105 (1998), http://www.scholarship.law.wm.edu/wmborj/vol7/iss1/3.

14. General Order No. 38, quoted in "The Enemy Within: Copperheads and the Knights of the Golden Circle," Ohio Civil War 150, http://www.ohiocivilwar 150.org/omeka/exhibits/show/the-enemy-within/of-snakes-and-men/clement -vallandigham (accessed September 26, 2011).

15. Herbert Mitgang, ed., *Abraham Lincoln: A Press Portrait* (Chicago: Quadrangle Books, 1971), p. 240.

16. Gideon Welles, quoted in "Henry W. Halleck (1815–1872)," Shotgun's Home of the American Civil War, http://www.civilwarhome.com/halleckbio.htm (accessed September 26, 2011).

17. Sandburg, *Abraham Lincoln*, p. 509.

18. "Fighting at Chancellorsville," *New York Times*, May 5, 1863.

19. "List of Killed and Wounded at the Washington Hospitals," *New York Times*, May 9, 1863.

20. Bruce Catton, *This Hallowed Ground* (Edison, NJ: Castle Books, 2002), p. 250.

CHAPTER TWO: CAMPAIGNS BEGINNING

1. Jack H. Lang, ed., *The Wit and Wisdom of Abraham Lincoln* (New York: Greenberg, 1941), pp. 225–26.

2. Ulysses S. Grant, "The Army Moves To-morrow Morning," in *The War of the Rebellion: A Compilation of the Official Records of the Union and Confederate Armies*, vol. 36, pt. 2 (Washington, DC: US War Department, 1902), p. 352. Hereafter cited as *Official Records*.

3. Robert E. Denney, *The Civil War Years* (New York: Sterling, 1992), p. 399.

4. *Official Records*, vol. 36, pt. 2, p. 403.

5. Ibid.

6. Shelby Foote, *The Civil War* (New York: Vintage Press, 1986), 3:150.

7. Henry Steele Commager, *The Blue and the Gray* (New York: Fairfax Press, 1982), p. 688.

8. Ibid., p. 689.

9. Bruce Catton, *A Stillness at Appomattox* (New York: Doubleday, 1953), p. 78.

10. Carl Sandburg, *Abraham Lincoln: The Prairie Years and the War Years* (New York: Harcourt Brace Jovanovich, 1982), p. 508.

11. Bernard A. Olsen, *Upon the Tented Field* (Red Bank, NJ: Historic Projects, 1993), p. 234.

12. *Wikipedia*, s.v. "Battle of the Wilderness," http://www.en.wikipedia.org/wiki/Battle_of_the_Wilderness (accessed September 30, 2011). Other sources, including Bruce Catton's *Grant Takes Command* (Boston: Back Bay Books, 1990), corroborate these numbers. Confederate losses are estimated.

13. Ulysses S. Grant, *Personal Memoirs of U. S. Grant* (Old Saybrook, CT: Konecky and Konecky, n.d.), p. 460.

14. Olsen, *Upon the Tented Field*, p. 236.

15. Catton, *Grant Takes Command*, p. 216.

16. Grant, *Personal Memoirs*, p. 473.

17. Ibid.

18. James M. McPherson, *Tried by War: Abraham Lincoln as Commander in Chief* (New York: Penguin, 2008), p. 221.

19. *Wikipedia*, s.v. "Battle of Spotsylvania Court House," http://www.en .wikipedia.org/wiki/Battle_of_Spotsylvania_Court_House (accessed September 30, 2011). Confederate losses are, as always, estimated.

20. Grant, *Personal Memoirs*, p. 495.

21. Catton, *Stillness at Appomattox*, p. 163.

22. Grant, *Personal Memoirs*, p. 503.

23. *Wikipedia*, s.v. "Overland Campaign," http://www.en.wikipedia.org/ wiki/Overland_Campaign (accessed September 30, 2011). James M. McPherson gives Union losses of 65,000 and Confederate losses of 35,000 in his *Battle Cry of Freedom* (New York: Oxford University Press, 1998), pp. 742–43.

24. "Casualties from Wilderness Battle," *New York Times*, May 9, 1864.

25. Olsen, *Upon the Tented Field*, p. 238.

26. Doris Kearns Goodwin, *Team of Rivals* (New York: Simon and Schuster, 2005), p. 620.

27. Sandburg, *Abraham Lincoln*, p. 510.

28. Ibid.

29. Lincoln's reading of this Bible passage, from 1 Samuel 22:2, is cited in Goodwin, *Team of Rivals*, p. 622.

30. Charles W. Johnson, ed., *The Official Proceedings of the First Three Republican National Conventions: 1856, 1860, and 1864* (Minneapolis, MN: Charles W. Johnson, 1893), pp. 176–77. Hereafter cited as *Conventions*.

31. Ibid., p. 178.

32. Ibid., p. 181.

33. Ibid., p. 187.

34. Ibid., pp. 188–89.

35. Ibid., p. 189.

36. Sandburg, *Abraham Lincoln*, p. 516.

37. *Conventions*, p. 190.

38. Alistair Cooke, *Alistair Cooke's America* (New York: Knopf, 1973), p. 216.

39. *Conventions*, p. 216.

40. See "The Eleven Resolutions," in ibid., pp. 225–26.

41. Sandburg, *Abraham Lincoln*, p. 517.

42. *Conventions*, p. 231.

43. Ibid.

44. Ibid., p. 232.

45. Ibid.

46. Ibid., p. 233.

47. Cooke, *Alistair Cooke's America*, p. 218.

48. David Herbert Donald, *Lincoln* (New York: Simon and Schuster, 1995), p. 506.

49. *Conventions*, p. 236.

50. Ibid., p. 237.

51. Sandburg, *Abraham Lincoln*, p. 523.

52. *Conventions*, p. 242.

53. Sandburg, *Abraham Lincoln*, p. 520.

54. Ibid.

55. "The Vice-Presidency," *New York Times*, June 9, 1864.

56. Foote, *Civil War*, 3:319.

57. Edward Longacre, *Worthy Opponents* (Nashville, TN: Rutledge Hill, 2006), p. 218.

58. Randy Golden, "The Battle of Rocky Face Ridge," http://www.ngeorgia.com/history/Dalton.html (accessed September 30, 2011).

59. Henry Steele Commager and Erik Bruun, eds., *The Civil War Archive: The History of the Civil War in Documents* (New York: Black Dog and Leventhal, 2000), p. 660.

60. Golden, "Battle of Rocky Face Ridge."

61. Ibid.

62. Ibid.

63. Bruce Catton, *This Hallowed Ground* (Edison, NJ: Castle Books, 2002), p. 340.

64. Robert E. Denney, *The Civil War Years: A Day-by-Day Chronicle of the Life of a Nation* (New York: Sterling, 1992), p. 406.

65. Ibid., p. 409.

66. Longacre, *Worthy Opponents*, p. 258.

67. Albert E. Castel, *Decision in the West: The Atlanta Campaign of 1864* (Lawrence: University Press of Kansas, 1992), p. 225. New Hope Church casualties also from ibid.

CHAPTER THREE: OMINOUS ROADS AHEAD

1. Shelby Foote, *The Civil War* (New York: Vintage Press, 1986), 3:442.

2. Bruce Catton, *This Hallowed Ground* (Edison, NJ: Castle Books, 2002), p. 330.

3. Noah Andre Trudeau, *The Last Citadel* (Baton Rouge: Louisiana State University Press, 1991), p. 19.

4. Ulysses S. Grant, *Personal Memoirs of U. S. Grant* (Old Saybrook, CT: Konecky and Konecky, n.d.), p. 516.

5. Bruce Catton, *A Stillness at Appomattox* (New York: Doubleday, 1982), p. 198.

6. Trudeau, *Last Citadel*, p. 54.

7. Bruce Catton, *Grant Takes Command* (Boston: Back Bay Books, 1990), p. 327.

8. Ibid., p. 330.

9. Catton, *Stillness at Appomattox*, p. 206.

10. Ibid., p. 191.

11. Excerpts from Lincoln's Great Central Fair speech in Doris Kearns Goodwin, *Team of Rivals* (New York: Simon and Schuster, 2005), p. 629, and Catton, *Grant Takes Command*, p. 295.

12. Trudeau, *Last Citadel*, pp. 65–66, and Catton, *Grant Takes Command*, p. 305.

13. Ibid.

14. Trudeau, *Last Citadel*, p. 66.

15. Goodwin, *Team of Rivals*, p. 629.

16. Trudeau, *Last Citadel*, p. 67.

17. Goodwin, *Team of Rivals*, p. 630.

18. Trudeau, *Last Citadel*, p. 66.

19. Goodwin, *Team of Rivals*, p. 631.

20. Ibid.

21. Joseph A. Califano Jr., *The Triumph and Tragedy of Lyndon Johnson: The White House Years* (New York: Simon and Schuster, 1991), p. 250.

22. Robert Dallek, *Flawed Giant: Lyndon B. Johnson and His Times, 1961–1973* (New York: Oxford University Press, 1998), p. 60.

23. Stephen W. Sears, *George B. McClellan: The Young Napoleon* (New York: Da Capo Press, 1999), p. 357.

24. According to James M. Cornelius, curator of the Abraham Lincoln Presidential Library and Museum, $1.00 in 1864 US currency would be worth about $40.00 in the early twenty-first century, which means that the current equivalent of a major general's salary would be about $240,000.

25. Sears, *George B. McClellan*, p. 363.

26. Ibid., p. 252. The full title of the document is *Report of Maj. Gen. George B. McClellan, U.S. Army, commanding the Army of the Potomac.*

27. Ibid., p. 361.

28. Peter Vredenburgh, quoted in Bernard A. Olsen, *Upon the Tented Field* (Red Bank, NJ: Historic Projects, 1993), pp. 246–47.

29. William T. Sherman, *The Capture of Atlanta and the March to the Sea* (Minneola, NY: Dover, 2007), p. 53 (chapters 15 through 20 of Sherman's memoirs). Kennesaw was spelled with one *n* during the Civil War. Most newspaper accounts also use one *n*.

30. Catton, *This Hallowed Ground*, p. 340.

31. Albert E. Castel, *Decision in the West: The Atlanta Campaign of 1864* (Lawrence: University Press of Kansas, 1992), p. 42.

32. Sherman, *Capture of Atlanta*, p. 56.

33. Ibid., p. 51.

34. Castel, *Decision in the West*, p. 313.

35. Ibid., p. 319.

36. Sherman, *Capture of Atlanta*, p. 57.

37. Catton, *This Hallowed Ground*, p. 341.

38. Castel, *Decision in the West*, p. 321.

39. Horace Greeley, quoted in David Herbert Donald, *Lincoln* (New York: Simon and Schuster, 1995), p. 513.

40. Ibid., p. 516.

CHAPTER FOUR: SUMMER OF DISAPPOINTMENTS

1. Edward Longacre, *Worthy Opponents* (Nashville, TN: Rutledge Hill, 2006), p. 8.

2. Ibid., p. 61.

3. Albert E. Castel, *Decision in the West: The Atlanta Campaign of 1864* (Lawrence: University Press of Kansas, 1992), p. 30.

4. Longacre, *Worthy Opponents*, p. 271.

5. Castel, *Decision in the West*, p. 358.

6. Ibid., p. 352.

7. Ibid., p. 353.

8. Ibid.

9. Bruce Catton, *This Hallowed Ground* (Edison, NJ: Castle Books, 2002), p. 342.

10. Ibid., p. 343.

11. William T. Sherman, *The Capture of Atlanta and the March to the Sea* (Minneola, NY: Dover, 2007), p. 68.

12. Charles Bracelen Flood, *Grant and Sherman: The Friendship That Won the Civil War* (New York: Farrar, Straus, and Giroux, 2005), p. 255.

13. Sherman, *Capture of Atlanta*, p. 68.

14. Castel, *Decision in the West*, p. 380.

15. Ronald H. Bailey, *Battle for Atlanta: Sherman Moves East* (Arlington, VA: Time-Life Books, 1985), p. 95.

16. Ibid., p. 134.

17. Carl Sandburg, *Abraham Lincoln: The Prairie Years and the War Years* (New York: Harcourt Brace Jovanovich, 1982), p. 530.

18. Catton, *This Hallowed Ground*, p. 345.

19. "Fighting around Atlanta," *New York Times*, July 24, 1864.

20. "News from Atlanta," *New York Times*, July 26, 1864.

21. "General Sherman Confident of Success," *New York Times*, July 26, 1864.

22. Sherman, *Capture of Atlanta*, pp. 83–84.

23. Castel, *Decision in the West*, p. 428.

24. Bailey, *Battle for Atlanta*, p. 134.

25. Castel, *Decision in the West*, p. 434.

26. Sherman, *Capture of Atlanta*, p. 86.

27. Catton, *This Hallowed Ground*, p. 346.

28. Flood, *Grant and Sherman*, p. 255.

29. James McPherson, "No Peace without Victory," *American Historical Review*, February 2004.

30. "Fighting near Petersburg," *New York Times*, July 31, 1864.

31. Robert Hunt Rhodes, ed., *All for the Union: The Civil War Diaries and Letters of Elisha Hunt Rhodes* (New York: Vintage, 1985), p. 159.

32. Ulysses S. Grant, *Personal Memoirs of U. S. Grant* (Old Saybrook, CT: Konecky and Konecky, n.d.), p. 521.

33. Rhodes, *All for the Union*, p. 162.

34. Ibid.

35. Shelby Foote, *The Civil War* (New York: Vintage Press, 1986), 3:459.

36. Rhodes, *All for the Union*, p. 163.

37. Charles C. Osborne, *Jubal: The Life and Times of Jubal A. Early, CSA* (Chapel Hill, NC: Algonquin Books, 1992), p. 298.

38. Bruce Catton, *A Stillness at Appomattox* (New York: Doubleday, 1953), p. 220.

39. Grant, *Personal Memoirs*, p. 523.

40. Noah Andre Trudeau, *The Last Citadel* (Baton Rouge: Louisiana State University Press, 1991), p. 107.

41. Ibid., p. 109.

42. Ibid.

43. Ibid., p. 126.

44. Bruce Catton, *Grant Takes Command* (Boston: Back Bay Books, 1990), p. 321.

45. Grant, *Personal Memoirs*, p. 527.

46. Henry Steele Commager, *The Blue and the Gray* (New York: Fairfax Press, 1982), p. 708.

47. James McPherson, quoted in "At Washington's Gates," *Civil War Times*, June 29, 2007.

48. "News from Petersburg," *New York Times*, August 2, 1864.

49. David Herbert Donald, *Lincoln* (New York: Simon and Schuster, 1995), p. 529.

50. Catton, *This Hallowed Ground*, p. 349.

51. Andrew S. Coopersmith, *Fighting Words: An Illustrated History of Newspaper Accounts of the Civil War* (New York: Free Press, 2004), p. 208.

52. James M. McPherson, *Tried by War: Abraham Lincoln as Commander in Chief* (New York: Penguin, 2008), p. 106.

53. Joshua Wolf Shenk, *Lincoln's Melancholy: How Depression Challenged a President and Fueled His Greatness* (Boston: Houghton Mifflin, 2005), p. 193.

54. James M. McPherson, *Battle Cry of Freedom* (New York: Oxford University Press, 1998), p. 767.

CHAPTER FIVE: NATURAL MILITARY CONSEQUENCES

1. Adolf A. Hoehling, *Damn the Torpedoes: Naval Ironclads of the Civil War* (Winston-Salem, NC: J. F. Blair, 1989), p. 105.

2. Christopher Martin, *Damn the Torpedoes! The Story of America's First Admiral David Glasgow Farragut* (New York: Abelard-Schuman, 1970), p. 240.

3. Shelby Foote, *The Civil War* (New York: Vintage Press, 1986), 3:497.

4. Hoehling, *Damn the Torpedoes*, p. 109.

5. Martin, *Damn the Torpedoes!* p. 252.

6. Hoehling, *Damn the Torpedoes*, p. 114.

7. Ibid., p. 111.

8. Ibid., p. 113.

9. Martin, *Damn the Torpedoes!* p. 258.

10. Hoehling, *Damn the Torpedoes*, p. 115.

11. Ibid., p. 119.

12. Ibid.

13. Foote, *Civil War*, 3:506.

14. "News from Mobile Bay," *New York Times*, August 9, 1864.

15. Ulysses S. Grant, *Personal Memoirs of U. S. Grant* (Old Saybrook, CT: Konecky and Konecky, n.d.), pp. 528–29.

16. Ibid., p. 529.

17. Ibid., p. 528.

18. Roy Morris Jr., *Sheridan: The Life and Wars of General Phil Sheridan* (New York: Crown, 1992), p. 1.

19. Ibid., p. 183.

20. *The War of the Rebellion: A Compilation of the Official Records of the Union and Confederate Armies*, vol. 37, pt. 2 (Washington, DC: US War Department, 1902), pp. 301, 329; Morris, *Sheridan*, p. 184; and Catton, *A Stillness at Appomattox* (New York: Doubleday, 1953), p. 275.

21. Bernard A. Olsen, *Upon the Tented Field* (Red Bank, NJ: Historic Projects, 1993), p. 260.

22. Robert Hunt Rhodes, ed., *All for the Union: The Civil War Diaries and Letters of Elisha Hunt Rhodes* (New York: Vintage, 1985), p. 170.

23. Olsen, *Upon the Tented Field*, pp. 264–65.

24. Catton, *Stillness at Appomattox*, p. 286.

25. Charles C. Osborne, *Jubal: The Life and Times of Jubal A. Early, CSA* (Chapel Hill, NC: Algonquin Books, 1992), p. 394.

26. Carl Sandburg, *Abraham Lincoln: The Prairie Years and the War Years* (New York: Harcourt Brace Jovanovich, 1982), p. 514.

27. Geoffrey Perret, *Ulysses S. Grant: Soldier and President* (New York: Random House, 1977), p. 332.

28. James McPherson, *This Mighty Scourge: Perspectives on the Civil War* (New York: Oxford, 2007), p. 113.

29. Noah Andre Trudeau, *The Last Citadel* (Baton Rouge: Louisiana State University Press, 1991), p. 146.

30. Ibid., p. 152.

31. Ibid., p. 156.

32. Catton, *Stillness at Appomattox*, p. 320.

33. Ibid.

34. Bruce Catton, *Grant Takes Command* (Boston: Back Bay Books, 1990), p. 353.

35. Charles Bracelen Flood, *1864: Lincoln at the Gates of History* (New York: Simon and Schuster, 2009), p. 251.

36. Ibid.

37. Excerpts from letter of Senator John Sherman to W. T. Sherman, in Albert E. Castel, *Decision in the West: The Atlanta Campaign of 1864* (Lawrence: University Press of Kansas, 1992), p. 445.

38. William T. Sherman, *The Capture of Atlanta and the March to the Sea* (Minneola, NY: Dover, 2007), p. 95.

39. Ibid., p. 97.

40. Ibid.

41. Ibid., p. 98.

42. Ibid., p. 100.

43. Ronald H. Bailey, *Battle for Atlanta: Sherman Moves East* (Arlington, VA: Time-Life Books, 1985), p. 140.

44. Sherman, *Capture of Atlanta*, p. 101.

45. Ibid., p. 142.

46. Catton, *Stillness at Appomattox*, p. 323.

47. James M. McPherson, *Tried by War: Abraham Lincoln as Commander in Chief* (New York: Penguin, 2008), p. 240.

CHAPTER SIX: TURNING THE TIDE

1. *Official Proceedings of the Democratic National Convention, Held in 1864 at Chicago* (Chicago, IL: Times Steam Book and Job Printing House, 1864), p. 3.

2. Ibid.

3. Ibid., p. 4.

4. Ibid.

5. Doris Kearns Goodwin, *Team of Rivals* (New York: Simon and Schuster, 2005), p. 654.

6. *Official Proceedings of the Democratic National Convention*, p. 5.

7. Ibid., p. 11.

8. Ibid., p. 21.

9. Ibid.

10. Ibid., p. 24.

11. Ibid.

12. All quotes from the Committee on Resolutions' planks, in ibid., p. 27.

13. Ibid.

14. Ibid., p. 29.

15. Ibid.

16. Ibid.

17. Ibid., p. 30.

18. Ibid.

19. Ibid., p. 43.

20. Ibid., p. 44.

21. Ibid.

22. Ibid., p. 46.

23. Ibid., p. 58.

24. John C. Waugh, *Lincoln and McClellan: The Troubled Relationship between a President and His General* (New York: Palgrave Macmillan, 2010), p. 205.

25. Ibid.

26. All quotes from McClellan's letter, *New York Times*, September 9, 1864.

27. Albert E. Castel, *Decision in the West: The Atlanta Campaign of 1864* (Lawrence: University Press of Kansas, 1992), p. 495.

28. Ronald H. Bailey, *Battle for Atlanta: Sherman Moves East* (Arlington, VA: Time-Life Books, 1985), p. 144.

29. Ibid., p. 144.

30. Castel, *Decision in the West*, p. 503.

31. Figures from fighting on August 31 in ibid., p. 503, and Bailey, *Battle for Atlanta*, p. 146.

32. William T. Sherman, *The Capture of Atlanta and the March to the Sea* (Minneola, NY: Dover, 2007), p. 103.

33. Bailey, *Battle for Atlanta*, p. 150.

34. "The Fall of Atlanta," *New York Times*, September 5, 1864.

35. Ibid.

36. Sherman, *Capture of Atlanta*, p. 105.

37. Ibid.

38. Ibid., p. 106.

39. Bruce Catton, *Grant Takes Command* (Boston: Back Bay Books, 1990), p. 360.

40. Bruce Catton, *This Hallowed Ground* (Edison, NJ: Castle Books, 2002), p. 352.

41. "Fall of Atlanta," *New York Times*.

42. "The Political Prospect," *New York Times*, September 7, 1864.

43. Ephriam Douglass Adams, *Great Britain and the American Civil War* (New York: Russell and Russell, 1958), p. 233.

44. Andrew S. Coopersmith, *Fighting Words: An Illustrated History of Newspaper Accounts of the Civil War* (New York: Free Press, 2004), p. 212.

45. Ibid., p. 212.

46. Castel, *Decision in the West*, p. 546.

47. Jefferson Davis, *The Rise and Fall of the Confederate Government* (New York: D. Appleton, 1881), p. 472.

48. Sherman, *Capture of Atlanta*, p. 119.

49. David Herbert Donald, *Lincoln* (New York: Simon and Schuster, 1995).

50. Ulysses S. Grant, *Personal Memoirs of U. S. Grant* (Old Saybrook, CT: Konecky and Konecky, n.d.), p. 534.

51. Roy Morris Jr., *Sheridan: The Life and Wars of General Phil Sheridan* (New York: Crown, 1992), p. 194.

52. Ibid., p. 200.

53. Robert Hunt Rhodes, ed., *All for the Union: The Civil War Diaries and Letters of Elisha Hunt Rhodes* (New York: Vintage, 1985), p. 175.

54. Ibid.

55. Ibid., p. 176.

56. Bruce Catton, *A Stillness at Appomattox* (New York: Doubleday, 1953), p. 299.

57. Rhodes, *All for the Union*, p. 177.

58. Morris, *Sheridan*, p. 202.

59. Shelby Foote, *The Civil War* (New York: Vintage Press, 1986), 3:555.

60. Bernard A. Olsen, *Upon the Tented Field* (Red Bank, NJ: Historic Projects, 1993), pp. 270–71.

61. Catton, *Grant Takes Command*, p. 364.

62. Morris, *Sheridan*, p. 202.

63. Catton, *Grant Takes Command*, p. 363.

64. Rhodes, *All for the Union*, p. 178.

65. Grant, *Personal Memoirs*, p. 536.

66. Carl Sandburg, *Storm over the Land* (Old Saybrook, CT: Konecky and Konecky, 1942), p. 550.

67. Ibid., p. 551.

CHAPTER SEVEN: THE GAME OF ALL OR NOTHING

1. Stephen W. Sears, *George B. McClellan: The Young Napoleon* (New York: DaCapo, 1999), p. 383.

2. Doris Kearns Goodwin, *Team of Rivals* (New York: Simon and Schuster, 2005), p. 662.

3. Tom Wheeler, *Mr. Lincoln's T-Mails: The Untold Story of How Abraham Lincoln Used the Telegraph to Win the Civil War* (New York: Collins, 2006), p. 116.

4. Noah Andre Trudeau, *The Last Citadel* (Baton Rouge: Louisiana State University Press, 1991), p. 220.

5. Goodwin, *Teams of Rivals*, p. 663.

6. Ibid. p. 664.

7. Trudeau, *Last Citadel*, p. 221.

8. Ibid., p. 222.

9. Ibid., pp. 242–43.

10. Ibid.

11. Ulysses S. Grant, *Personal Memoirs of U. S. Grant* (Old Saybrook, CT: Konecky and Konecky, n.d.), pp. 213, 542.

12. Ibid., p. 542.

13. Bruce Catton, *A Stillness at Appomattox* (New York: Doubleday, 1953), p. 322. "Ad libitum," in this sense, means "free access to feed."

14. Roy Morris Jr., *Sheridan: The Life and Wars of General Phil Sheridan* (New York: Crown, 1992), p. 210.

15. Philip Sheridan, *Personal Memoirs* (New York: Charles L. Webster, 1888), pp. 68–69.

16. Ibid., p. 75.

17. Ibid., p. 80.

18. Catton, *Stillness at Appomattox*, p. 312.

19. Sheridan, *Personal Memoirs*, p. 81.

20. Ibid., p. 80.

21. Bernard A. Olsen, *Upon the Tented Field* (Red Bank, NJ: Historic Projects, 1993), p. 282.

22. Ibid.

23. Ibid.

24. "Victory!" *New York Times*, October 21, 1864.

25. Shelby Foote, *The Civil War* (New York: Vintage Press, 1986), 3:574.

26. Sheridan, *Personal Memoirs*, p. 92.

27. Ibid., p. 91.

28. "The Truth about Sheridan's Ride," Bivouac, http://www.bivouacbooks .com/bbv2i3s4.htm (accessed November 2, 2011).

29. Ibid.

30. Ibid., and Thomas R. Lounsbury, ed., *The Yale Book of American Verse* (New Haven, CT: Yale University Press, 1912), pp. 339–41.

31. "I Like Ike" was the slogan of Dwight D. Eisenhower's presidential campaign in 1952. Eisenhower overwhelmingly defeated Democrat Adlai Stevenson in that election.

32. Robert Hunt Rhodes, ed., *All for the Union: The Civil War Diaries and Letters of Elisha Hunt Rhodes* (New York: Vintage, 1985), p. 188.

33. Carl Sandburg, *Storm over the Land* (Old Saybrook, CT: Konecky and Konecky, 1942), p. 610.

34. Ibid., p. 611.

35. Harry J. Maihafer, *War of Words: Abraham Lincoln and the Civil War Press* (Washington, DC: Brassey's, 2001), p. 222.

36. Sandburg, *Storm over the Land*, pp. 611–12.

37. David Herbert Donald, *Lincoln* (New York: Simon and Schuster, 1995), p. 544.

38. John C. Waugh, *Reelecting Lincoln: The Battle for the 1864 Presidency* (New York: Crown, 1997), p. 354. See also Sears, *George B. McClellan*, pp. 385–86.

39. Olsen, *Upon the Tented Field*, p. 283.

40. Rhodes, *All for the Union*, p. 188.

41. "Glorious Results Yesterday," *New York Times*, November 9, 1864.

42. Maihafer, *War of Words*, p. 222.

43. Ibid., p. 223.

44. Ephriam Douglass Adams, *Great Britain and the American Civil War* (New York: Russell and Russell, 1958), p. 239.

45. Jefferson Davis, *The Rise and Fall of the Confederate Government* (New York: D. Appleton, 1881), p. 517.

46. Ibid., p. 515.

47. Waugh, *Reelecting Lincoln*, p. 358.

48. Bruce Catton, *This Hallowed Ground* (Edison, NJ: Castle Books, 2002), p. 354.

CHAPTER EIGHT: THE NEXT FOUR YEARS

1. Henry Steele Commager, *The Blue and the Gray* (New York: Fairfax Press, 1982), p. 751.

2. Bruce Catton, *Grant Takes Command* (Boston: Back Bay Books, 1990), p. 403. After the war, Butler became a Republican member of the House of Representatives. He later switched political parties for the second time—he had started his political career as a Democrat—and became governor of Massachusetts as a Democrat in 1882.

3. Carl Sandburg, *Storm over the Land* (Old Saybrook, CT: Konecky and Konecky, 1942), p. 347.

4. Ibid.

5. William T. Sherman, *The Capture of Atlanta and the March to the Sea* (Minneola, NY: Dover, 2007), p. 162.

6. Ibid., p. 160.

7. Ibid., p. 164.

8. Ibid., p. 163.

9. Bruce Catton, *This Hallowed Ground* (Edison, NJ: Castle Books, 2002), p. 354.

10. Charles Bracelen Flood, *Grant and Sherman: The Friendship That Won the Civil War* (New York: Farrar, Straus, and Giroux, 2005), p. 264.

11. Sherman, *Capture of Atlanta*, p. 175.

12. Frank E. Vandiver, "Civil War Words and Music," in *1001 Things You Should Know about the Civil War* (New York: Grammercy, 1999), p. 236.

13. Ibid., p. 175.

14. Edward Longacre, *Worthy Opponents* (Nashville, TN: Rutledge Hill, 2006), p. 294.

15. Catton, *This Hallowed Ground*, p. 358.

16. C. Brian Kelly, *Best Little Stories of the Blue and Gray* (Nashville, TN: Cumberland House, 2006), pp. 190–92.

17. Ibid.

18. Sherman, *Capture of Atlanta*, p. 185.

19. James M. McPherson, *Tried By War: Abraham Lincoln as Commander in Chief* (New York: Penguin, 2008), p. 254.

20. David Nevin, *Sherman's March: Atlanta to the Sea* (Alexandria, VA: Time-Life Books, 1986), p. 120.

21. Shelby Foote, *The Civil War* (New York: Vintage Press, 1986), 3:758.

22. Longacre, *Worthy Opponents*, p. 303.

23. Ibid.

24. Nevin, *Sherman's March*, pp. 259, 261.

25. Catton, *This Hallowed Ground*, p. 373.

26. Ibid., p. 377.

27. Flood, *Grant and Sherman*, p. 297.

28. Jan Morris, *Lincoln: A Foreigner's Quest* (New York: Simon and Schuster, 2000), p. 167.

29. Catton, *This Hallowed Ground*, p. 382.

30. Catton, *Grant Takes Command*, p. 440.

31. Bruce Catton, *A Stillness at Appomattox* (New York: Doubleday, 1953), p. 329.

32. Earl Schenck Miers, *The Last Campaign: Grant Saves the Union* (Philadelphia, PA: Lippincott, 1972), p. 168.

33. Foote, *Civil War*, 3:815.

34. Ronald C. White Jr., *Lincoln's Greatest Speech: The Second Inaugural* (New York: Simon and Schuster, 2002), p. 76.

35. Carl Sandburg, *Abraham Lincoln: The Prairie Years and the War Years* (New York: Harcourt Brace Jovanovich, 1982), p. 662.

36. Ibid.

37. Ibid., p. 663.

38. Ibid.

39. Ibid.

40. Doris Kearns Goodwin, *Team of Rivals* (New York: Simon and Schuster, 2005), p. 702.

41. All quotations from the Second Inaugural Address are from Paul M. Angle, *A Pictorial History of the Civil War Years* (Garden City, NY: Doubleday, 1967), p. 212.

42. James Tackach, *Lincoln's Moral Vision: The Second Inaugural Address* (Jackson: University Press of Mississippi, 2002), p. 143.

43. Bruce Catton, *The Civil War* (New York: Tess, 2009), p. 584.

44. David Herbert Donald, *Lincoln* (New York: Simon and Schuster, 1995), p. 568.

45. White, *Lincoln's Greatest Speech*, p. 192.

46. Ibid., p. 190.

47. Ibid.

48. Goodwin, *Team of Rivals*, p. 701.

49. White, *Lincoln's Greatest Speech*, p. 195.

50. David Alan Johnson, *Betrayal: The True Story of J. Edgar Hoover and the Nazi Saboteurs Captured during WWII* (New York: Hippocrene Books, 2007), p. 272.

EPILOGUE: NEVER DEAD

1. Jan Morris, *Lincoln: A Foreigner's Quest* (New York: Simon and Schuster, 2000), p. 197.

2. David Herbert Donald, *Lincoln* (New York: Simon and Schuster, 1995), p. 546.

3. Ibid.

4. William Faulkner, *Novels, 1942–1954* (New York: Library of America, 1994), p. 535.

INDEX